The Collected Writings

(*so far*) of Rick Wormeli

Crazy Good Stuff I've Learned about
Teaching Along the Way

Association for Middle Level Education
Westerville, Ohio

AMLE.

Why do I teach?

I teach to dispel the dark and remind the universe that we are not inconsequential. I teach because it's infinitely compelling to watch dynamic souls punch through their not-so-elastic cocoons of childhood, daring the community to accept their forward motion. Brushing complacency's dust from everyday ideas and objects by viewing them through children's eyes opens our own, and it connects us to that golden, "What if…?" superhero in our earlier selves. I teach because setting a constructive example for my students generates a greater ethic in me than I can achieve without their example or provocation. I teach because I am deeply, unrepentantly grateful for life, and the most potent way I know to express that gratitude is to build a world worthy of the next generation, then give them the tools to make it their own.

—Rick Wormeli [From a teacher/author poster
distributed by Stenhouse Publishers 2012]

Contents

Grading

Conclusion

Introduction

If someone told me back in the 80s when I attempted to write my first professional education article that we'd be here today with enough critical mass for a book of collected writings, I would have said, "You and Doc Brown went to the wrong future in the Delorean, Marty. There's no way I could write anything that people would want to read." Similar to the set-up in the *Back to the Future* film, it's a little over 30 years ago that I started teaching. I still can't believe people read what I write about it.

In order to be a teacher, we need a little bit of ego. We get up in front of a bunch of students and presume that what we have to say and do with them that day is important enough to demand their attention, and we assure them that the content they learn will serve them the rest of their lives. Wow, that's pluck, but we also realize the tenuous order teachers establish with students is achieved only with their cooperation. At any moment, our students can get up and leave the classroom or create a disturbance that prohibits our teaching. Fortunately for our lesson plans, students have been indoctrinated to sit still and be cooperative since kindergarten. It still takes a lot of confidence on our part, however, to assume our thoughts are worthy of others.

It's similar when writing education articles: We need enough audacity to imagine that our words are worth editing and printing, and even more importantly, that practitioners will find value in reading them. We also need to accept the strange dichotomy of writing, too. On one hand, it's a lonely job: there's no one else here in the room with me for hours on end. On the other hand, it's very crowded in my head because I'm

having imagined conversations with teacher and author heroes as
I write:

> Will you, John Norton, think this is worth passing on to others?
> Holly Holland, do you think this is professional enough and has heft?
> John Lounsbury and Gordon Vars, does this live up to the promise
> for what you and others so bravely fought all those years ago? Chris
> Toy, will you take this and make it better as you do so capably?
> Debbie Silver, is there enough poignancy and a bit of humor to
> connect with my audience? Carol Ann Tomlinson, you write vividly;
> what do you think of the metaphors I used? Researchers and subject
> experts, have I respected what you bring to the table that we need to
> hear? And what about the real audience, you who teach and who lead
> teachers: You work with real students in complex classrooms and you
> have little time to waste reading material you already know or that
> does not advance your cause—Will this writing be of value to you?

It's loud with all of you talking in my head, but I can't write without
the noise.

The most helpful moments for me professionally are those that synergize
teaching and writing about teaching. It turns out that I sort my thinking
by writing. As a result, I'm a better teacher for having written about a
topic, and I'm a better writer for having taught the topic, an interaction
many others find useful as well. Writing is a deeply personal endeavor,
but it's basically thinking convergently and divergently at the same time
as we teach others what we know, which, of course, is the way we come
to know it ourselves. One of the authors I most admire, William Zinsser,
observed in his 1988 book, *Writing to Learn*, that we can write our way
into an understanding of anything. I think that's what I've been trying
to do for the last 30 years—figure out teaching by writing about it.

Sometimes the teaching experience is so resonant human-to-human
that we achieve a "Flow" moment causing me to feel like I'm going to
pop unless I write about it. You know the feeling: It's when everything
works. We've lived up to the expectation and trust students place in us
to be inspired souls guiding their path. We and our students both find

meaning in our enterprise, including true enjoyment just being together, sharing a common interest in the subject and bettering ourselves, maybe even revealing a previously unknown talent. Throw in some genuine laughter or revised thinking, and we've hit the jackpot. Some of the essays included in this collection are riding the tails of such comets.

This book of collected writings includes many the columns I wrote for Association for Middle Level Education's (AMLE) *Middle Ground* magazine, plus online work, two pieces written for ASCD's *Education Leadership*, and a commencement address I delivered this past year. Many of those original *Middle Ground* columns became fully developed chapters in my books published by Stenhouse and AMLE, including *Meet Me in the Middle: Becoming an Accomplished Middle-Level Teacher* (2001), *Day One and Beyond: Practical Matters for New Middle-Level Teachers* (2003), *Fair Isn't Always Equal: Assessing & Grading in the Differentiated Classroom* (2006), *Differentiation: From Planning to Practice Grades 6–12* (2007), and *Metaphors & Analogies: Power Tools for Teaching any Subject* (Stenhouse, 2009). I encourage you to read them in their entirety for further thinking on the topics and practical tips.

These collected writings cover quite a range of topics, from building teacher creativity, motivating students, and conducting field trips to planning for the last weeks of school, assigning homework, evaluating the honor roll, and designing lectures. There are pieces on memorization, English Language Learners, meaning-making, tiering, grading, metaphors, class discussions, and more topics pertinent to everyday classroom teaching. The goal for each one was to be practical, but we can't be effective without being principled. Recognizing this, there are plenty of places where I implore the reader to consider the larger context of what he does so he is purposeful, not haphazard, in his techniques.

The writings begin with the most important aspect of a teacher's success: ongoing professional growth beyond initial teacher preparation programs. "The Professional Side" is filled with writings on building sense of teacher self, ways to improve, the compelling nature of revising one's thinking in light of new evidence, and setting the tone for highly accomplished practice, not just getting by. It's an invitation to be a great teacher, not someone just showing up to get a paycheck, and it shows teaching as personally and intellectually engaging. Hopefully, it cultivates respect and expectation for readers, whether they are brand new or seasoned veterans.

The second section on motivation and connection reminds us that we can't teach students unless we can reach those students. Here are some of the largest worries for both new and seasoned teachers, and I wanted to provide some practicality in these areas right away. In fact, without discussing motivation from the beginning, readers will respond to many of the other ideas in the book with, "That's a nice idea, but what do you do if students don't care?" We need to get this out in front, or that other material will seem like mere puffery for a too-perfect world that doesn't exist.

The third section begins all those cool ideas about learning that we can incorporate into our lesson plans and thinking. It's one practical and creative idea after another. The emphasis is on what we know about students, how they best learn, and what that means for the classroom. Within that category, of course, come differentiation and literacy, and I address them in the chapters that follow closely behind.

A case could be made for everything in the teaching techniques chapter to be within the "Providing Effective Learning Experiences" chapter, but these essays all focus more on the logistical and thoughtful execution of the teaching plan rather than what's going on with students. Their point of view is a teacher's rather than a student's. Assessment and grading are huge and quite provocative topics, so I wanted to end with this deeply enticing material. There's practicality here, but also candor, perhaps pushing many readers' "buttons" a bit. This is good: It furthers the conversation we need to have.

Here's a quick notation if you read the essays in sequence: Some of the essays on a particular topic are placed near each other but were actually written years apart. As a result, you will find repetition in places where I incorporated earlier declarations and strategies that still rang true years later in subsequent pieces. Please forgive me, and I hope that perhaps an idea you encountered earlier will have new meaning for you in the later context. And, while I'm coming clean, you may encounter some versions of columns that were later fleshed out into chapters in some of my previous books.

I didn't want this collection to be a museum display, so I've gone through each one and updated it so that it might be helpful to educators today and next year as well, and the year beyond that, and maybe even for the next decade or two. After that, I expect readers to write their own essays, or, eh, I mean beam a holographic version of their 3-dimensional template for human meaning construction augmented by the DuFour/Marzano Constant with infinite revision capacity for the current diversity matrix to the faculty dashboard for reciprocal analysis. Or something like that.

No teacher is perfect, and gosh, I'm a living example of that every day. We come close, however, by vigilant attention to professionalism, which includes knowing our craft well, and using it in compassionate and courageous ways in our schools with students and colleagues. Remember, too, that 90% of our success is mindset: We *get* to do this, not *have* to do this. Teaching is not a "gotcha!" enterprise in which we present content and merely document students' mistakes along the way. We're out for students' success, and with it, comes our own. Let's enjoy the new discoveries about teaching we'll make this year and next, but let's also make sure to pass along the insights to the generation of educators and policymakers who follow us. Yeah, it's that audacity thing.

In deepest gratitude for every reader over the years and for those yet to come,

Rick Wormeli
January 2013

The Professional Side

Building Teachers' Capacity for Creative Thinking

For most of the grading period, one of Mrs. Weaver's students does not do his homework. In her third phone call to his parents about the problem, they say that there's nothing they can do about the issue. They claim that she's not doing enough to teach their son responsibility. Mrs. Weaver finishes the call in frustration. She rubs her temples and declares, "There's nothing more that I can do here. He doesn't do his homework, and there's no parent support. I can't teach him."

Translated, Mrs. Weaver is really saying, "I've exhausted my imagination." She thinks she's tried everything she knows, and she precludes everything she might generate. Is this burnout or just someone in need of a creativity boost?

It's not overtly taught in many teacher-prep programs, but learning how to think creatively is key to not only student success, but teacher longevity as well. Teachers encounter situations every day that require creative thinking. Consider their internal monologues:

- My whole lesson today is based on accessing those three websites, but the school's Internet is down, so what can we do instead?

- Small groups are not working in my class, yet I know they're important for many students' learning. How do I get these students to stay focused on their group tasks?

- I've backed myself into a corner explaining an advanced science concept, and it's not making sense to me, let alone to my students. What should I do?

- Angelica doesn't understand the concept after my explanation, but I don't know any other way to teach it. What will I do?

- I'm supposed to differentiate for some of my students, but I don't see any time to do it.

- My school's electronic gradebook system doesn't allow me to post anything but norm-referenced scores, and I want to be more criterion-referenced in my grades. What can I do?

- Because I'm a veteran teacher, I've been asked to be the rotating teacher using a cart and moving from classroom to classroom each period, so the new teacher can have his own room and not have so much to deal with his first year. How will I handle this?

Given that teaching requires so much creativity and problem solving, it's amazing that we don't spend more time building capacity for such thinking, nor do we require demonstrations of it in our teacher evaluation system.

Consider, too, that teachers are told in multiple ways each year not to think for themselves. In many schools, they are handed the curriculum rather than invited to participate in its creation. They are told of new policies that dramatically change current practices without time or structure to make the transitions carefully. Their opinions on controversial education issues are not often sought by policymakers.

Some schools make the mistake of mandating a scripted program in certain subjects with no option to adjust it according to students' needs. Some administrators spend the majority of their building "walk-throughs" with pacing mandates in hand, making sure everyone in the same subject at the same grade level is on the same page on the same day of the week. Teachers are warned to plan accordingly because: the paper supply will run out in January; the master schedule cannot be changed to accommodate a compelling guest speaker; they can't incorporate a new "app" in their lessons because it promotes the use of personal technology that school hasn't sanctioned; new students are three grade levels below grade-level proficiencies, but they have to do well on the final exam anyway; no, they can't take that field trip with the class because they only get one per year; and besides, that would take too much time away from preparing for the annual state or provincial exam.

Such declarations come across as teachers can't be trusted to make professional decisions. As offensive as this sentiment is to teachers, it's actually a wise caution if teachers have never developed their capacity to reason and think divergently. We all want the pilot who thinks "outside the box" when the plane's navigational system fails at 35,000 feet, and we want teachers to think in unusual ways if the regular curriculum or lesson plan isn't working. Inducting, deducting, revealing logical fallacy/consistency, making connections, and analyzing situations: We want those trusted to create the future via today's students to perform these tasks well. School reformers do better to train teachers to think and act creatively than they do spending time and money teacher-proofing instruction.

Ironically, some teachers who want more autonomy to be creative are often suspicious of colleagues who achieve it. Teachers providing imaginative lessons with students are annoying to some teachers who don't, and unhealthy comparisons follow: "Stop being so creative," a coworker comments. "You're making me look bad."

Creativity in teaching falls flat in schools with complacent and intellectually entrenched staff. It thrives in schools with staff who regularly revise their thinking in light of new evidence. In creative schools, teachers frequently access professional development opportunities. We affirm their professional inquiry via personal action research projects, PLCs, subscriptions to professional journals, and participation in listervs, webinars, Nings, and wikis.

Unfortunately, in some schools it comes across as "uncool" to be known as someone who contemplates cognitive neuroscience, pedagogy, assessment, instructional practice, critical analysis, learning theories, or who promotes serious contemplation of ideas. This anti-intellectualism is understandable; it's survival: We don't like to do what we are not good at doing. This isn't a sign that teachers are intellectually bereft; it's a sign that they haven't been given the resources and autonomy to develop their intellectual side. They shoot down new ideas and research analysis because they aren't sure what to make of the new information, and it takes less energy to dismiss a new idea than it does to think carefully about it.

This is a real problem: Someone at a department or team meeting says, "Did anyone read Kovecses' research on cognitive linguistics in last month's *Middle School Journal*? There were three points he made that really changed my thinking about how students learn vocabulary." Already there are some faculty members who are rolling their eyes and hoping the curious reader will quiet down so they can move on to other business, like whether or not school is closing early on the last day before the holiday. Think of all the great concepts, tips, and skills that no one passes on to others because they are afraid to come across as too Joe or Jane Professional Know-It-All.

The problem is that these initially unwilling teachers are actually thoughtful people, and if they heard the ideas, they would enjoy the conversation. They would think seriously about trying the ideas in their own classes. Without administrative and collegial encouragement and a risk-taking, contemplative school culture, teachers don't have the skills or motivation to think intellectually about what they do, yet it's vital to student success and our evolving profession.

Intellectual explorations are positive things. Teachers who question policies, offer new research to consider, share compelling professional reading with others, post regularly on professional Listervs, and think critically about teaching practices should be affirmed and supported, not made to feel like the goody-goody at the front of the room keeping everyone from recess because they are excited about amphibians and have one more question to ask about tree frogs in the Amazon.

There are multiple ways principals can build teachers' capacities for creative and critical thinking in daily teaching. Principals can invite teachers to:

Learn content or a new skill outside of your subject discipline.

Ask teachers to take a course in logic, divergent thinking, mind-mapping, synthesis, reasoning, analysis, law, politics, or rhetoric. Perhaps they'd like to start a forensics or debate club at the school, or participate in an adult version of one. Maybe they want to learn to play a new musical instrument and participate in an adult orchestra or band. They can start their own blog, write feature stories for the local paper, or participate in a local writers' support group. They might wish to learn a foreign language or three, or finally make good on that promise to themselves to start sculpting or painting. They can participate in a small group studies at their church, synagogue, or mosque, and they can experience a ropes initiative course, similar to Project Adventure and Outward Bound. Doing something new and outside one's field of study is a great catalyst for personal creativity.

Build instructional versatility.

Teachers can't be creative with what they don't have. They improve creativity when they have a variety of skills and content on which to draw. Invite them to walk into their lessons with at least three ways to present content and to have more than an inkling of what they'll do for students who learn the material in the first ten minutes of class and do not need the rest of the lesson as planned. Ask them to invite students to submit alternative perspectives and procedures for the material they are presenting and to learn five new learning models or five more uses of an iPad before the end of the school year.

Of course, with all of these, helpful principals find ways to finance additional training and subscriptions to professional journals for faculty, and they arrange the master schedule and provide substitute teachers, so teachers can study and work together to increase their instructional repertoire. Principals even read instructional articles and pass them along to teachers who may not have had the time to read them.

Reconsider what you have around you.

Sitting in an empty parking lot, could your math teacher teach students all they needed to know about Algebra? Dirt floor, wooden bench, thatched hut: If this were your history teacher's classroom, could she teach students the differences between Middle Ages and Renaissance artwork?

When I was a classroom teacher, one of the biggest liberators for my own thinking was to recognize that some of the greatest teaching tools are all around us. I didn't need to put all my hopes for effective teaching into getting the latest techno-toy from Carolina Biological Supply so much as I needed to think creatively about everyday objects as my teaching tools. Could I get the idea of homeostasis across to students using only elements found in the cafeteria or library? How about communicating the definition of "gestalt" when comparing different linoleum patterns on the floor and ceiling tiles of our building?

And how cool is it that an item seen every day will be there to remind students of the analogous concept every time they see it? It becomes a constant study guide and reinforcer. Someone who lives near the Mississippi River delta whose teacher compared that delta to the branching bronchial tubes leading to the alveoli in the lungs will see the Mississippi as one big trachea leading to the shipping ports (alveoli) where one good (product) is exchanged for another (carbon dioxide-oxygen exchange). Teachers offering lackluster lessons may need a principal's help in making connections between content and everyday objects and routines.

Practice creative thinking.

On a regular basis, invite faculty to explore hypotheticals: If [insert scenario here] was the teaching situation, what would a creative and highly effective teacher do? We get better at thinking creatively by actually thinking creatively, so let's practice it frequently. If teachers do this, they draw upon it when they really need to think creatively in their classrooms. They can identify awkward and difficult situations similar to those beginning this column and brainstorm successful responses with colleagues. It's amazing what such conversations trigger in teachers' minds when really teaching and planning.

Education expert Doug Reeves often reminds his readers that true professionals are not instantly good at just-learned strategies. They need to practice them to become proficient. We learn new strategies best through practice, reflection, revision, and more practice and reflection, not by reading or hearing about it once and giving it a single shot. Let's practice creativity in difficult situations, reflect on it, then practice some more.

Brainstorm—a lot.

Brainstorming builds idea fluency. Look at the clock on the wall: What is it doing? It's marking time. It's mocking my goal to prepare the school budget by this afternoon. It's decorating the office, but it's also tormenting students down the hall as they count down to the final bell, and it's representing human evolution beyond other life-forms on earth. What is it not doing? It's not setting any speed records, nor is it declaring justice for the oppressed. It's not lobbying for tax reform, nor is it introducing new technology to the world, nor compiling a list of the year's best movie one-liners.

From the sublime to the ridiculous, invite teachers to list all that comes to mind when brainstorming, and tell them to feel free to embellish ideas with occasional coloring outside the lines. For example, we might ask teachers: What are all the ways to motivate a reluctant student to read a particular book? They respond:

- Give background on the story before reading so he understands what's happening.
- Teach him the difficult vocabulary he'll encounter.
- Share the major themes first and see if any of them resonate with his own life.
- Show him the movie version.
- Bribe him.
- Have someone give testimony about the book's impact on them.
- Compare the book to one he's already read and liked.
- Let him blog or draw responses to his reading instead of writing to a prompt in his hardcopy journal.
- Show how reading the book will transform his life in some way.
- Point out current events that parallel the story's conflicts.
- Let the student interview the author about how and why he wrote the novel.

Twelve ideas were quickly listed in here by a single person: With colleagues in the building or from an online community, we could double that amount easily. More choices means more chance to find optimum solutions.

Sometimes divergent and occasionally nonsensical excursions while brainstorming lead to more powerful ideas, but it's hard to identify successful responses unless we practice brainstorming for its own sake. To improve at brainstorming, ask teachers to do it daily or at least weekly. Principals can do it, too: Take the time to brainstorm five or more options for how to respond to a poor performing teacher, which parents to ask to lead a new steering committee, how to get facility concerns across to a building manager so she makes them a priority, how to get up to speed personally on the latest in assessment practices, and whom to ask for donations for new technology needs.

Regularly do automatic tasks and let the mind roam.

Encourage teachers to go for a walk or run, drive a long distance without listening to music, take an extended shower or bath, wash a lot of dishes, mow the lawn, weed the garden, paint a room, crochet, watch birds for 45 minutes, swim freestyle slowly, or tread water.

Seriously, these are activities that build creativity. In these moments where our bodies and our minds are on automatic pilot with a routine or repetitive task, the gate that normally keeps our minds from wandering too far is lifted; imagination gets oxygen. We see issues in other parts of our lives, including teaching, more clearly. Heretofore unseen insights gain footholds, and we visualize ourselves and others responding constructively. We see parts and the whole, we recognize relationships, and we dream of what could be. This is not simplistic mumbo jumbo: Many of the best ideas in the history of our world occurred to inventors while their minds were occupied on other pursuits. Do yourself and your teachers a favor and extend the same opportunity to your creative self.

Accept life's complexity.

It's rarely a singular textbook series that turns around a school's math test scores. A commonly accepted teaching strategy doesn't always work the same way for every teacher. Reserving Shakespeare only for high school or Collins' Hunger Games only for 8th grade demonstrates unreasonable rigidity and limited thinking. Teachers should know that the student with many missing assignments in a row should not be given zeroes for all of those assignments without a sincere investigation into what went wrong. Simple black and white, either/or thinking rarely enables creativity to flourish. Ask teachers to re-consider traffic patterns and new pavement composition instead of repeatedly filling the same potholes.

Read.

Invite teachers to read everything about their subjects and teaching young minds that they can, including professional books and journals, blogs, news articles, and research. Against the backdrop of all that content, teachers make more connections and draw upon a larger reservoir of responses. This reading often provides not just a new strategy, but the trigger for something teachers invent ourselves. It's hard to be creative when the only catalyst is our own perspective; a teacher's professional reading provides shared catalysts. Don't forget: Portions of faculty and department meetings can be dedicated to reading professional material.

Listen.

The theater of the mind cultivates personal creativity. To spark imaginative thinking, ask teachers to access information via non-visual experiences. This way the mind has to fill in the perceptions which in turn, activate other parts of the mind. Our mind's eye is an amazing thing, so nurture it: Using our iPod or car CD player, we can listen to fiction and non-fiction writing. We can listen to downloaded podcasts and debates, replays of Sunday news shows on C-SPAN radio, and to radio shows that provide in-depth exploration of important topics, not just sound bites. Particularly thoughtful radio shows include those on NPR: Science Friday, Talk of the Nation, Tell Me More, Fresh Air, Morning Edition, All Things Considered, the Kojo Nnamdi Show, and The Diane Rehm Show.

Open instruction to professional critique.

Are there teachers who come across as accessible and inviting of critique? Are there others that thwart all attempts at access and assistance? In a culture where everyone invites critique from colleagues, parents, and students, teachers can develop their "teaching senses" more quickly, and as a result, plan better for students whose needs deviate from the norm. This is much better than closing their classroom doors and rationalizing that their teaching must be okay because no one is complaining about their assignments.

Remember, too, that there is a constant interaction between the teacher and the "critiquer." This is where most of the transformation occurs: not only in the information offered by the one critiquing, but in the back-and-forth between the two people involved. This is hard, of course, because to accept a new idea, teachers have to first admit what they were doing was ineffective or wrong. Yet, what goes unlearned by students because teachers weren't open to critique?

Actions speak louder than words, of course, so one of the most effective ways to get teachers to be open to critique and to respond to it constructively is to demonstrate both as the building leader. Consider opening multiple avenues to critique of you as principal as well as how to respond constructively to critique that is both positive and negative of you. Be sure to give testimonials to faculty about how critique feels, how valuable it is to your job performance, and how it led to new insight. Faculty need permission to be a bit uncomfortable with critique at first. It's natural. They also need encouragement for the give-and-take that improves their versatility.

Design multiple access points and meaning-making experiences for students.

This brings out a teacher's creative side. The more access points a mind has to a concept, the better the mind understands and retains the concept. If a student has both the sound and the visual of his teacher describing the Treaty of Versailles, he reads two compelling commentaries on lessons learned from its negotiation, and he participates in class discussions of its impact on today's political relationships, he can recall the information more vividly than studying the Treaty via one avenue alone. Having teachers design multiple access points for students cultivates their creativity.

We can't stop at access, however. Students have to process the information for meaning as well. If 8th grader Yuri gets the chance to reenact the debate between Germany and the Allies as they drew up their declarations of peace at the end of World War I, he's even more engaged and retains the memory much longer and more accurately. Meaningful learning most often happens when students "recode" learning for themselves.

A great technique for helping students do this is simulation, which is multi-sensory: As Yuri tries in a debate to convince Germany to accept responsibility for the war, to disarm, and to make reparations, or alternatively, to protect Germany from these concessions, his mind is on fire and he learns. Help teachers see the possibilities here—maybe a little role playing simulation in the midst of a faculty meeting?

Metaphor construction is another excellent method for personal recoding for students: "Mr. Puckett," C. J. says, "what you just described happening in the U.S. Congress with everyone pressuring their party members about this health care bill is just like my parents' locking pliers: The grip is tighter the more torque is applied, but there's a trigger release that relaxes everything when the job is done."

Help teachers see the power of metaphors for meaning-making by constructing powerful ones yourself, then inviting teachers to see if they fit the situation or if they require adjusting to be more meaningful. Play with metaphors in your work with faculty: Is it hall duty or hall opportunity? Are grades compensation or communication? What's a bottleneck to the building's new initiative? Do we need a new way of referring to core and non-core subjects?

Do activities with no associated extrinsic rewards.

In *Drive*, Daniel Pink reminds us, "Rewards, by their very nature, narrow our focus." (p. 44) If teachers are only creative in the classroom because it might mean more pay, they probably won't be very imaginative.

Creativity happens more often because people are curious, not because it satisfies financial incentives. Yes, we do some things in order to increase our salary step or receive a bonus, but creativity is usually a casualty of such approaches.

Invite teachers to write articles and blogs on topics they enjoy, not just on topics that pay, and share with faculty your own efforts in this area. As they have time and interest, encourage them to participate in training and teach a class about which they are curious—ELL, gifted, computer programming, library/media services, learning disabilities, drama—and they'll find new creative selves. Over the years in my own classroom, I have requested students with learning disabilities and/or Asperger's syndrome to be placed in my classes, if possible, so I can learn more about them and develop effective responses to their needs, not because I thought it would look good on my resume. As strange as it sounds, removing the pressures of extrinsic rewards boosted personal creativity in the classroom.

No lipstick on the mirror

Remember the urban legend about the problem of 8th grade girls practicing their kisses on the washroom mirror? The principal assembled the suspect pucker practitioners in the washroom and asked the custodian to demonstrate for the girls how he cleans the mirrors each evening. The custodian then dipped the toilet brush into the toilet bowl water and used it to scrape the lipstick from the mirror. 'Problem solved: No lipstick appeared on the mirror again. Wouldn't it be nice to be able to generate such clever responses to daily issues in the school building?

We can do this, but creative muscles atrophy without use. We can't leave creativity to only when we have time; life happens quickly, and learning is too complex in today's schools. We need to build teachers' capacity to generate creative responses on the fly. It takes practice and humility, however. Actors are often told that they will never make it if they are unwilling to look ridiculous, and Margaret Wheatley is correct in her educators' corollary: We can't be creative unless we're willing to be confused. Rest assured, being unsure can lead to positive learning states in both teachers and their students.

And Mrs. Weaver's issue with the student who didn't do his homework and lacked parent support? She spent time thinking creatively. It took at least four different strategies plus two new ones learned by consulting with friends on-line, but the student's doing homework steadily now, and it's showing in his achievements. Mrs. Weaver has moved to another concern: an 8th grader confided in two friends that she thinks she's a lesbian, but one of those friends posted it on Facebook, and the 8th grader is very upset. She wants to transfer to another school as a result, and her classmates aren't sure how to respond to her or the friend who posted the secret. With sensitivity, deep knowledge, commitment, and creativity, Mrs. Weaver helps these students navigate these occasionally turbulent waters. Thankfully, she has the inclination and capacity to do so.

Endnotes

This is a more extended version of a column written originally for the Association for Middle Level Education's Middle Ground *magazine. This version published by the National Association for Secondary School Principals in* Middle Level Leader *in May 2012 has more examples and strategies and is written from the perspective of the principal or teacher leader who is helping teachers develop their creative selves. You can access the article at*

http://www.nassp.org/tabid/3788/default.aspx?topic=Building_Capacity_for_Creative_Thinking

Making the Most of Professional Development

Today's classrooms are more diverse and teacher accountability is on the rise, so professional development is more important than ever. We must make every moment count.

Long-Term or short-term?

Although embedded, long-term professional development experiences are the ideal, they are not always possible. They can be expensive and difficult to maintain throughout multiple years—especially if the district locks into one or two presenters and must work around their schedules.

A single-day activity, conference, or Skype session can have tremendous impact on teachers and student achievement—especially if it includes pre-session and follow-up activities as well as a support network. Examples include:

- Preliminary study and discussion of the identified topic and the presenter's materials.
- An initial presentation followed by classroom observation and analysis.
- Book studies and discussion groups.
- Professional learning communities or teacher action research groups.
- E-mail correspondence with the presenter.
- Follow-up Listserve conversations with the presenter and participants.
- An initial presentation followed by the presenter's return to the school a month or year later to answer questions.

If the professional development experience is sustained, everyone talks about it rather than letting it collect dust on a shelf.

The right presenter

When choosing the appropriate professional development opportunity, look for presenters who've been on the front lines. They don't have to be currently practicing teachers, but their materials and methods must be grounded in today's reality. This is not to say that consultants who've never worked in a classroom have little to offer us; many of them are excellent presenters who can transform teaching practice. Just make sure the presenters understand how their strategies translate in real classrooms. We want to walk away with big ideas, specific practices, and inspiration for great things in teaching.

Investigate to ensure the presenters practice what they preach. Be wary of presenters who promote active learning in the classroom yet lecture for two hours. Be suspicious of presenters who teach us how to write yet do not write themselves. Of course, we look for seminars that include time to work in small groups, to reflect on provocative ideas, and to question and apply ideas. These are all characteristics of excellent training experiences.

However, "sit and get" experiences are valuable. I know this will make some of you cringe, but give it some thought before you judge it too harshly. If I am attending a 75-minute workshop, I want to spend the majority of that limited time learning directly from the speaker, not brainstorming ideas with tablemates or participating in a 30-minute role-play experience that does not advance my understanding of the topic. Every moment discussing applications with a partner is one less moment of content from the speaker, and I came for that content. My fellow participants and I can process the content later. "Sit and get" experiences resonate—especially if participants' minds have been primed by reading the speaker's materials in advance. At least 80% of the training experience should be in direct interaction with the presenters and their knowledge.

Participant savvy

To be professional, honor the presenter and get more out of the workshop by sitting in the front half of the room. Yes, even if your department buddies sit in the back row, be the grownup and sit near the front.

Consider how you record your thinking during the workshop or seminar. "Tweeting" observations and reflections in real time during the presentation is a great way to encapsulate "silver bullet" ideas you want to carry forward. It also keeps you attentive to the workshop. As a presenter, I don't consider participants posting reflections online during my workshops disrespectful. When participants post their reflections on Twitter, Facebook, or a blog in real time, they carry more of the content with them when they leave. (This might be something to consider when working with students in our classrooms.)

If you realize the workshop is not what you thought it was and there's a concurrent workshop that might better meet your needs, quietly pack your things and leave. Do it without guilt. Good presenters know how valuable your time is and that miscommunication sometimes happens. They won't take offense. You're doing more for your students by attending the other session than by sitting in a workshop you don't need. If you can, however, try to ascertain the appropriateness of the workshop in its first few minutes, not halfway through.

After the experience

Smart administrators ask those who attend conferences and seminars to do some form of turnaround training of the content for the rest of the faculty. This not only enables everyone to benefit from the conference, it helps hold conference attendees accountable. Processing the content so you can present it to others clarifies your own thinking as well. It's win-win.

Letter to presenter. If you get a chance, send a short letter to the presenter a few months after the session describing how you are implementing or struggling with the ideas. This helps you maintain commitment to the new ideas, and it can clear up misunderstandings or muddled thinking. It's also helpful to plan your next steps in pursuit of these new ideas. With whom will you partner on these new ideas and when will you converse about them? What structures and further PD would help you fully explore and implement the new ideas?

Listserve. Is there an associated Listserve you can join? The online community has exploded in the past 10 years. Every education association, including AMLE, has online discussion groups, Listserves, Moodles, wikis, and more that provide useful information and allow us to process that information meaningfully. And it's available 24-7. Every specialty area—choir directors, athletic directors, technology teachers, foreign language teachers, speech and language specialists, art teachers, and more—has an online community. Participation in these communities is one of the best things we do for ourselves professionally.

Book Study. What about book studies? Identify a study facilitator or rotate leadership among the department or grade level. If the faculty is not doing a formal book study, start one of your own. If it's awkward to meet at school, meet at a local coffee place or in someone's home. Local businesses and parent-teacher groups provide money for multiple copies of professional books for teachers. Some book publishers and stores offer bulk discounts if the books are for local teacher professional development.

Make it happen

Given the dynamic changes in course content and in our knowledge of how the mind works, teachers are obsolete if they don't evolve professionally. In truth, it's ongoing professional development that leads to improved student achievement. Waiting for the administration or school district to do our professional development isn't even treading water. We have to take our professional development into our own hands. As self-renewing professional educators, we make PD happen every day. As a result, our teaching improves and our students and communities are well-served.

Conference Etiquette

While attending national and regional education conferences, some teachers skip concurrent and keynote sessions so they can shop, catch a harbor cruise, or go out to dinner with friends. This is inappropriate and disrespectful to the folks who put the conference together.

If you hit "workshop overload" and need to do something different for a session, replace a session with something that's related. Visit the exhibitors and get ideas for the classroom; have coffee with a colleague and discuss ideas; go for a walk outdoors to clear your mind; or post your responses to conference content online or in a professional reflection journal.

Behave appropriately during the workshops themselves. For example, if it looks like the session is going to finish early, don't roll your eyes and grumble when someone asks a question that requires several more minutes of discussion. We teach civility and patience to tomorrow's leaders; we can extend both to our colleagues.

Don't monopolize the speaker's time with more than one or two questions. Try to keep questions to ones that most folks would find merit in asking. Save questions about specific situations in your own practice for conversations after the workshop.

Don't bring in strong smelling food and food wrapped in plastic that makes loud noises when unwrapped. Turn off all cell phones and pagers. If you've brought a stack of papers to grade or a newspaper to read, put them away when the presenter begins.

During the presentations, do not have conversations in the back of the room.

When something is being distributed down the rows, take only one.

Follow the presenter's lead. If she asks you to quietly reflect on something, do it. If she invites volunteers to come forward to help her demonstrate something, get out of your chair and walk forward. Active participation will help you remember the content longer.

The Power of Twitter

To be honest, I'm a relatively late convert to the usefulness of Twitter. Initially, I thought it was major "time suckage" I could not afford. Today, I marvel at the insight and practicality gained through participation in the "Twitterverse," and I wonder how much goes unachieved in classrooms because teachers don't use Twitter's easily accessible resources. Let's learn the basics and make the case for classroom teachers (and their principals) to incorporate Twitter into their professional lives.

Getting started

Twitter is free and easy to use—it took me fewer than 30 seconds to be up and running.

At www.twitter.com, type in your name, e-mail, and a password. That's it. You can enhance your account by uploading a picture or logo, and posting a short descriptor of yourself that will display any time someone wants to find out more about you or verify you are the Amy Smith they are looking for. You can be as humorous or as straightforward as you want to be in these descriptors. You can include professional certifications, interests, favorite quotes—anything you want others to know about you. This information also helps people decide whether they want to follow your posted comments. Here's an example of a profile:

> "Blogger and Nationally Board Certified middle school science teacher at Niels DeGrasse Tyson Middle School, Herndon, VA. Father, husband, 'Trekker,' member of Middletalk Listserve, AMLE, and deft guacamole connoisseur"

Make your profile your own!

Whom to follow

Many of your favorite authors, education leaders, and celebrities are on Twitter. Type anyone's name in the search box and see. If the searched name comes up, click on it, and it will take you to the brief Twitter profile. If this is the person you are seeking, click on the "Follow" box, and you will now receive postings from them. And just as cool: You can read through all of their earlier postings, too. This is a gold mine of great information from our education thinkers and shakers!

Through Twitter, you can feel a connection to people in a wide variety of fields. Many influential educators and organizations post commentary daily or weekly, and their insights inform our own corners of the world as they invite personal contributions to the larger profession. Reading the short 140-character comments is helpful enough, but entering into conversation with these people takes it to a whole new level. We progress thoughtfully in ways we never imagined we would. Figure 1 offers a sampling of the inspiring, education-focused thinkers and doers on Twitter that are worth following. Figure 2 suggests organizations worth following.

So why participate?

Because we are allowed 140 characters for each message, spaces included, we must be focused and get to the point right away. To be that efficient, we try to get clever in our wording and abbreviations; we clarify and condense what we're really thinking. Creativity loves constraint!

Twitter is very organic. We can retweet (pass along) any message we receive to all our followers, and in turn, they retweet what they find interesting or valuable to their followers. Quickly, teachers and leaders from around the world are aware of our inquiries and insights, and they can build on them and send helpful responses.

We can even place a hashtag (#) in our messages with a word or few words indicating the topic, and now everyone can use the hashtag to follow the string of conversation among all the Tweeters. The point-counterpoint chain of thought in these conversations is invaluable. Rodd Lucier's @Educhat is the place to start exploring education conversations on Twitter.

We get "push back" on our ideas, too, as Tweeters respond to comments, present conflicting research, pose "What if…?" questions, and connect us to colleagues with alternative viewpoints. It's done constructively, and for many, it's cultivated professional relationships outside Twitter.

Attachments. With the click of a button, we can attach links to useful articles, inspired projects, photos, websites, videos, and anything else of common interest that the 140-characters limitation prohibits. When we hear or see good ideas in education while teaching, talking in the teacher's lounge, surfing the web, or reading professional material, we can easily pass these more in-depth descriptions and graphics to others. As a result, we are more likely to share ideas in the spur of the moment. Teachers become more creative and resourceful as their toolkits grow.

This immediacy is dramatic. In a given minute on Twitter, educators post the links to live streaming video of Venus passing across the Sun, a famous author's keynote address, an orchestra's riveting performance of Edvard Grieg's work, a tour guide's explanation of sculpture in Florence, Italy, a surprise discovery under ice in the Antarctic, or the final moments of World Cup soccer.

Perspective. When we witness the actions and thoughts of education colleagues across the nation and around the world, we see the larger picture of what we do, and we realize we are not alone. Sometimes our egos get in the way of good teaching, and we think we're teaching in the most effective manner possible. Then someone opens our minds to other possibilities, and we get humble and inspired at the same time. Teachers who interact with the larger profession have healthier responses to new program initiatives. With the perspective of how others are handling the same issues in their communities, we find camaraderie and solutions.

Twitter is a powerful blowtorch against the clanging walls of echo chambers we have so carefully built around ourselves. As we begin this new school year, let's take a moment—a lot of them—to connect with one another and become something more than we can achieve alone. It's natural for modern students; it can be the same for their teachers.

Figure 1

Educators and Thinkers on Twitter

- Tom Whitby–Blogger, technology guru, conduit, professor of education *(@tomwhitby)*
- John Norton–The ultimate connector and thinker *(@middleweb)*
- Todd Whitaker–Education leader, author, motivator *(@ToddWhitaker)*
- Valerie Strauss–Provocative and helpful education writer for The Washington Post *(@valeriestrauss)*
- Diane Ravitch–Queen of education reform, particularly when it comes to high stakes testing *(@DianeRavitch)*
- Larry Ferlazzo–Author, teacher, and among the most prolific and useful Twitterers for educators on the Internet–really! *(@Larryferlazzo)*
- Stephen Krashen–Author, reformer, researcher, literacy expert *(@skrashen)*
- Carol Jago–Prolific and thoughtful writer, English teacher *(@CarolJago)*
- Donalyn Miller–Blogger and the book whisperer *(@donalynbooks)*
- Brenda Dyck–Teacher instructor, technology integrator, writer *(@bdyck)*
- Will Richardson–Author, blogger regarding social web tools effect on learning *(@willrich45)*
- Paul Thomas–Provocative thinker, education professor *(@plthomasEdD)*
- Pasi Sahlberg–Author, education change activist *(@pasi_sahlberg)*
- Jill Spencer–Author, leader, consultant *(@JillSpencer)*
- Chris Toy–Author, leader, consultant *(@cmtoy)*

- Patti Kinney–NASSP Middle Level Director, author *(@kinney_nassp)*
- Steven W. Anderson–blogger, Edublogs Twitterer of the Year, #Edchat co-creator *(@web20classroom)*
- Alan November–Author on technology *(@globalearner)*
- Daniel Pink–Author, speaker *(@DanielPink)*
- Andrew Rotherham–Writer of School of Thought for TIME, blogger, analyst *(@arotherham)*
- Steven Johnson–Author of Where Good Ideas Come From, among others *(@stevenbjohnson)*
- Deborah Meier–Writer, activist *(@DebMeier)*
- Bill Ferriter–Teacher, PLCs, technology integration *(@plugusin)*
- Jen Robinson–One of the most helpful bloggers about children's books, including young adult, you'll ever find *(@JensBookPage)*
- Sir Ken Robinson–Author, creativity focused, thinker, (TED Talks speaker) *(@SirKenRobinson)*
- Alfie Kohn–Author, speaker *(@alfiekohn)*
- Teri Lesesne–It doesn't get better than Teri for young adult literature, *(@ProfessorNana)*

Figure 2

A Few Organizations That Are Worth Following

- Association for Middle Level Education *(@AMLEnews)*
- iCivics *(@icivics)*
- The National Writing Project *(@writingproject)*
- National Association for Secondary School Principals *(@NASSP)*
- National Board for Professional Teaching Standards *(@NBPTS)*
- Politics K-12 *(@PoliticsK12)*
- Alberta Assessment *(@AACinfo)*
- Teaching Channel *(@TeachingChannel)*
- TEDTalks Updates *(@tedtalks)*

Teacher Health

I really should write a maintenance request to fix the ceiling tiles and weather stripping in my classroom. They've been broken and ugly for months. The forms are in the front office. Oh yeah, I remind myself, go talk to Ray about that great mock trial thing he does. He's not teaching right now, he might be available. Nah, he's on the other side of the school. Maybe tomorrow. I put down the essay I was going to grade and grab another half-donut, then lean back and stare blankly out the window at the returning spring. Yeah, tomorrow will be good to do all that.

I can give the students those last six grammar worksheets and spend some time grading. I'm too tired to come up with something creative this week. Oh jeez, don't forget about those three parents who've been calling, and those two students' recommendations you promised to write. I wonder if the clinic has an empty bed for napping. Hey, maybe there won't be any students staying after school today for extra help, and I can go home early to take a nap. It doesn't matter, I realize: there's an in-service today.

If we're not careful, we can become cynical blobs. Blobs that get stuck in a rut with little motivation to be anything else. Our Physical Education Department Chair at Rachel Carson Middle School, Paul Helstrom, quotes Newton's Law: "A body at rest tends to stay at rest. A body in motion tends to stay in motion. Good health is simple physics." So, if I could overcome physics, then I'd be a heck of a teacher. My lack of energy, therefore, is merely accepting the laws of physics, I rationalize. Yeah, right. I've sunk to a new comfort zone. And quality teaching has been left behind.

A teacher's health directly affects the learning of his or her students. It's directly proportional—the better the health of the teacher, the better the instruction and the better the learning. I believe teachers and administrators who want to improve student achievement would be wise to improve the emotional and physical health of their faculties.

How many times do we put off talking to a colleague about a student or a lesson plan because it's just too far to walk, especially at the end of our day? How many times do we wait until we get a critical mass of paperwork before we walk the long road to the front office? Look at the times we sit in a chair to teach rather than stand, thereby forfeiting proximity to students that would keep them attentive and would enable us to monitor their learning. Look at our tired bulletin boards that overstay their welcome for weeks because we just don't have the energy to do anything about them. And one of the worst ones for me as an English teacher: How many ways can I put off grading that stack of 148 compare/contrast essays? Yeah, that stack, the pile next to the other five piles of things to grade.

We could... If we were in good mental and physical health, I think we could: create those creative and high-energy lessons on factorization, the progressive era, tertiary colors, or biomes. We'd return those phone calls, chase down and schedule guest speakers, prepare manipulative materials, create interactive and instructional classroom displays, and we'd even study the latest in our subject areas and update our instructional practices. We wouldn't find in-services as invasive or poor uses of time. We'd be more willing to collaborate with others because we wouldn't be in survival mode trying to protect what little time and energy we have. We wouldn't be threatened by administrative edicts; we'd make constructive responses to those with which we disagree. Teacher lounge cynicism that often creeps into conversations would be replaced by teachers planning overnight subject celebrations (How about a "Science-apalooza"?) In short, we would be the kind of teachers we want our own middle school children to have.

A growing concern

It's hard not to notice the deteriorating health of some teachers. In some places where I do presentations, schools are in danger of reconstitution due to low student performance. In these and other schools that are experiencing low student achievement, about half the folks sitting in front of me are significantly overweight, exhausted, and/or bitter. To be honest, given some of the dire conditions in which they teach, I'd probably have physical or mental issues, too. I can't help but think that my presentation on differentiated instruction will make no impact because the teachers just don't have the energy to do things differently. If their classrooms are teacher-centered because they physically can't have it any other way, students must come to them. Whatever wonderful and highly effective lessons they might like to employ may be denied the light of day because of the teachers' poor health.

Sadly, I also see this with a number of teachers in schools that don't have the angst of reconstitution worries or severely challenging students. I see it even in myself sometimes. Though I'm not in horrible shape, I'm not in good shape either. I procrastinate and whine with the best of them.

Teacher health should be a growing concern for us, especially as more and more pressures are added to teacher's lives in forms of larger class sizes, standards accountability, increasing curriculum, and the increasing role of teachers in administration, such as with site-based management. A second, yet just as significant, factor is the example that we set for our students who are most impressionable concerning good health values. We should be demonstrating to them that proper exercise, healthy eating habits, and constructive management of stress do not end when we are out of school; they are a lifestyle.

Achieving teacher wellness

"A teacher's overall wellness is achievable," says Helstrom. Movement is vital. For example, "The best thing for most headaches," he says, "is a brisk walk. He reminds folks that, while it's nice to park in the farthest spot in the parking lot and walk in from there, it's not exercise.

Exercise. "Exercise requires us to do something planned for just that—exercise. To be effective, it needs to be five days a week, each session 30 minutes in duration." With such minimal efforts, says Helstrom, teachers will feel better about themselves and they'll regain focus. "Good exercise and diet makes people optimists. Endorphins are released and suddenly everything's not as bad as we thought. We see the possibilities in things."

Besides sharpening our minds, good exercise and diet dramatically cut teacher absenteeism, something every middle school principal should consider in these substitute-short days. In addition, Helstrom says there's research demonstrating that exercisers actually budget time better. "They build routines and habits. It becomes a ritual. They make better use of their time. "

Helstrom has several ideas for getting folks out of non-exercise ruts. The first hurdle is motivation. Helstrom advises teachers to get support in the form of walking clubs and lifting partners. The expectations of partners create a positive peer pressure to keep us going.

Set small goals. Being consistent is another step to success. It's hard to do that, he says, when we try to rush the changes. His advice: set small goals: "Try walking four days a week for twenty minutes, then the next week choose one day and walk for thirty minutes. Ninety percent of it is taking the first step."

Charting. Helstrom advises teachers to chart everything they put in their mouths. It's an objective way to analyze diet. Once done, he tells us to make small changes. "Eliminate one soda per day. Increase fruits by one fruit serving a day." Moderation is the key, he says. My wife has learned this, and I'm always jealous the day after we go out to a restaurant. She cuts her meals in half then takes them home to enjoy for the next day's lunch.

We can also chart exercises—how far, how long in duration, how much we did—not pounds. "I know people who are a little heavy but are in great shape, and I know people who are very slender and are in terrible shape. It's not the weight, it's the health that's important," says Helstrom. He adds that we need to have a variety of exercises in order to be successful. "It's easy to get bored or make excuses because of weather or location. Have back-up plans."

To Paul's ideas, I add others:

Water. Switch to water. Reduce the number of soda machines. I used to think that I could get through my pile of papers to grade as long as I had diet Coke to drink. It was the caffeine that would help, I reasoned. Wrong. Caffeine dries you out. While it might provide an initial stimulus, it leaves you with tired thinking in the long run. When I switched to drinking bottled water while grading papers, I stopped getting so sleepy. I made it through more papers in the same amount of time.

I once spoke with several Trailways bus drivers about how they stay awake on those cross-country trips. Every one of them said they drank lots of water and ate a lot of fruit to keep alert. The same is true for our classroom tasks. Besides, the extra water is good for you, especially in our often poorly ventilated classrooms.

Faculty meeting fare. At faculty meetings, stop the flow of cookies, cake, pastries, and chocolate muffins. Sure, some of these things every once in a while are fine for you. The problem is that they seem to be the rule, not the exception. If we want our faculty to be attentive in faculty meetings, then we need to do everything we can to make sure people are not falling asleep, especially at the end of the day when the adrenalin of the day is ebbing. Sugary items may put some folks into dreamland. How about providing only healthy munchies instead? Put out trays of crackers and cheese, vegetable sticks, salsa, pieces of fruit, whole grain breads, unbuttered popcorn, sunflower seeds, leafy salads, and bottles of water.

People might just remember everything that's said in the meeting. If it's going to be an hour or more, how about stretches every thirty minutes? It'll seem silly at first, then people will see how awake they are even at the end of the meeting and marvel why they hadn't done movement exercises before.

Use school facilities. As part of faculty orientations each year, have the PE department take the faculty through a tour of the workout facilities at the school, including where staff would be able to shower and change clothes out of sight of the students. Also include how to work the weight lifting machines, whom to contact for advice, and some basic stretching exercises before and after workouts. They might even want to publish a map of local walking and running routes. Emphasize that exercise doesn't have to come at the end of the day, either. A good workout in the middle of the day during a planning period may be a better use of time than sitting around answering e-mail or sleepily grading papers. The workout results in more oxygen getting to the brain, which increases thinking ability and provides energy to finish the day strong. If we have short class periods, we can still fit in thirty minutes of exercise and fifteen minutes of a cool down and shower.

Stress management. Do repeated in-service training for staff on stress management, an important component to most wellness programs, and your insurance carrier might have qualified professionals who will provide coaching and strategies. Coping with the stresses of the job is where we spend a lot of our energy. This training can come as five-minute mini- presentations during faculty meetings, in a faculty intranet folder on stress, printed suggestions in teacher mailboxes, or something more formal. Topics might include dealing with paperwork, massage, meditation, use of music in learning and working, humor, yoga, exercise, dealing with conflict, decision making, time management, and setting priorities.

Incentives. I've been asked on several occasions about teacher incentives for various programs. On each occasion I've mentioned increased salary and time. Teacher salaries are a topic for another column. Time, however, is worth mentioning here. It's one of the most highly valued things an administration can bestow, and it promotes good health. Administrators can offer faculty the gift of time in creative ways. With advanced notice, administrators can offer teachers an extra period off during the school day. This might mean an administrator covers a class, a substitute teacher might be redirected during free periods during the day (or hired for a day just to offer teachers that need that extra period off). These periods can be spent by the teacher reading, exercising, taking a nap (a practice I highly recommend), enjoying an extended lunch period, listening to music, writing letters, or working on their first book. The point is that teachers use it for something regenerative without worry about their students.

Administrators can also give the gift of time by not spending time making general announcements at faculty meetings that could be put in writing. Faculty meetings should be places where we do things we can only do when we are together. If administrators are concerned with folks really reading the material, they can distribute the list of announcements at the meeting, give time for reading, then ask if there are any concerns or questions. If they want to present a new idea to the staff, they can send out some advance reading material ahead of time. We need to get right to the discussions or substantive presentations of the meeting, not bogged down in the details of the testing schedule slated for three months from now. Imagine half-hour faculty meetings, followed or preceded by another presentation from a guest speaker on a cutting edge topic. That's a good use of time. Faculty meetings are vital in successful middle schools. We should get together and establish ourselves as an informed and collegial group on a regular basis. We just need to make sure we're focused on things for which we are truly called together.

Clubs. Start those indoor or outdoor walking clubs for staff. We have them at our school. Every day around 4:00, I see folks from our administration and clerical staff clothed in workout suits laying tracks around the school. They've figured out what constitutes a mile, and they walk briskly through the course while conversing with one another about anything that comes to mind. These folks set goals for miles walked and pounds lost. It's inspiring.

If you have tennis courts nearby, create a tennis roster. List everyone's name, phone number and level of play for those that want to be on the list. When folks get a free afternoon, they can consult the list and set up a match with someone from their same skill level. You can do the same thing with golf, basketball, bowling, running, and swimming. How about a faculty swimming night at the local recreation center?

Fun runs. At Frost Valley YMCA in the Catskill Mountains of New York state, we used to hold a Fun Run every camp session. In it, everyone from campers to staff totaling over 700 people used to move around a specified track in whatever manner they wished—run, walk, waddle, skate, hop, wheel (as in wheelchairs), and so on. We'd play music with a good beat and make it a fun time. As people finished, we had other activities set up such as Frisbee throws, pounding nails into logs, rolling inner tubes, listening to storytellers, crazy exercises and relays, and wild games. There were also nutritious snacks and drinks as well as places just to chill out and sit under a tree. Some folks played guitars in the corner of a field and some folks painted pictures. We were not only physically active, but mentally active as well. The fun runs affirmed that which we were teaching the kids: being together and doing something physically and mentally active is fun and healthy. The fact that we did it regularly sent a clear message that wellness was important.

Lifestyle change. Okay, it's time to get off my duff and stop being such a hypocrite. I'm not going to wait until I have a heart attack to make a lifestyle change. I can exercise while watching television, I can stretch between classes, and I can stock my school refrigerator with water. I can prepare healthy snacks for the week during the preceding weekend. I can get my students to stand up and do a crazy exercise halfway through each class. I can schedule personal reading time for me, and I can sign up for those classes at the local museum that I have been coveting. I can learn how to give a good massage to my wife, I can try a few low-calories recipes, and I don't have to finish every meal with something sweet. And through all of this, I can watch my students learn more because I have the energy and inclination to not just survive the day, but to excel at what I do. Expending energy on exercising and eating right actually gives me more energy. It's not a sacrifice. It's building a future—one for me in my later years, and one for my students right now as they get the foundations for healthy adulthood. 'Need to take something to the front office? Give it to me. I'll swing by there on my way to the gym. Here, have an apple.

The Courage It Takes

There's a great story about General Westmoreland that reminds us what can happen if we are brave with each other. It may or may not be an urban legend, but the general was reviewing a line of paratroopers and spoke to three of them.

"Son," he said to the first one, "Do you like to jump out of airplanes?"

The paratrooper grinned before responding enthusiastically, "Yes, sir! It's an adrenaline rush, sir!"

The general nodded approval and moved to the next soldier. "Son, do you also like to jump out of airplanes?" he asked.

"Yes, sir," the soldier said. "I've dreamed of doing it all my life, sir. If you get the opportunity, you should try it sometime. It's like nothing else in this world!" The general smiled and moved to the final soldier. "And how about you, son?" he asked. "Do you like to jump out of airplanes?"

The soldier saluted and responded so quickly and confidently that it took the general by surprise. "No, sir!" The general paused, then stepped closer to the soldier and looked him in the eye. "Then why are you a member of this paratrooper division?" he asked.

Again, the soldier didn't hesitate. "Because I like to hang with guys who do like to jump out of airplanes, sir!"

Courage is contagious. When those around us demonstrate courage, it's easier for the rest of us to be brave. And if we are brave together, imagine what we can accomplish!

I first recognized the potential of this possibility when I was talking with a student of mine who was a member of a violent gang. We were talking about the increasing number of gangs in our community. During the conversation, he turned to me and said, "You know, Mr. W., gangs are only as strong as the town lets them be."

I was stunned. He was correct, but I had never considered the idea. Instead, I had been wallowing in troubled desperation over the growing violence among students. His comment spurred months of personal reflection, however. I wondered: What's not working for these children who join gangs, and what leads them down such a horrific road? In what kind of community do I want to raise my own children, and what am I going to do to create and maintain it?

I attended several in-service trainings and conferences on gangs and youth violence and found kindred spirits in the participants. With each conversation with these similarly-minded people, dealing with the issues that drive students to gang affiliation, solutions on how to dissolve gangs in our town, and returning neighborhoods to healthy places to raise children seemed more and more possible. Today, things have improved, but we are not finished, and there's no room to waver in our diligence.

Deciding what's important

The mindset needed to take on gangs and other issues in our schools is expressed compellingly by rock band manager James Hollingworth, aka Ambrose Redmoon, a paraplegic: "Courage is not the absence of fear, but the belief that something else is more important than that fear." Reflecting on our everyday classroom practices with students and interactions with colleagues, what might we consider so important that it trumps our fears of rejection, embarrassment, breaking rules (hidden or not), or ruffling others' feathers?

- How about choosing a different novel if the one mandated by the English department isn't working with a particular student?

- How about risking embarrassment by confronting (in a constructive manner) a colleague who is doing something with students that takes a lot of class time and a lot of school resources but usually results in little or no student learning?

- How about suggesting the school rededicate itself to teacher-advisory programs, including offering training for teachers and readjusting the master schedule to provide opportunities to conduct the advisories, even if a faction of faculty members doesn't support it?

- How about being a seasoned teacher who admits to colleagues that he doesn't know how to teach a particular student and would like some assistance?

- How about giving up the classroom we've had for years and taking the roving, classroom-teacher-with-a-cart position so that a new teacher can have your room and one less thing to worry about during her first years in the profession?

No one said courage was easy. Yet colleagues and mentors throughout our careers have bravely taken such risks. The least we can do, then, is dedicate ourselves to courageous acts of teaching and collegiality, even when we don't feel like we're up to the task.

Let's admit to students that we aren't really sure what the author meant symbolically, what really happened during a particular moment in history, whether or not a politician is misleading us, what an object is made of, or if our teaching strategy is the best way to teach.

Let's get out of our students' way and not limit them to our imagination. If we're doing it right, every subsequent generation will be superior to the current one. If students only learned what we teachers know, society would grind to a halt. The goal is always that students will write a better paragraph, conduct a scientific experiment more wisely, compose more efficient computer code, and sing more beautifully than we can. Are we committed enough to let them?

Let's ask students questions to which we don't already know the answer.

Let's circle in our lesson plans the places we see our expertise in the nature of young adolescents expressed, and if we don't see it there, let's redesign those lessons so we can.

Let's prove to students every day that they have roles in our classrooms and that they make good company.

Let's decide, as author and educator Annette Breaux suggests, that in some situations with students and colleagues, it's better to be kind than to be right. We can be right tomorrow.

Let's give more than mere lip service to the idea that what is fair isn't always equal, even if pushing for fairness leads to unpopular decisions.

Let's teach in ways students best learn, not in the ways we best learn.

Let's invite parents to the classroom to observe us and give us feedback.

Let's make sure students ask at least one more question each day than we do. Whoever asks the most questions does the most learning.

When disciplining students, let's follow discipline expert Jim Fay's advice and ask short questions like, "What did you do?" "How did that work for you?" and, "How will you rebuild our trust in you?" instead of providing long admonishments. Let's not suggest solutions for discipline problems to students, but instead guide them through questioning to their own discoveries. Students should work harder than we do when it comes to their discipline.

Let's teach in whatever way we would teach if students weren't required to come to school and we had to persuade them every day that our subjects are worth their personal investment.

Let's remain open to correction from others.

Let's not automatically turn to the next page in the textbook because it's the next page of the textbook, but because that page best serves the students we are teaching. And if the next page isn't as good as the one 57 pages later, let's go to the one 57 pages away without guilt.

Let's prove every day that academic struggle is virtuous—a compelling road to future success—not weakness, and that failure can teach us in ways consistent success cannot. In many situations, therefore, failure is not only an option, it's preferred. We can't chase it away or sweep it under the rug.

Let's videotape ourselves and ask a group of colleagues to sit with us as we watch it and analyze our teaching against standards of excellence.

Let's contribute to already-in-progress conversations on our favorite online Listserves without worrying about repeating what others have said or asking dumb questions—we've all been there, and those of us who read your postings would like the chance to extend the forgiveness we've received from others.

Let's ask the larger questions of teaching every year: What do we know about young adolescent minds that we didn't know 10 years ago and how is that knowledge used in our work with today's students? How are our current structures limiting us? Whose voices are unheard in our discussions? What is the purpose of schools? What should we be teaching? Are we teaching in ways that students learn? Are we closing the gap between knowing what to do and actually doing it?

These and other acts of courage provide the momentum about which Robert F. Kennedy spoke years ago:

Each time a person stands up for an ideal, or acts to improve the lot of others, or strikes out against injustice, he sends forth a tiny ripple of hope, and crossing each other from a million different centers of energy and daring, these ripples build a current that can sweep down the mightiest walls of oppression and resistance.

Acts of courage

Courage in schools can't be left to chance. If we are not at a point in our careers where we can be courageous, let's do whatever we can to help others be courageous. Our current and future students depend on at least some of us swapping fear for potential right now.

Consider doing a common, yet wonderful staff development activity: Write your personal list of what you would do if you were truly brave. As you record your thoughts, remember that you don't have to do the tasks alone, and in fact, you'll be more successful by sharing the journey, if for nothing else than bravery's contagious nature.

Here is one act of courage on my part—to put forth for educators' scrutiny, my own personal list of what I would do if I were brave. It's dangerous for me to share this list because you may disagree with me, judge me, or refuse to read anything else I write. If you respond to me about any of these items, it may force me to rethink that idea, and change can be scary.

Nevertheless, I shall not take the timid route when so much is at stake. After reading the list, I hope you'll create your own list to rally your energy in the new school year. Here are my top 20 brave acts to take:

1. Adjust the school's master schedule to support best practices, not sacrifice best practices to support the master schedule.

2. Make it easier to let ineffective and toxic teachers and principals go. Some folks have misidentified their strengths or misjudged the date of their retirement.

3. Ask principals who demand that next week's lesson plans from all teachers be submitted for review each Friday to present their own plans for next week for teachers' review each Friday. Before I'm misquoted, however, know that I fully support struggling teachers submitting their plans for review, professional learning communities exchanging plans for collegial review and coaching, and proven veterans submitting plans at least once a year, so the principal knows what's going on in his or her school.

4. Help change teacher evaluation systems so that those principals with little or no teaching experience in a teacher's subject or grade level do not do the majority of teacher evaluations for that teacher. To critique and evaluate teachers, we must be up-to-date on the subject being taught.

5. Choose to teach the students no one else wants. They are the ones who bring out our true teaching colors, who most inspire our creativity and efforts. In our democracy we teach all students, not just those easiest to teach. It's a feather in our cap to be considered the answer to a problem.

6. Revamp most of our country's grading systems. They do not accurately portray what happens in standards-based, differentiated classrooms.

7. Open teacher practices to public scrutiny. Brave educators must have frequent opportunities to publicly defend their thinking on educational issues, formally and informally, rather than living safely behind the closed classroom door. When we must articulate what we do, it becomes real and actionable, something we constantly reference, not an abstraction.

8. Question No Child Left Behind, Race to the Top, Response-to-Intervention, the Common Core State Standards and every other federal, state, provincial, or local education mandate from any political party in power from now until we retire if we have concerns about it.

9. Mandate all students and their teachers get residential, outdoor education experiences of a week or more every year, including ropes initiatives courses. Adults and students come back changed for the better, closer to who we really are, critical thinkers, and appreciative of learning and each other.

10. Promote a law that we cannot take students out of PE or the fine or performing arts to double up on their math or reading remediation for state exams. For many of our students, it is these other subjects that give them hope and a way to succeed, and for all of us, it is these subjects that give meaning and dimension to much of what we learn in other subjects.

11. As a white Caucasian born in America with little about which to complain, I will remain attentive to racism in schools and even go around the country sensitizing colleagues and communities, both white and of color, citizens and noncitizens, about racism and how to end it.

12. Openly and compassionately discuss with colleagues controversial subjects such as intelligent design vs. evolution, recording zeroes or 50s, and tenure.

13. At local events and in the local paper, speak up about what's going on in schools.

14. Publicly question shows like Survivor, American Idol, and Weakest Link, which go against every fiber of nurturing teachers. We battle every day against sentiments like, "You are not worthy to be with us" and "We want you off the island because you are incompetent." These are the antithesis of what middle schools are about. Peter Yarrow got me going on this one.

15. Decrease the number of standards we have to teach. We cannot physically, emotionally, and intellectually teach all that we are supposed to teach in the time allotted. Removing standards isn't watering down; it's actually increasing what students learn.

16. Accept the reality and research about adolescent sleep patterns and attentiveness and start all middle and high schools at 9:30 in the morning or later.

17. Require reading be taught as a separate and intense course to all students at least up through their sophomore year of high school.

18. Work in impoverished and low-performing schools.

19. Work in affluent and high-performing schools.

20. Every year, take specific steps to battle the greatest threat to student achievement: poverty.

Ralph Waldo Emerson said, "A hero is no braver than an ordinary man, but he is braver five minutes longer." For our students' and communities' sake, let's take the opportunities in the school year ahead to dare greatly and be brave five minutes longer.

Questioning the Status Quo

Rock the boat. She won't sink. In fact, she'll sail farther. Complacency becalms and even endangers the casual sailor. Educators can't afford anything less than vigilant attention to progress, regular examinations of all we do.

In healthy schools, everything is up for discussion: Do we announce to students, "In order to get an A on this project…" or do we announce, "In order to master this concept…" before listing criteria for success? Do we think our class's bell curve grade distribution is acceptable even though it indicates that about half our students performed poorly? Does everyone's getting As and Bs indicate we are somehow lenient?

Question the common practices.

Do you really believe that:

- Homework assigned over a school holiday results in learning?

- Adolescents can learn without moving every 15 to 20 minutes?

- Students will understand and retain concepts with which they have no prior knowledge?

- School assemblies in which a small group of students receives academic awards motivate their classmates to strive for the same recognition?

- Students' social interactions are unproductive?

- Multi-page writing assignments are more rigorous than one-page assignments?

Research, cognitive theory, and years of experience indicate otherwise. Effective educators do what works, not what's easiest. If we don't use a practice we know is highly effective and we have nothing better to offer, we may not be able to look ourselves in the mirror or face our colleagues or students' parents, let alone our students with integrity. Our responses to these questions matter; our students are in these grade levels only once, or so we hope.

Shake it up

Because it's easy to get caught up in protecting our way of doing things, let's make it an annual practice to unlearn. Many of us have been teaching the same lesson for 10 years or more when we should have been teaching 10 or more different sets of students in the ways each set learns best.

We can't get too comfortable with routine and assumptions if we want to be effective. Let's not automatically turn to the next page of the basal text because it's the next page of the basal text. If we determine the page is an effective next step for our students' learning, then we turn to it, but not without consulting our professional knowledge of the topic and the needs of our current students.

Teaching is not telling, nor is it presenting, yet so many of us stop there. "Hey, I taught it," a teacher says, "It's up to my students to learn it." Nothing could be farther from the truth. Teaching requires us to not only present concepts and skills, but to enable students to make sense of them and to bring meaning to them. We don't just deliver others' truths, we present them and help students determine their validity and create truths of their own.

An ineffective teacher's curriculum presentation might look something like this: am leabc f bicn nmt v. The student sees it as incoherent. He buckles down and memorizes the information using a mnemonic device, but easily forgets the information once he's taken the test.

Here's a highly effective teacher's presentation of the same curriculum written as nonsense above, based on an analogy used by David Sousa in his 2003 book, *How the Brain Learns* from Corwin Press: amle abc fbi cnn mtv. We see that it's the same curriculum, but the effective teacher changed the pacing of its delivery so students could make sense of it and bring meaning to it. Our communities—and our students—don't need a teacher-proof curriculum in which everyone is on Chapter 9 at Week 12, they need thoughtful, strategic thinkers at the helm.

Question your practices, but also question the curriculum every year. Reflect on what is truly essential and enduring, not just nice to know. Discuss the what and how of your teaching with your colleagues. Each of us emphasizes something different in the same units we teach, so why not hear what others find salient and compare notes? Professionals don't operate in isolation, and nothing is absolute.

Remember, however, that the greatest testimony to our effectiveness as teachers is not what we teach, but what students carry forward with them in June. If we're teaching for long-term retention, then we employ best practices and teach a developmentally appropriate curriculum. We may or may not like rap music, for example, but we'll assign students to write a rap song about a math topic if we think it will help them learn the topic.

Front and center

We also have to make visible what we do in middle schools. That means we occasionally write letters and guest columns for local papers. We get in television and radio news reporters' contacts folders as a resource for education stories. We speak up at school board presentations, and we write letters to state legislators. We invite parents into the classroom every day and make them feel welcome when they are there. We want these parents to be the ones talking at sporting events and grocery stores about what's going in schools, not the parents who've never set foot in our classrooms.

We can make ourselves available to local Rotary Clubs or business gatherings for presentations on the state of affairs in the local schools. We can display students' products around the community: literary magazines, science projects, artwork, or history writing in local Jiffy Lube stores, dentist offices, the local library, the shopping mall, or Pizza Hut. How about having student essays published in local papers or student artwork and poetry on the movie screens in local theaters, so patrons can see what's happening in the schools?

Curriculum is a manifestation of an ever-changing construct—society. If the foundation is ever shifting, the building on top of it can never stop moving—a dizzying experience at the very least. It's no wonder so many middle level educators prefer to stand outside and just accept what spills to the street. It's safer, but we can't always play it safe.

Compelling disequilibrium

Everything is up for questioning, even Federal government mandates and claims by education reformers. Do we believe that testing students annually will result in improved teaching and learning? Does everything that works in teaching have scientifically based research behind it? Is it worth narrowing the curriculum to the test-specific subjects as so many states are doing? Is everything on standardized tests truly what's important for intelligent, contributing citizens?

This process of creating positive and contributing citizens is more than singular pursuit of test scores. The analysis of curriculum and practice that comes with reform efforts is healthy, but some federal mandates send us down roads we don't want to travel. Let's get a seat at the table and work toward making the best decisions. It starts with speaking up.

Educator and author Margaret Wheatley is right. A vibrant, progressing organization avoids equilibrium because a system that has achieved equilibrium is at rest. It no longer requires input or resources, and it no longer produces anything. In conflict, such as when a system or organism responds to stimulus, there is growth. The system is reaching out, pulling in, reaching out again, adapting, and progressing. The call for middle level educators, then, is not to push for consistent stability, but to facilitate compelling disequilibrium.

Education's ultimate goal is the application of compassion and courage to what is learned. Students and teachers must be free to question and decide. To teach that philosophy, we must live it. We teach what is important, not just possible. Yes, it's a race among competing ideologies, but we don't have to feel like we're losing ground because we changed direction. We get bogged down when we close our minds to new insights. We actually progress in our schooling enterprise when we solicit more than one perspective.

A worthy course

Remember the classic poem about the six blind men who touch different parts of an elephant? Each one feels only one part of the elephant such as a leg, ear, or tail and claims that his one perspective is the complete truth about what makes an elephant. Combining their perspectives would result in a truer picture. Our collective wisdom is more accurate than one person's perspective. We can redress ineffective practices only if we can cooperatively discuss those practices.

The time to question the status quo and to progress is now. What we do with students today has real effects on what happens just ten years from now. The boat isn't coming into port, though; it's going out to sea. That's what boats are meant to do. We can breathe new vitality into our schools by questioning all we do. We must not settle for the status quo. Ours is a course worth charting.

Spring Cleaning Our Teaching

Spring is a time to assess, clean, and de-clutter our houses and our classrooms. It's also a good time to do the same with our teaching.

Throughout our profession, we must periodically clean our instruction house by candidly examining what we do, identifying what works, and discarding any clutter that impedes our mission. Let's face it, there are some teaching strategies that we use just because we've always used them or because they're easy, but we don't really know whether they work. In fact, we know some of them don't work but we use them anyway because we don't have anything better. So as we weed our teaching garden this year, let's be brutal.

Some strategies don't work in our classrooms because of our teaching styles or the types of students we serve. Those are not the strategies we're talking about here. Instead, we're talking about teaching practices that are past their prime, if they were ever in their prime. These strategies do not have enough anecdotal testimony or factual research evidence to support their continued use. In fact, they actually may slow student learning if for no other reason than they waste time when another more effective strategy could be used. Using ineffective strategies often gives everyone a false sense that learning is happening when it isn't.

Cleaning house

Here are a few of those ineffective strategies it's time to remove from our teaching:

Unwavering adherence to pacing guides. School and district pacing guides are usually written by knowledgeable and experienced teachers; teachers are wise to follow their suggestions. The problem, of course, is that students come in all shapes, sizes, learning challenges, cultural backgrounds, prior knowledge, and readiness levels. There is no such thing as the perfect pacing guide, and nobody can lift something from one situation, move it over, set it down in another situation, and expect it to work exactly the same way. In fact, it's uniformed and arrogant for a school district or textbook publisher to declare that their pacing guide will meet every classroom reality within their borders.

As responsive educators, we must use our expertise to adjust curricula so students learn. If we perceive some students are learning the material more quickly than others, we don't mire them in busywork while their classmates catch up. If students are struggling, we don't press ahead to the next unit just because it's Tuesday and we're required to be on page 45.

We should consult the wisdom of the pacing guide but maintain enough autonomy to break from it occasionally and serve our students without fear of retribution. A teacher who follows a strict pacing guide regardless of its impact on students is copping out. He needs a swift and commanding reminder of his role in the classroom: to teach so that students learn, not simply to present the curriculum.

Homework that does not advance our cause. Some teachers, including me earlier in my career, assign frivolous homework assignments that really aren't related to what we're studying in the classroom. For example, some of us assign decorating history notebooks as homework. If students decorate the notebook so that it extends their knowledge or proficiency in history, that assignment might be justified, but this is rare.

Homework assignments must correspond to the standards we're teaching. I have yet to see "The student will decorate his or her history notebook in an exemplary manner" on any state's list of history standards. Assessing students on such assignments makes school more about doing the teacher's bidding than about learning. Even worse, some teachers have the audacity to lower or raise a student's history grade because he did or did not do this non-history assignment.

The purpose of homework is to allow students to practice, reinforce, and extend their learning—that's it. Every assignment should be substantive and advance our cause. This is not a knock against using artwork as a way to learn or practice content. In fact, artwork assignments that require critical thinking of content are an effective homework assignment. Recreating a scale model of Sumerian city-state out of foam board (or drawing the plans for one) complete with written explanations as to how we know today where everything was then and how the layout of the city-state expresses the culture of the period is an effective assignment.

Let's be very clear about what we're teaching and make sure our homework assignments teach that objective specifically.

Alphabet books and acrostic poems. Most alphabet books and acrostic poems are endurance projects. Students struggle to find topics that start with each letter and write or draw something about it. Very few of us learn from, let alone find meaning in writing 26 different descriptions or drawing 26 different pictures about a specific subject. It's a lot of wasted paper (or Web space), time, and energy that results in little, if any, learning.

Think of doing one right now regarding something you might be learning yourself. For example, create an acrostic poem for "Inquiry Method." Does forcing some descriptive word for each of the letters help you learn and remember the inquiry method in a substantive way? Meaningless assignments garner resentment, not real learning.

Asking students to summarize each chapter of a fiction novel. Don't kill the story for students. Imagine being asked to stop every 20 minutes while watching a movie or enjoying a favorite rock band's concert to write a cogent distillation of the salient moments so far. Better that students first capture the whole experience, then go back and focus on key moments.

Assuming all students have reviewed content because we called on a few students to answer recall questions. Some teachers over-rely on vicarious learning. They assume that because one student parroted the formula for converting Fahrenheit to Celsius, every other student knows and can apply it.

This is not an acceptable assessment or summarization experience. Every single student must respond to every single prompt. Ask them to record their responses on small dry-erase boards, half-sheets of paper, or index cards if you have to, but get something from every student. A quick "hunt and peck" by calling on a few individuals is not a sufficient sampling from which to conclude anything about the class.

Telling students to study for the test. This endeavor is simply a waste of our planet's oxygen. Most students need actionable steps to take, not generic directions to study. In middle school, they often don't know how to study.

Rereading a chapter in a textbook is not sufficient. We need to give students more assistance. Ask them to categorize information, summarize in innovative ways, find three similarities and two differences between concepts, draw a mind-map, create a graphic organizer, create notecards of facts about the topic, create a chapter outline, make a deck of Rummy cards and actually play the card game, or any other structured interaction with the test's content.

Heck, give them the test questions if they are in the constructed response format and ask them to write their best responses to the questions as practice. If it's a math test, of course, reserve the right to change the number values and decimal locations on each problem so no one can just memorize answers for the actual test.

Relying solely on talking. Most students are visual learners. Most teachers, however, use talking as their primary teaching tool. They rationalize, "I said it, so students must have learned it." Wrong.

This disconnect is a huge miscalculation. If it's important enough to teach, it's important enough to display visually. To emphasize a point, we should present it large and bold enough for everyone to see. We can do this by providing photos, drawing arrows among the sections of the graphic organizer, writing the major points on the overhead or computer screen, displaying animated or real-life videos of what we're describing, and by asking students to visualize particular moments in the process we're teaching.

Putting a lot of curriculum on a test. Here's what was tested on Friday's Spanish test: conjugation of three irregular verbs, basic vocabulary associated with sports and music, reading Spanish text and answering questions in Spanish, pronunciation of 20 words, spelling of 20 other words, and writing descriptive paragraphs in Spanish. Adam's grade: C+. How does a C+ provide specific feedback, document Adam's progress, or inform his teacher's instructional decisions regarding any one of those objectives on the test? It doesn't. It's a mish-mash.

In his 2006 book, *Classroom Assessment & Grading That Work*, Robert Marzano explains the problem of grades or scores being associated with more than one trait being tested. Adam could get a score of 3 on one topic but 13 on another topic for a total score of 16, for example, whereas Adam's friend, Wilbur, gets a 7 on the first topic and a 9 on the second topic, earning Wilber the same score of 16. Their scores are equal, but when analyzed they reveal very different performances. The more we aggregate into one score, i.e., the more curricula we pile into a test, the less useful and accurate the student's score. It's more valuable to give frequent tests with less curriculum on each, or at the very least, give multiple scores on each test, each score corresponding to one topic.

Prohibiting students from reading a book this year because a teacher in their future may teach it as well. I have taught Shakespeare in middle school for years, and for years high school teachers have complained that they don't have anything new to teach those students when they arrive in their classroom a couple of years later. Then, after having my students in their classes, those same teachers send follow-up e-mails thanking me for preparing the students so well and the experience in their grade level was much better as a result. What happened?

Middle school students process Shakespeare at one level of life experience. They get caught up in the compelling drama and universal themes. They see themselves in the scenes, laughing at the absurdities of mistaken identities, celebrating with the truly humble and good as they conquer the swaggering tyrant, and commiserating with youth whose lives have been torn asunder by unfair parents. Shakespeare speaks to them, and they marvel at how someone from so long ago can provide such insight for today. The door is opened.

When they get to high school, they've got two or three more years of life experiences under their belts. They are different people as sophomores than they were as seventh graders. They bring new perspectives from their lives, and teachers can illuminate greater complexities than before.

I worry about high school teachers who say there is nothing left to teach a student who read Hamlet at age 11. Do these teachers have nothing more than superficial expertise? Every time we reread a complex story we find new treasures, especially if we've grown between the readings. Students gain a tremendous amount by reading complex stories in more than one teacher's class and in more than one grade level.

By the way, it goes the other way as well. Middle school teachers must contend with students who've already read books we wanted to teach in middle school. Do we complain about it with the elementary teachers? No. We take students' advanced knowledge and do something even more flexible and challenging with it.

Watching videos for the whole class period. Sadly, some teachers show videos—often videos students have already seen—so they can grade papers during class.

Even if the videos are connected to the curriculum, which they are often not, teachers should stop periodically and create some interaction with the video content. It's the way material gets into long-term memory. Waiting until the end of a lengthy video to answer a few comprehension questions does not promote student learning. School is for doing things that we can do only when we are gathered together in the company of the teacher's expertise and the building's resources.

Good luck with your spring cleaning. Enjoy rediscovering ideas you forgot you had and renewing the excitement a sense of organization and insight can provide. It's amazing how much better we see paths to our goals when we remove the clutter. When there's no competition from the weeds, student achievement rises and blooms as the tallest flower in the garden.

Movin' Up to the Middle

At the beginning of each middle school year, teachers stand near their classroom doors and greet arriving students. They smile, shake a few hands, and direct the wide-eyed students to their seats, remarking to themselves, *They're getting shorter every year.*

By June, after a year of body growth, intense hormones, intellectual sparring, and distancing themselves from anything "so last year," these young adolescents are dramatically different beings. But even as educators pause to acknowledge the newly competent students standing before them who can hold their own in political debates and band competitions, a crop of fresh young faces once again demands its turn at bat.

And this is where it gets interesting.

Those important middle years

The way we handle life in later years can often be traced back to specific experiences in middle school; it's that transformative. Robert Balfanz, a principal research scientist at Johns Hopkins University, presents compelling evidence that the middle school experience has direct correlation with graduation rates, particularly in high-poverty environments.[1] And everyone from classroom teachers to the National Governors Association recognizes the powerful influence that high school graduation has on individuals' capacities to build meaningful lives and create workforce readiness.

It's interesting, too, how some adults revert to adolescent responses when stressed by conflict, failure, and risk taking. If we learn to handle issues constructively during these formative years, ages 10–15, we tend to respond positively to challenges later on. So, if high school success, navigating the larger world, and discovering the direction we want our lives to take all have roots in young adolescence, why would anyone leave the transition into this impressionable phase to chance?

Give me five

Five mind-sets for educators are key to designing successful transition programs for incoming middle school students.

1. **Understanding students' concern about belonging**

   Belonging is one of the primary concerns for new middle-level students; addressing it is crucial for a successful transition. Teachers and administrators should assure students that their classes are a good match for their readiness, that their teachers understand them, and that they have roles to play in their own success.

   Design classrooms and hallways with student interests in mind, with student work prominently displayed. Find ways to help students see themselves "doing middle school." For example, the year before they enter, invite students to shadow a middle school student for half a day. If that's difficult to arrange, show rising middle schoolers "A Day in the Life of a Middle School Student," a video that you've guided current middle school students to create for the incoming class. Let rising middle schoolers discuss middle school life with current middle school students. To make new students comfortable, conduct these conversations in students' elementary classrooms, not at the middle school.

   In the first few weeks of school, give new middle schoolers meaningful tasks that foster a sense of belonging, such as doing the morning announcements, maintaining and operating classroom technology, and assisting in lesson delivery. This creates purposeful inclusion. Students at this age balk at superficiality and find it distancing, the opposite of belonging.

Joining clubs and organizations goes a long way to creating belonging as well. Team-building activities and participation in outdoor experiences, such as a ropes initiative course, are helpful here. A note of caution, however. Students are hungry for academics in their first few weeks of school. Contrary to stereotyped assertions about students at this age, day after day of get-to-know-you and team-building activities wears thin if students don't get to study specific course content as well. Set a can-do tone and high expectations early on by teaching intense course content during this time. Students will transition more readily if they feel that they're doing real middle school work, not just summer camp.

2. Empathizing with students

Given the fact that a year in a middle school student's life is a much larger percentage of his or her overall life than it is for an adult; and given all the growth taking place—the mistakes, conflicts, insights, joy, tension, wisdom, and risk taking; and given that students lack the perspective that comes from life experience, it's no wonder that students experience their first year of middle school as intense and tumultuous. Every day is the end, or beginning, of all life as they know it.

Middle schools with the best transition programs are the ones in which faculty members are in touch with their inner, young adolescent; these educators can empathize with students because they remember what it was like when they were that age. This empathy helps teachers understand students' major worries: homework, demanding teachers, bullying, and getting lost. Schools should build practical advice for handling each one of these concerns into their transition programs.

To promote empathy and respond constructively to new students, it's helpful to think of your middle schoolers as having arrived in a new country in which they don't speak the language and don't know the customs. In fact, many strategies that are effective with transitioning new English language learners work equally well for helping incoming middle school students (see "20 Double-Duty Strategies").

3. **Understanding the characteristics of the age group**

   Can everyone on your faculty identify what makes a middle school developmentally appropriate for young adolescents? Many educators have little to no training in the specific needs of these learners. This lack of knowledge can limit the success of transition efforts and student learning.

   Consider how teachers are meeting the physical and mental needs of this age group in the months before and after the first day of school. In the area of physical characteristics, girls mature faster than boys. In both genders, bones grow faster than muscles, so coordination is a big issue. With all the growth comes almost ceaseless appetite. The explosion of hormones coursing through the body causes increased development in sexual features as well as worry over body changes. There is an increased need for good hydration and nutrition.

   Or consider various characteristics of students' maturing brains. The prefrontal cortex is not fully developed in most 10- to 15-year-olds. As a result, the navigating tools for academics and life are not completely "online" yet. These include decision making, impulse control, moral and abstract reasoning, planning, understanding consequences of words and actions, and other executive functions. There is an increased tendency toward addictive behaviors[2] and pleasure seeking.

   Middle schoolers are fiercely curious and independent, yet almost paradoxically, they crave social connection. They make insightful, candid observations about their learning, themselves, and the adults who guide them. They realize for the first time how wrong or misinformed adults can be, and they're not sure what to make of it. They move from concrete to abstract thinking, becoming skeptical about some things—"I want the school board to prove to me how knowing algebra will make me a better adult"—yet swallowing without complaint the ridiculous—"If I don't forward that chain letter to 13 of my friends, I'm going to fail the civics test on Friday."

Despite their natural egotism, young adolescents are extremely compassionate toward those who are less fortunate. Middle schoolers also make many connections among topics, recognizing and using patterns, relationships, metaphors, and nuance; and they enjoy asking questions to which there are no answers. They sort and apply complex data, solve problems, and argue from more than one position; and they are fascinated by real-world applications, morality, and justice.

Where in our transition programs do we respond to these needs and strengths?

4. Focusing on the positive

The world excites these students, and they are eager to explore it, so it's jarring for them to spend the first week of school listening to an endless litany of edicts. With each information session on rules and limitations, wise teachers offer something positive that middle school students can do, even something as simple as being able to check out 10 books at a time from the library instead of the limit of two they had in elementary school.

Because middle schoolers seem so young, some teachers make the mistake of thinking they are less competent than they really are. They may not have experience in everything, but they're quick learners. Show them how to set up accounts on the school server, for example, and they'll post their own work, weave in content applications from multiple classes, create stylized presentations, and participate in problem-based wiki groups within the first week. Explain that there's a shortage of lab equipment, and they'll figure out the best way to maximize everyone's time using it.

Opening doors like this aids students' transition, so open them frequently and clearly. When scheduling a guest speaker, ask students to make the first contact with the speaker. Invite students to participate in planning an evening education event for parents, landscaping a portion of the school's property, or redesigning the school's website. Occasionally, ask students what kind of practice with today's topic would most benefit their learning; assign one of their suggestions as homework that evening.

It's also useful to teach students self-regulation, although they display this quality unevenly at this age. Marching as a class to the cafeteria for lunch and back, with the teacher monitoring their every move, is insulting. Teach students instead how to monitor themselves: What do they need to do to maintain a civil, learning atmosphere for others while they move through the hallway? Although it's fine to correct students' behavior, the goal is to build autonomy, not dependence.

For example, if chaos erupts when a visitor enters the classroom, suspend the lesson for a moment and discuss solutions to the problem. Have the class practice those constructive responses, including asking a volunteer to cause a fake interruption while the class maintains focus on the lesson. If students don't have the necessary supplies for the day's lesson, help them determine how they can continue their work until they get the necessary supplies instead of simply letting them off with, "Take the zero." For adults and middle schoolers alike, self-efficacy aids transition.

5. Building hope

The only reason students raise their hands to answer a question, turn in assignments, or participate in the world is because there's hope for a positive outcome. Without hope, a child will throw down the ball and go home— and we can't teach a child who is not physically or emotionally present. Let's put hope into every day. This is not a syrupy greeting card sentiment— it's visceral. *Maybe the teacher won't know what a jerk I was on the bus this morning, and I can start the day again in first period,* Kellan hopes. *Why did I just say that to Melissa?* Adam worries. *Can I fix this? Will she text me about it?* And moments later, Lakiesha chants in her internal monologue, *Please tell me I left my science notebook in my locker and not at home; please, please, please!* Middle school hallways are filled with such longings: *Maybe English class won't be so bad today,* or, *Maybe I'll get taller; my dad did when he was my age.* To young adolescents, hope is oxygen.

Interestingly, parents and teachers often offer warnings instead of hope as their way of preparing students for middle school. Students do better with a clear picture of what to expect, advice on how to handle potential issues, and assurance they will be OK. This hope has a real effect on school performance.

When students are late for class, for example, they should expect a teacher response that preserves their dignity rather than demeans them in front of others. If students can't get their computer program to function so they can finish an assigned task within the class period, the teacher should provide additional resources and time for them to accomplish the task. If students break the trust by missing an assignment due date or cheating on a quiz, teachers need to identify clear avenues the students can take to rebuild that trust, including a finite window for being on probation for the infraction.

Moreover, if students struggle to control impulsive behaviors, such as making inappropriate noises, sending text messages during a lesson, or making snide remarks, these behaviors should not affect their grade for content knowledge. Being rude is not mentioned in the curricular objective "Understands oxidation." Academic grades should only report what's in the curriculum. When teachers can separate impulsive, immature behavior from academics, there's hope for students.

Preparation first

Louis Pasteur reminds us that "chance favors the prepared mind." We can prepare our students' minds for every success by being both proactive—for example, by focusing on experiential learning—and interactive, for example, by offering team-building experiences. We create a real future on the basis of what we do with today's young adolescents, not what we do to them. Working together, we build personalized tools for safe passage.

20 double-duty strategies

Teachers can use the following strategies, which help English language learners transition to an English-speaking environment, to aid all new students in their transition into middle school.

1. Speak clearly.
2. Repeat important words and information several times.
3. Extend time periods for responding to prompts as necessary.
4. Avoid using idioms, colloquialisms, and shorthand references unless you're going to take the time to explain them.
5. Point to what you're referring.
6. Label things in the classroom and hallways, such as "Computer Lab 2," "Student flash drives," "Mrs. Silver's stapler—Please return to her."
7. Provide specific models and hands-on experiences.

8. Use visuals during instruction, such as pictures, illustrations, graphs, pictographs, and real objects.

9. Demonstrate what you mean, rather than just describe it. For example, use a scientific balance when explaining equal values right and left of the equation sign in algebra. When teaching parallel sentence structure in English, write the model sentences parallel to each other on the display board.

10. Make students feel that they belong and have a role to play in classroom learning. Find something in a student's background that connects to the topic you're studying and incorporate it into the lesson. Have students take on leadership positions, and ask them to demonstrate their talents.

11. Use think alouds to model sequences of tasks.

12. Use cooperative learning groups, with more seasoned students partnering with less seasoned ones.

13. Find ways to enable new students who may be tentative about their abilities to demonstrate their intellectual skills and maintain dignity.

14. Give students quick and accurate feedback. An English language learner might say in halting English, "This correct paper?" Reply in affirmation, "Yes, that is the correct paper. Thank you." A middle schooler might ask, "Am I doing OK?" Respond, "Yes, you're doing well, and here's how I know. …"

15. Spend time building background knowledge. If you're about to teach students about magnetic fields, for example, let them play with magnets, pouring iron shavings near the poles to watch their pattern of dispersal or gathering. Before teaching students about irony, orchestrate an ironic happening in the classroom and ask for comments.

16. Stay focused on how students are moving toward their own learning goals—not on how they're doing in relation to other

students. We do students a disservice when we compare them with their peers or try to motivate them by parading others' success in front of them. English language learners and middle-level students desperately want to be successful.

17. Recognize the difference between conversational and academic language and understand that students need help with both. Go out of your way to explain terms like *similar, math exercise, vocabulary, compare, instead of, not only,* and so on.

18. Take the time to learn about students' interests and cultures. This engenders good will and enables you to make connections in the curriculum.

19. Teach new content through a medium or topics that students already know. In the case of English language learners, this means teaching content in or making connections to their native language whenever possible. In the case of all middle schoolers, it means building on familiar knowledge.

20. Remember that students are *individuals* worth our time and energy. Labels such as *English language learner, gifted and talented, hearing impaired, gamer, Goth,* and *gang member* blind us to the individual underneath.

Tips for great transitions

- Invite incoming students to begin school a half or full day earlier than returning students. On these days, students can get their schedules and lockers, move from class to class, meet their teachers, experience a short lesson in each subject, get a list of supplies from each teacher, get their school server accounts, purchase items with school logos, and practice opening and closing their lockers—without having to worry about getting hassled by an older student or arriving late for class. Incoming students will start school knowing at least some of the ropes.

- If your middle school asks students to use lockers, take a locker door with a combination lock to feeder elementary schools in the last few months of school. Let students practice opening and closing the lock as much as they want for at least a week. This activity ranks as one of the most helpful experiences in student surveys.

- Ask elementary teachers to forward to middle school staff, if possible, observations and comments regarding every student they teach. Make it manageable—a single page or less. Comments can include students' strengths, motivators, family factors that affect learning, potential issues, and anything else that might be helpful.

- Send a letter of congratulations to all rising middle schoolers on their last day of elementary school. J. F. Drake Middle School in Auburn, Alabama, does this every year. The letters are addressed directly to each child and include students' team assignments and the dates of their Drake Summer Camp session, a transition program for both students and parents held during the summer.

- Have your leadership team visit with students in their elementary schools the year before the students enter middle school. Retired principal Patti Kinney of Talent Middle School in Talent, Oregon, notes that 5th graders pose concerns freely during these sessions, such as, "My sister says that when she was in middle school there was [insert distorted rumor here]." These sessions can clear up inaccuracies and help students see administrators as accessible and supportive. A similar program in the evening for parents is just as important. Rising middle schoolers at Talent Middle School are also invited to major middle school events.

- Invite elementary and middle school teachers to switch jobs for a day. Each gets a sense of how the other school works in terms of daily operations, content, and both student and teacher expectations. This information not only will be of value to teachers as they work with their own students, but it will also help them provide clearer advice about transitioning to parents.

- Repeatedly connect with parents. Send the middle school newsletter home to parents of rising middle schoolers. Invite new parents to serve on school committees, and provide clear lists of volunteer opportunities. Meet with new parents the year before their children enter middle school and periodically throughout the first year.

- Have all staff members wear "Ask Me" badges for the first two weeks of school. The badges nudge students to ask questions from safe and accurate sources of information.

- Include healthy doses of humor. Humor lowers stress and creates camaraderie. Students need license to laugh at themselves and life.

References

[1]Balfanz, R. (2009). *Putting middle grades students on the graduation path: A policy and practice brief.* Westerville, OH: National Middle School Association. Retrieved from www.nmsa.org/portals/0/pdf/research/Research_from_the_Field/Policy_Brief_Balfanz.pdf

[2]Wolfe, P. (2010). *Brain matters: Translating research into classroom practice* (2nd ed.). Alexandria, VA: ASCD.

Endnote

This article was originally published in 2011 in Educational Leadership, *68(7), 48–53. Printed with permission from Association for Supervision and Curriculum Development.*

It's the Relationships That Matter

In those less-than-proud moments when our brilliant lessons fall flat and too many students seem to need those things we're not in the mood to provide, we can get cranky. Some of us even throw up our hands and lament not-so-tongue-in-cheek, "I could really teach if it weren't for all these kids!"

If we find ourselves tolerating rather than looking forward to our students, something is amiss. Students—whether standing before us or via a proxy such as homework or e-mail—are our priority. Educator and Invitational Schools originator William Purkey illustrates this when he substitutes the word "student" for "customer" in an excerpt from an L. L. Bean employee training manual:

> A student is not an interruption of our work...the student is the purpose of it. We are not doing a favor by serving the student...the student is doing us a favor by giving us the opportunity to do so.

Our classrooms are more than workplaces; they represent opportunities to serve and form relationships with students.

Showing you care

The adage "Students don't care how much we know until they know how much we care" is more than a simplistic Hallmark card sentiment. Almost everything that enters a young adolescent's mind goes first to emotional response centers rather than cognitive centers of the brain. So, right there, we've identified a major route to students' success: a positive connection between teacher and student.

The first thing we can do to cultivate healthy relationships with our students is to realize that most of what happens in our classrooms and hallways isn't about us, it's about the students. So many times during the day, we cut off students from experiences they need because we're thinking of our own concerns, not theirs.

When a student tells us a story we've already heard, we don't interrupt him, saying, "Yeah, I heard that from Joe this morning," as if we're trying to save both him and ourselves time and embarrassment. We listen patiently to the whole story because the important thing is the interaction, not the information.

Just as important is that we be purposefully inviting. Purkey claims that teachers open and slam doors every day, inviting and disinviting students. To invite students, consider placing your desk to the side or the back of the room. If it's centered in the front of the room, it's an unspoken message that the teacher is the most important person in the room; the students are secondary citizens and are disinvited to the learning table.

It's the same with classroom decorations. If most of the walls are filled with student work, at eye-level so all can see it clearly, they invite students to participate. If the walls are covered in the teacher's or school's work rules, announcements, cafeteria menus—then it's disinviting.

When students walk through the classroom door, welcome them by name. Hearing their name may be the only proof these students have that they are worth having their name remembered by a respected adult. Imagine if more than one adult in the building said each student's name during the day. The clear message to students is: you belong here.

Let students know they make good company. Lean toward them, keep eye contact, and ask follow-up questions about their discussions with you, even if you don't care about their new pet or the performance of their favorite sports team. Follow up with a comment a few days later to show what they said was worth remembering.

Don't forget that the person you see in front of you is not yet complete. We can't hold their digressions and experimentation against them. Students can dress "Goth" and still graph equations. Be the wise adult who doesn't accept the facade students present to the world as the final declaration of who they will become. Be mindful of the gold inside and that what we do today with students will likely impact their growth for years.

Convincing students that we believe in them is critical to these relationships. To prove our trust in students, we can

- Catch them doing things right.

- Applaud their risk taking.

- Allow them to choose how they will demonstrate mastery every so often instead of taking our tests.

- Redirect one student to another for assistance.

- Ask students to coordinate the literary magazine publishing, escort guest speakers, plan and facilitate special events, run the school TV studio, maintain the class webpage, and coteach with us.

Positive reactions

Sometimes a student gets something wrong and we have to address it immediately, but we don't want to destroy a positive relationship. Here are five ways to negate students' responses without shutting them down:

- Use empathy or sympathy: "I used to think that, too. Then I read the paragraph at the bottom of p. 65, and it changed my mind. Let's take a look at it." Or, "That's very reasonable. I see how you arrived at that conclusion. Let's take a look at the data again to see if it's accurate."

- Change the rules so their responses are correct: "That's the answer to the question on rotation I'm going to ask in a few minutes. Hold on to that while we look at planet orbits for a minute."

- Ask for more information: "Tell me more about that." By explaining themselves, students may recognize the error in their thinking and save face.

- Affirm risk taking: "Yes, that's the kind of thinking we're looking for, but you're not quite there, so we need to explore further. Thanks for having the courage to break the ice and get the ball rolling."

- Redirect to another student: "Mack, can you offer evidence to support or refute what Melanie just said?"

Don't forget the 10-minute rule. After every negative interaction with a student, try to circle back and have a positive interaction within 10 minutes to rebuild that personal bridge. You can ask a question to which she knows the answer, affirm the student as an expert in some area, or sincerely thank the student for something she did unrelated to the negative incident.

At each turn, allow students to see that you are there to push for their success, not to document their errors. Instead of writing, "This is very disappointing. You have no evidence for your claims and your thinking is sloppy. See me!" try writing, "I'm having trouble finding the evidence for your claims. Can you show me where it is?"

While adults can separate comments about assignments from being comments about them as individuals, middle school students often cannot. They think that negative comments on their projects reflect on them as people.

Another thing we can do to build successful relationships with students is to be well-prepared each day. That means we respect students enough to present the best lessons for the topic, not just something to get through the day. We remember promises made, keep up with the latest ideas in education and what we're teaching, and we express sincere interest in sharing the subject with students. Passion for our discipline goes a long way with young adolescents.

Cultivating relationships

As we survey our students toward the end of the school year, we discover many of them have risen from being one more paper to grade to being fascinating, deeply moving individuals of their own accord. We've established ties with them. We've grown closer to some who initially irritated us, and we're regretting the short time we have left with them. We can't leave our relationships with students to chance.

Some teachers think that dealing with emotions in the classroom is somehow "soft" and takes away from their academic cause. Wrong. When there's angst in our lives, we are easily threatened by others. When we are at peace, we extend ourselves to others in a nurturing manner. There is nothing soft about cultivating good relationships with students; to avoid something so pivotal to academic success is close to malpractice.

Let's embrace the truth that we teach more than the state or provincial standards. Those standards and the humanity we promote are achieved by cultivating healthy relationships with students. I'll leave you with a quote from Elsbeth Murphy's book *Chalkdust* (1979), "If I had been a kid in my class today, would I want to come back tomorrow?" Let's make sure students can answer "yes" every day.

Motivating Students to Step Up

Cameron works intensely for 20 minutes on a single math problem, but then he cracks a smile and exclaims, "Got it! I used a different property, and it worked!"

In another class, Gina's knotted brow suddenly relaxes as she plugs in the right code sequence to get her graphic design software to depict a three-dimensional solid rotating on two different axes. It took her

22 minutes to figure it out, but she's excited to solve an initially daunting problem.

In these first post-solution moments, both students are awash in moderate euphoria. They both look up to their teachers and say, "Give me another one."

The reward for hard work is more hard work. University of Kentucky Professor of Educational Psychology Tom Guskey mentioned this premise in a workshop I attended back in the early 1980s, and its veracity has deepened in the years since. We're hardwired to explore complex ideas and to do challenging yet productive tasks.

Absent some kind of brain damage, every student is motivated. It's wrong for us to label academically disengaged students as lazy. Languid, apathetic students whose most common response to classroom inquiry is "Huh?" are focused feverishly as they triumph over different levels of online gaming that afternoon or practice for a regional athletic competition next weekend.

Students who declare homework assignments "dumb" and forget to do them will run a classmate's election to student council campaign with impressive attention to detail or spend hours building sets for the school musical. So what's going on when teachers lament that they can't get students to come for after-school help on tests, do their homework assignments, participate in class, or care about their learning?

In his video, "How Difficult Can This Be? The F.A.T. City Workshop— Understanding Learning Disabilities," learning disabilities expert Rick Lavoie reminds us that motivation is only doing to the best of our ability what we are already capable of doing.

Consider for a moment: If we perceive we can do it, we are inclined to do it; but if we don't perceive ourselves as capable, we hesitate or avoid tasks. So, it's easy to see why students might be reluctant to try new math algorithms, incorporate new art techniques, apply physics principles, or experiment with rhetorical analysis, especially if they have learning challenges. Perceived competence plays a significant role in motivation.

Asking for more

I once asked students to create comic strips about a historical event. I told them not to worry about their artwork, adding that I used stick figures for human drawings myself and that would be fine here. I was grading them only on the accuracy of the historical content expressed in their characters' caption bubbles.

The comic strips were awful. The drawings in each panel were quickly scribbled, dashed off just to satisfy the assignment. The content in the caption bubbles was also limited; its quality matched that of the simplistic drawings. Students demonstrated little enthusiasm for any element of the assignment.

For the first time in my career, I invoked my now oft-used explanation for diverging from the posted pacing guide: I temporarily suspended the curriculum. To teach the curriculum effectively later, I had to address a noncurricular issue today.

During this 30-minute temporary suspension, I taught cartooning skills using seven books I found on the topic. We learned how to draw cartoon heads, eyeballs, and hands in motion, emotions, perspective, and much more. Many of the students took the books home and practiced on their own.

I reassigned the comic strips. This time the comic artwork was excellent and so was the caption content. The students were proud of their cartooning and excited to create something that looked so professional. They figured the quality of the caption bubbles full of historical content should match the quality of the artwork. As a result, the content was much more sophisticated, complex, and thorough.

Motivation doesn't come by doing low-quality tasks easily. Instead, it comes when we do high-quality work with effective tools and training. Weirdly, I thought I was being kind by letting students "off" from skilled cartooning requirements, but the kinder act was to require students to do well on a demanding task and give them the tools to rise to the challenge.

Getting results

Daniel Pink *(Drive: The Surprising Truth about What Motivates Us, 2009)* and others tell us that paying employees excessive salaries doesn't necessarily improve their output. Will paying teachers more than $100,000 motivate them to work harder to improve their students' test scores?

Rather, we find that employees, including teachers, who experience autonomy (power to choose which tasks are done and how they are done), mastery (real competence in their field), and purpose (see themselves in active roles to improve the world) in their jobs are more effective in their jobs and achieve better results.

It's the same with young adolescents. They crave autonomy, competence, and meaning. Let's circle in our lesson plans where our students experience each of these:

- Where do they have choice in which direction to go or how to go about doing a task?

- Where have we provided direct feedback about students' growing competencies and adjusted learning experiences when necessary competencies aren't there?

- Where have we moved from sense-making to meaning-making with students, helping them see how content transforms their lives and they, in turn, transform the world?

Uninformed teachers rely too much on grades and grading policies as motivation and classroom management tools. Students do assignments and participate in learning for far more reasons than the fear or lure of the grade book. Some teachers are hesitant to allow retakes of tests because they think students won't study for them the first time they are given. These educators are well-intended, but they have some catching up to do on motivation research.

Really, we know better. Classrooms that promote the perform-feedback-revise-perform-feedback-revise cycle are not only motivating, they are far more demanding and preparatory for the working world than are classrooms in which students get only one shot at learning.

Closing the gap

It's time to vanquish the notion that our students aren't motivated or that we don't know how to motivate them. We know exactly how to motivate students, but there's a gap between knowing what to do and actually doing it. Let's close that gap, not just by increasing complexity, providing tools, building competence, and making meaning, but with as many motivational elements as we can muster.

With motivation, we must be proactive, interactive, and reactive. Our instruction must be developmentally appropriate. We must cultivate positive teacher/student relationships. And, we must respond and adjust to students' needs as they arise. Most teachers who struggle with student motivation haven't had time to get up to speed on developmentally appropriate instruction, and they fall back on unproven notions of how to motivate others, or their students suffer from poverty, illness, or some other aspect over which teachers have little control.

Motivation is not something we do to students; it's how we help them reveal to themselves. Eventually, we achieve the ultimate testimony from a student stepping out the door each morning: "I can't wait to get to school today."

Here are 18 strategies that motivate young adolescents. Make them more than just nice things to try if you "have time." Incorporate them in all your planning.

1. **Provide structure.**

   Minds crave structure. Provide parameters and models, reveal text structures, and identify the inner workings of concepts and objects. Ask students to complete graphic organizers so they can see how concepts fit together. Provide templates early in the learning and then slowly wean students off them. Providing structure early in the learning is inviting, but later it can be limiting.

2. **Offer new audiences.**

   Any audience other than the teacher is immediately attractive to students. Students will stay late to work on projects that are going to be on display in the community. Give students opportunities to do plays for elementary schools, decorate Jetways and walls at airports, and provide artwork for dentists' waiting rooms.

3. **Make an emotional connection.**

   Almost everything that goes into students' minds goes to emotional response centers first. Be enthusiastic about topics and watch students give themselves permission to be enthusiastic as well. Orchestrate moments of anger, anxiety, joy, excitement, and surprise to create personal response in students and help them retain content in long-term memory.

4. **Show your passion.**

   Many of us become interested in something because someone we respect is also interested in the topic. Do book talks about favorite books and watch those books fly off the bookshelves into students' hands. Enjoy a subject and watch students enjoy it as well.

5. **Have a growth mindset.**

   Carol Dweck distinguishes between students with a fixed intelligence mindset who believe that intelligence is innate and unchangeable and those with a growth mindset who believe that their achievement can improve through effort and learning. She shares in the January 2009 issue of NASSP's *Principal's Research Review:* "Teaching students a growth mindset results in increased motivation, better grades, and higher achievement test results."

   Ensure your lessons engender hope so students who realize they aren't ready for a complex task now, know that with time and perseverance, they will be ready in the future.

6. **Create curiosity.**

   Television producer Fred Friendly said back in the 1950s, "Our job is not to make up anybody's mind, but to open minds and make the agony of decision making so intense you can escape only by thinking." This is true for today's classrooms as well.

   Foreshadow what's to come. Introduce conflict to conventional thinking. Place mysterious packages in the room to create anticipation and curiosity. Wear a portion of a costume and incorporate it into the lesson that day. Ponder weird ideas aloud.

7. **Nurture cognitive connections.**

   Experts think in terms of relationships, connections, patterns, chunks; novices keep things in individual, discreet pieces. We are moving students from being novices to at least partial experts. Help students make these connections themselves and they'll be motivated to learn.

8. **Encourage creativity and divergent thinking.**

   Students crave novelty and creativity. Anomalies, non sequitors, surprising puzzle solutions, interesting recombinations of ideas and objects, Odyssey of the Mind activities, and exceptions to rules capture students' attention. It's okay to go out of your way to teach backwards. Ask students to use unusual props, conduct debates in which students must argue from the side opposing their own, and conduct risk-free experimentation with manipulatives, art, music, technology, and writing.

9. **Provide clear expectations and descriptive feedback.**

We're motivated by a clear picture of what we have to do. If it's unclear and we can't visualize the final product or step, we hesitate. In motivating classrooms, teachers are so clear with evaluative criteria, including exemplars and descriptive feedback, that students can tell you what they are supposed to be learning and where they are in relation to those goals.

10. **Use narrative.**

To capture and keep students' attention, use narrative often. It's entertaining, sure, but it also provides connection and structure for information, and our minds are attracted to these elements. Tell the stories behind the facts, and engineer narratives that make connections among disparate elements. Real or fantasy—it doesn't matter.

11. **Activate prior knowledge.**

When we create personal background experiences for students, then attach new learning to these backgrounds, we engage students. Consider how we marvel at artwork when we understand the story behind it or the techniques used to make it. Without that prior knowledge, the world is a gray, uninspired place and we are slow to engage in it.

12. **Encourage sleep.**

Sleep deprivation changes our personality and lowers our investment in even the most interesting of topics. Even worse, our minds make connections while sleeping, and without the connections made during those 8 to 11 hours needed by adolescents, their minds are less willing to make the effort to do so in the middle of class. Lack of sleep not only changes motivation, but also performance. In *Brain Matters* (2010), Pat Wolfe cites a 2003 study indicating that missing even one hour of sleep has detrimental effect. A slightly sleepy 6th grader performs in class just like a typical 4th grader. (p. 98)

13. Promote nutrition.

Proper diet does wonders for our emotions, physical energy, and neurotransmitters like serotonin and dopamine needed for cognition. Encourage students to eat nutritious meals. Breakfast and lunch should include complex carbohydrates, proteins, water, fruit, fish, lean meats, breakfast cereals rich in omega-3 fatty acids, multigrains, and whole grains.

14. Encourage exercise and movement.

The brain is very attentive to movement. Regular exercise increases oxygen flow to cognitive portions of the brain. It also releases protein IGF-1 which stimulates neural growth, according to Pat Wolfe (*Brain Matters,* 2010). Add movement to your instruction to get students' attention. A student can watch out of the corner of her eye if you just stand there, but if you move suddenly or in an unusual manner, her attention is drawn to you immediately. Incorporate movement in students, too. Include some form of physical activity every 10 to 20 minutes.

15. Orchestrate vividness.

Our minds are engaged by vivid experiences. The more vividness we orchestrate in our instruction, the less passivity we observe in our students. Appeal to more than one sense, use original resources and artifacts, incorporate education simulations, and engage students' emotions to increase vividness.

16. Find opportunities for self-definition.

Adolescents crave opportunities to figure out who they are. When we incorporate self-definition into learning, we engage them. Teach them about multiple intelligences while they study the Civil Rights movement. Let them choose favorite celebrities to portray when explaining phototropism. Invite them to reflect on their own moral beliefs when writing about population controls in crowded countries.

17. Extend wait times

Students are motivated when they know the teacher will wait for them to put together coherent responses. Extend wait times to eight seconds or more. Those extra silent seconds send a message that the teacher believes the student will do well. When someone believes in us, we can move mountains.

18. Get outside.

If I had my way, every student would spend two weeks camping or hiking each school year. A maturity and motivation come from survival in the wilderness that cannot be found anywhere else. Being in the wilderness for just one week can change students. They eat meals without complaint, and they do chores and homework without being told. They want others to see them as capable leaders. Superficial things about which they used to worry don't loom so large any more.

When Nothing Else Works

Ninety-eight percent of our students respond successfully to the myriad strategies we use to motivate and teach them every day: constructivism, differentiated instruction, cooperative learning, teacher-advisory periods, inquiry method, parent involvement, Socratic Seminars, simulations, games, vividness, demonstrations, WebQuests, and more.

But what about those few students who drive us crazy because we can't seem to motivate them?

Before you finally snap—in the middle of the lunch room, surrounded by 13-year-olds frozen in mid-bite as you loudly retract your previously unassailable conviction that all students can learn—let me assure you there is hope. Put down those ranch salad dressing pouches you were waving menacingly toward the back table of homework slackers and come with me. When all else fails, we still have options.

Consult experts

Ask for advice from a specialist such as the school social worker or psychologist, or perhaps another staff member with whom the student is doing well. Check the student's cumulative folder, too, for any advice from pervious teachers.

Seek advice from Teacher Assistance Teams (TATs). If your school doesn't have one, start one. The basic ideas is that teachers present a case study to a team of five or six teachers and administrators representing multiple grade levels and subjects. They, in turn, follow a well-defined, 30-minute sequence of analyzing the situation and creating a viable plan to resolve the issue.

In your presentation of the case, you share your concern about the student and explain what you have tried thus far. Your colleagues respond according to the TAT strategy and propose a plan. You try the team's ideas, updating them on an agreed-upon date.

Professional learning communities, critical friends groups, and action research groups can also offer methodical and collegial support when you are working with difficult students. Don't forget other adults in the child's life as well. Talk to the student's parents, first, of course, but then you can triple-team the student by enlisting the help and advice of other important adults in the student's life, such as a coach, minister, rabbi, or Scout leader.

Consider the root

Sometimes motivational issues have physiological roots. Students' minds may not be operating in such a way as to elicit interest or maturity in what we're teaching. If this seems to be the case, consider asking parents to take the child to the doctor for a physical exam, including blood tests. The doctor may detect medical factors that affect motivation, such as a chemical imbalance, a lack of certain hormones, or unusual stress of which we are not aware.

Diet also may play a role. The brain requires large amounts of water to function. Unmotivated students could become motivated simply by getting well-hydrated. Encourage students to drink a lot of water throughout the day and allow them to drink water in our classroom. Also be aware that young adolescents who eat a lot of heavy foods and sugars may become sleepy in the afternoon—another reason to teach good nutrition.

Sleep is a big physiological factor in motivation as well. Young adolescents usually require between 9 and 11 hours of sleep to function at peak levels the next day. Unfortunately, the adolescent brain doesn't secrete the chemical for sleepiness until late at night, and it continues secreting that chemical well into mid-morning hours, according to Barbara Strauch's research in her wonderful book, *The Primal Teen*. This can decrease motivation during early class periods and increase family angst in later evening hours.

Get trained

The expertise required to teach seventh grade is different than that required to teach eleventh grade or third grade. To motivate our students, then, we must be trained in what is developmentally responsive to students' needs.

If we do not understand the unique nature of our students, then it will be difficult to make our lessons compelling. For example:

- To be fully engaged in learning experiences, adolescents need to physically move about every 15 minutes. This relieves stress on the growth plates on the ends of the bones. In primary grades, it's about every 6 to 8 minutes.

- Adolescents crave opportunities to define who they are, to express themselves creatively, and to contribute to the learning, not just receive it. *Turning Points 2000* and AMLE's *This We Believe* list other "cravings" that are necessary to motivate students. Without such expertise, motivating young adolescents is a shot in the dark. The middle school concept rallies around these well-defined needs, and it is a significant factor in students' motivation or lack thereof. Implement the concepts including teacher-advisory programs and looping if you want motivated students.

- Spencer Rogers of Peak Learning Systems advocates using inertia to motivate students. He often relates the story of his wife wanting him to take out the trash while he's watching football. When he tells her, "Just a minute, after this play," yet doesn't take out the trash when the play is over, his wife resolves to overcome his inertia. She asks her husband for a kiss, and he dutifully gets off the couch to do this quick action. While kissing, she hands him the garbage from behind her back and says, "While you're up, will you take this out for me, honey?" And he does.

We can get our students doing something enjoyable, then throw in that less desirable activity they might not otherwise have done. An object in motion tends to stay in motion.

- If students are in denial about their lack of motivation, videotape them and then watch it with them, asking guiding questions about what they're doing and how it affects their learning and the learning of those around them. The stark reality-check might provoke them into action. It can be very motivating if Mom or Dad is invited to the viewing.

- If there is a chronic motivation problem, it may be appropriate for Mom or Dad to sit next to their student while in class for a day or more. This is drastic, but it's worked for me on occasion.

- Don't forget the power of multiple intelligences, either. We all gravitate toward our proclivities, and we tend to shut down when we're constantly exposed to intelligence areas that are not strong in us. If we provide plenty of experiences in a student's two or three strongest intelligences, we significantly increase the likelihood of his participation. Create those opportunities by capitalizing on how students are smart, not focusing on how smart they are.

We can offer students experiences using different learning styles, readiness levels, interests, teachers, modalities, or even different schools.

Meet students' needs

Middle school students want to belong (not be rejected) and to be powerful (have control). If a student is unmotivated, she may be feeling like she doesn't belong, or that she has no control over the situation. To motivate her, then, we affirm the student's important role and appropriate placement in the group regularly, and we find ways for the student to have a say in the learning.

We can capitalize on this need for involvement in a number of ways, such as allowing them to choose from among assignments, choose how assignments will be assessed, participate in more inquiry experiences, constructively advise the teacher, and help decide classroom rules.

In some cases, a behavior contract may work. This is an agreed-upon set of stipulations that will earn the student a reward if they are followed for a period of time. Students themselves describe the problem they're having and then follow it up with an agreed-upon action plan or set of behaviors to be achieved every day that solve the problem. The last part of the contract lists the reward the student will receive if she follows the contract.

Please note that while these contracts may work in the short term, they don't usually solve the problem in the long term—they rely too much on extrinsic forces. Intrinsic rewards such as having a role in the learning process, finding meaning, and experiencing competence endure. The contracts may, however, create some positive habits in students that plant the seed of potential full-time adherence.

Just ask

We can also cut to the chase by simply asking the student what would work. Students often have surprising insight if we just stop "chasing zebras" and listen. Sometimes a student of color doesn't do the work because he is afraid of looking too "white" to members of his own race. Some students are taking care of their four younger siblings each afternoon and evening while their parents work multiple jobs and are too exhausted to finish their homework. Some students are perfectionists who are afraid to try because they might make a mistake. If we are out of motivating options, it's professional to admit as much to the student and ask her to help you solve the problem.

Four keys

Motivating students is not as difficult as we sometimes make it out to be. While there are many motivational approaches for middle school students, they all work from four premises:

1. Good teaching motivates students. Make your lessons developmentally appropriate and the best they've ever been. Your students will thrive.

2. Just because a strategy doesn't work with an unmotivated student this week, it doesn't mean it won't work next week, three weeks from now, or with another student. Great teachers don't dismiss a strategy as useless because they tried it once and it didn't work.

3. Students aren't lazy. Those behaviors that come across as laziness are learned behaviors, results of something else we can address. Look beyond student comments like, "I just didn't feel like doing it," to what else is going on. Mel Levine makes a strong case for this in his book, *The Myth of Laziness.*

4. Nothing motivates like success. Practice new behaviors in short chunks and make substantive success readily attainable. If a student succeeds with a particularly difficult math problem, for instance, he often says, "Give me another one." The moderate euphoria that comes with new competence is very motivating.

Choosing only one of these approaches for the profoundly unmotivated student will probably not work; doing three or more in tandem usually will.

Your ceaseless advocacy for the student is key, however. Sometimes it's hard to look beyond the external surface these students offer us, but know they are "wired" from birth to want to succeed, participate, and be well thought of by others. Sometimes these desires have been subordinated or taught out of them by life. We can be the ones to reintroduce them to who they really are.

Living With and Teaching Young Adolescents: A Teacher's Perspective

This piece was written for one of AMLE's (then, NMSA) Month of the Young Adolescent, which occurs in October each year. It was meant to pull together a lot of ideas to give a clearer sense of what makes a young adolescent a young adolescent. It's often distributed to parents at back to school night, to teachers entering the classroom for the first time, and in undergraduate and graduate courses on teaching young adolescents. Some of this material came from Meet Me in the Middle, *some from other articles, and some of it is original to this piece.*

The middle level years are an extraordinary period of our human development. The only other time we grow as much physically, emotionally, and intellectually is from ages zero to two. But early adolescence is much more than just tripping over large feet and calling friends on the phone to discuss who likes whom. The ways we deal with conflict, relationships, and personal development as adults have direct connections to specific experiences we had between the ages of 10 and 14. We can create a very positive future, then, when we provide careful and compassionate experiences for today's young adolescents.

The truth about young adolescents

One of my middle school students is the oldest in her family. She cooks dinner and does laundry for her young siblings because both parents work at night. She also bathes her siblings and puts them to bed before starting on her homework. Last year, another student coordinated the building of an elevated sidewalk through a mud pit at the back entrance to a local school. In May, one of my students raised over $22,000 for the National Juvenile Diabetes Foundation. Other students at my school came in second for having the most soda cans recycled. Several students performed the National Anthem at a regional swimming Olympics program attended by thousands. One seventh grader was a volunteer performer at a Virginia plantation reenactment, and another was an opera singer who performed at the Kennedy Center.

Bragging? You bet. The great thing is that anyone who works with middle schoolers can probably make the same claims about students in his or her area of the nation. In transition from child to adult, these morphing humans are amazing doers and thinkers. Their comments can be profound, pithy, honest, absurd, and juvenile, all at the same time. They reveal developing wisdom, deep understanding, free spirit, and are a generation of thinkers in the making. They are a far cry from the inept persona some journalists assign to this stage of human development.

With good reason, my wife and I ask middle school students to babysit our six- and seven-year-old children rather than most high school students. Why? Young adolescents are ceaselessly conscientious. They are not apathetic in positions of trust. Doing the right thing matters to them. They want to be taken seriously so badly that they go overboard to make sure they are perceived as responsible. When I've taught students who had challenges at home or personal problems such as diabetes, other middle school students are often the most mature and tender sources of help.

The young adolescents in my school can analyze news articles that disparage their age group using logical fallacies such as false dichotomies or emotional appeal arguments. They can analyze President Hoover's political actions with big business during his term of office and compare them to today's issues with the famous Microsoft court case about monopolies. They can determine the exact amount of paint needed to completely cover an L-shaped office building minus the spaces for doors and windows. They can prepare entire multimedia presentations with proper presentation etiquette and student-enhanced digital photography worthy of any corporate boardroom. They can run their own television studios, and they can speak and sing in front of thousands. They can also tell you what personal pronoun is third person, plural, objective case.

In the next breath, however, young adolescents can be absurd, on purpose or by accident. Tough kids get their braces stuck in classroom pillows or glue their armpits so they can't raise their arms without ripping hair, both of which recently happened in my classroom. Seemingly sophisticated students laugh until they cry when someone passes gas during a test, and they all ask questions that were answered four seconds earlier. They get dramatic about budding romance, and they bump up against the rules society has imposed on them and have to face the consequences. Those of us who work with middle schoolers delight in seeing the world through their eyes. It keeps everything fresh. Our classes are full of humans in the making and we have a front row seat as coaches and referees. Never, however, do we use student indiscretions and confusions to paint the whole picture of the charges before us.

Numerous young adolescents who gave me nothing but frustration and less than acceptable work in their middle school years went on to become wonderful students in high school and college. Somewhere inside them they were germinating the seeds of what they could become. With each one, we look past the frustrating years, and we do not hold their current state of development against them. What would we have become if we had been held to the labels placed on us as young adolescents? We're farmers who trust that the crop will produce, even before the first seed has sprouted.

Though their accomplishments are often exceptional, most middle schoolers cannot be held accountable for adult-level expertise and expression, either. For example, I can't compare their first attempts at technical writing to that of accomplished technical writers in the field. We can barely do that with accomplished high schoolers. Nor can I get angry over their inability to express themselves coherently. They're closer to being children than they are to being adults. It was relatively recently that they were sleeping with the light on while wearing their favorite superhero pajamas, stuffed animals lining the beds. They laugh when people trip, and their tongues become lead when someone on whom they have a crush walks by. To expect them to perform at adult levels is cruel. We're there to do everything possible to ensure their success, not to critique inadequacies.

So how are they different?

As adults we sometimes forget that most young adolescents:

- Don't remember a world without iPads and SmartPhones.

- Have not known a time without electric cars and hybrid vehicles

- Assumed there have always been an African American and a woman Supreme Court Justice.

- No longer discern between homework and classwork; it's all practice or tasks assigned to be done at any point in the next 24 hours.

- Have never known movie tickets to be less than $10.

- Don't know what freshly run ditto paper smells like.

- Have no meaningful recollection of the Presidents Bush and Clinton, 9/11, or the Iraq war.

- Weren't alive when the space shuttle blew up or even when 9/11 happened.

- Have never known the world without AIDS, Ebola, or K-12 school shootings.

- Don't understand the expression, "You sound like a broken record." Many don't understand why anyone would buy music CDs.

- Think that roller skating has always been in-line.

- Think that every good children's book has been made into a movie they download at that exact moment for free.

Young adolescents are physiologically different from adolescents and those in late childhood. They undergo rapid physical, intellectual, and moral growth. They move from concrete to abstract thinking and from absurdity to rationality, and back again. They deal with tremendous pressures from peers, parents, and society, all the while searching for identity, purpose, security, and acceptance. These shifts produce strong emotions. Acting out, feeling hurt, defining authority by defying it, and alternating between being a child and being an adult all create situations that demand guidance from compassionate adults who have lived through those phases. Young adolescents crave:

- Positive social interaction with adults and peers.
- Structure and clear limits.
- Physical activity.
- Creative expression.
- Competence and achievement.
- Meaningful participation in families, school and communities.
- Opportunities for self-definition.

If we don't meet these needs at home and at school, young adolescents will become alienated, lack self-esteem and a sense of belonging, and choose destructive methods of coping, including delinquency and drugs. Early adolescence is the last point of effective intervention before their downward spiral toward self-destruction that can occur if we do not provide developmentally responsive learning environments for these students. Children between the ages of 10 and 14 need neither the protected coddling of elementary school nor the alienating subject departmentalization of high school. They need a bridge between the two levels, something that is age appropriate, focusing on unique intellectual, social, emotional, moral, and physical needs. Young adolescents are forging autonomy and identity. Their physical changes are so rapid that they often don't have time to adjust. Discomfort or embarrassment occurs. They are needy, moving from extreme egotism to thoughtful humility. They are champions for what is fair to the point where that's all that matters in some conversations. And just to make it exciting, they are all maturing at different rates with varying degrees of intensity.

Parents and schools working with young adolescents

Today's middle school classrooms can include students' parents in every step of the middle school experience. Current technology, innovation, and invitations improve upon yesterday's middle school approaches to parent communication. We're only on the first rung of a ladder with many new opportunities for parent-teacher communications. Online posting services are one of the most amazing phenomena to hit middle schools in the past few years. Teachers can post daily, weekly, and monthly homework, tests and quizzes, project directions, maps, student work, vocabulary lists, chalkboard notes, and much more.

Moms and dads should realize their continuing—but different—role. Don't let the middle school years be the time to let your child "fly solo." Some parents back off from their children's lives when their children enter middle school, claiming that their children need to meet consequences on their own—good or bad. Experience and collective wisdom from those who've passed this way before, however, all disagree with this. Rather, they teach us that early adolescence is a time to actually increase parental involvement, not reduce it. Parents wouldn't stop mid-stride from teaching 11-month-old Kenny how to walk when he was a toddler; they shouldn't back off from helping him develop strong character and academic success in his early adolescence. It's important for young adolescents to know that an adult's being in their presence is time well spent. It's affirmation that they count for something.

Educating and raising healthy young adolescents

Eighty percent of all jobs our students will one day hold haven't been invented yet. Experts say, in fact, that the overall amount of knowledge that exists is doubling every 10 to 12 months, whereas it used to double every decade, then every few years. Futurists add that current young adolescents might commonly live to be 120. Our young adolescents do not need teachers who see themselves solely as dispensers of all there is to know about particular subjects. They need dynamic adults offering a solid core of current knowledge but ones who create the ability and inclination to learn more in the years ahead. We have to respond to an evolving future before it happens. John W. Gardner was right when he said, "All too often we are giving young people cut flowers when we should be teaching them to grow their own plants." Content preparation isn't enough. Benjamin Franklin once said, "Tim was so learned that he could name a horse in the nine languages, [but] so ignorant that he bought a cow to ride on." Future employers and the community want more than individuals who can cite facts and figures. Companies want employees who can also self-educate, solve problems, anticipate needs, collaborate with others, think for themselves, and behave ethically.

The modern middle school approach has developed four important components that distinguish it from the traditional junior high school.

First, it incorporates some form of an advisory program so that every student is a part of a small group of students (less than 20) assigned to an advisor. Such a program develops close relationships between students and adults and gives them a sense of belonging and an advocate.

Second, it features interdisciplinary teaming wherein a core of academic teachers is assigned to the same group of students. These teachers have a common planning period, so they are able to respond collaboratively to the needs of individual students, meet jointly with parents, and design instructional units that relate the subjects to one another and to life.

Third, they utilize varied approaches to instruction in conducting a rigorous curriculum that also addresses students' own questions and focuses upon real life issues, calling for their active engagement in problem solving while mastering fundamental knowledge and skills. Lots of hands-on activities are possible in a flexible block schedule under the direction of the team. Service projects and varied learning strategies meet their needs for creative expression and meaningful participation in our communities.

Finally, they include exploratory programs and enrichment experiences that capitalize on the innate curiosity of young adolescents, exposing them to a wide range of academic, vocational, and recreational subjects for career options, community service, and enrichment. Here they may discover aptitudes, talents, and interests that will impact the rest of their lives. Exploratory areas include foreign languages, home and family living, technological arts, music, art, speech, drama, careers, consumer education, creative writing, intramurals, interest clubs, and other activities.

Middle school teachers are committed both to young adolescents and to their subject area. They have very high expectations for all students, not just those who show promise early on. They assess learning authentically, frequently, and in such a manner as to diagnose and teach, not just document deficiencies. They find academic and physical competitions for students to enter and then coach them on how to study. They teach them how to cope with disappointment and with success, give them positions of real responsibility, and require them to do some things in which they are not entirely sure of themselves, standing by their sides every step of the way. They affirm positive risk taking and include everyone who wants to participate. All students who want a speaking part in this year's Shakespeare play, for instance, receive one, even if it means we have to split a longer speech into two speeches.

Attitude can turn a blob of sand into King Arthur's castle. The reality is that teachers and parents of young adolescents teach more by what they are than by what they say. Young adolescents often do not separate the teacher from his or her attitude—the teacher is the attitude. Students are looking for hope. The adults in their lives inspire them to do the right thing. They exemplify the virtues they teach. They model making a positive contribution to the world and being of service to others. They strive to merit respect. And they enjoy themselves while doing it! Good spirit is contagious.

Assessment and accountability for young adolescents

Middle school teachers are judicious in how time is spent in the classroom. They do things with young adolescents that can only be done when everyone is together. They don't waste precious time on activities that can be done at home or ones that enable teachers to grade papers while students do busy work. Accountability pervades the whole middle school concept. Because we are so committed to becoming aware of student strengths and areas for improvement, then taking specific action and establishing high, rigorous goals as a result of that knowledge, today's middle school is far more demanding than yesterday's junior high school ever was. The use of authentic and alternative assessments alone qualifies for intense accountability towards a high standard. The feedback and responsibility are clearly delineated. Students and teachers are pushed towards excellence, not mediocrity.

When being assessed, young adolescents respond well to real audiences. When someone "in the outside world" witnesses middle school students' efforts, they become highly motivated. For instance, I get nearly 100% participation from all 140 of my students on our class literary magazine when they know those magazines will be displayed in hospital and dentist waiting rooms across our community. Whenever possible, middle schools and parents should use real audiences for middle schoolers' work—real scientists can review student science projects; members of the community can review student literary and news magazines in offices; the town historian can give feedback on student community histories; and a local landscaper can work with students to landscape their school grounds. If they know their science essays or art projects might be hanging in the local Jiffy Lube or the dentist's office, students become accountable to their community, friends, and family. They put more effort into achieving the high standards we've set.

As we assess young adolescents, we use frequent and formative feedback. Good assessment of young adolescents' work should never be saved for the end of a unit. We evaluate along the way, giving students feedback on their performance while they're learning. Football coaches don't wait until the football game is over to tell their players what they were doing wrong. An end-of-unit grade on a six-week project does little to motivate young adolescents. Multiple confirmations of success or redirection motivate students, however. Peer critiques, self-critiques, and think-alouds motivate students.

Much of a young adolescent's academic success is influenced by readiness in reading comprehension. Reading comprehension, however, has more to do with students' background and readiness than it does with the mere ability to decode or define words. Teachers and parents who want students to understand and remember concepts spend time creating background experiences prior to intense study. Before giving students a reading assignment, for example, we can show them pictures or video excerpts to provide context. We can ask them to role-play, hear testimonials, watch demonstrations, listen to stories, do simulations, or participate in a relevant field trip. The reverse is true as well: before we take them on a field trip, students do several readings about their destination so that they have a readiness to benefit from the location. The idea is to create some familiarity about content before engaging in it at a challenging level. If done, young adolescents remember the material and can use it intelligently.

In today's middle schools, we try to fulfill Oscar Wilde's declaration that the goal of every teacher is to put himself out of a job. Good teachers and parents of young adolescents find ways for everyone to experience depth and competence, no matter where their standardized test scores fall. No one is left to the shallows, and no young adolescent will be considered less than worthy of intellectual challenge.

Conclusion

Teaching young adolescents is one of the most demanding and rewarding jobs in life. We must apply extremely varied instructional strategies in concert with substantive content and skills, all while navigating hormonal storms and identity expeditions from humans at their most awkward stages. The mental dexterity and commitment to excellence of middle school teachers is beyond reproach. Middle school teachers are on the front lines, shaping a very real tomorrow.

I love being on those front lines. Teaching young adolescents is a combination of serving in the Peace Corps, organizing an amoebae circus, competing in the decathlon, being a salesman, and vying for an Academy Award. In no other job do you laugh aloud, ignite someone's imagination, bring peace, pose conflict, kiss frogs, quell fears, affirm goodness, stand amazed, and read a crumpled love note that assures the end of the world by 3:00 that afternoon. And that's just the end of first period. I wouldn't miss it for anything. After teaching for two decades, I believe that the world is going to be a better place for these individuals' substantive contributions. Middle school teachers are the bridge between the past, present, and future, not just the bridge between elementary and secondary levels. We are many things to many people, but most of all, we, along with their parents, are the significant others in the lives of these vulnerable young people.

Want to really affect the future? Spend time with a young adolescent. While reflecting on his life as a father of a young adolescent at 2:00 a.m. one weekday last year, a father wrote the following letter to his child's middle school team:

"Watching my son grow up is so bittersweet. My influence is waning fast, my conversations with him increasingly are—I don't know—inconclusive. I compare my interactions with my 13-year-old to my interactions with my 7-year-old. With my younger son, I dominate his entire horizon; with Matt, I'm mostly just blocking his view of the TV set.

Is this his form of self-protection? Is he insulating himself from me? It's easy to imagine the worst, to view this egocentrically, and think this is about me. It's not, I know. But still it's important to me to want to be a central part of his life. So I flip-flop between casual, superficial stuff and wanting to talk about "big stuff." The former have become easier and more comfortable while the latter have become more strident and ineffective.

I can tell by a glance how receptive he might be to my attempts to pull him back into my world. If I time it right, I can catch him open-minded early on a weekend morning with the offer of a trip to McDonald's. Sometimes, we get into serious discussions then—but always he draws the invisible bounds around his world, and cordons off certain things he reserves for himself.

I've come to learn, as I'm sure millions of parents have before me, that his world and mine no longer overlap the way they once did, and that it's OK. I've learned that Matt having his own world, distinct from mine, is a critical part of his development as a person. Invading it is not okay. As a parent, I have an obligation to protect him even when it is the last thing in the world he thinks he may need. But in order to protect him, I have to know what's going on in his world. No wonder parents fill their kids' schedules with sports and music lessons! It's totally about trying to control their world, to shape it in a certain direction one feels comfortable with. And the line between this control being acceptable and dysfunctional is hard to define and varies from child to child.

Anyway, it's late at night, and I set out to make a point in far fewer words than I've already written. My point was this: I subconsciously let go of a lot of my need to understand everything about his world outside of my own after the first few times I visited his middle school. Much more than with his elementary school, I feel like I have partially turned over the reins of his development to his middle school teachers and staff. I intuitively trust the school to be as caring, as concerned, as supportive and attentive with Matt as we have been as parents.

It is the natural order of things that he separate himself from us somewhat at this point in his life, to go about the difficult business of finding himself. By letting go, by giving him freedom to explore, I see he relaxes, and I can occasionally feel him reaching back to make sure I am still there. And every once in a while, among the casual responses I get to my attempts to hug him, he'll hug with me back with such a fierceness that it brings tears to my eyes, and I know we're going to be fine. Thanks, Matt's middle school teachers, for being such a key part of Matt's extended family, his community, and his parenting. There are few I would trust with such an important-to-me role, fewer still who could pull it off so well." — John, parent of a middle school student

Can Teachers Be Friends with Students?

On Larry Ferlazzo's website October 25, 2011, Brad Patterson asked: *"Can we be friends with our students? Where do we create barriers? How about social-media wise? I'm interested to hear about your experience, lessons learned, regrets, what you would offer as advice for new teachers."*

Larry asked me to write the first of three separate posts responding to Brad's question. While the other posts addressed the social media aspect of the question, I tackled the issue of how teachers and students view their relationships with each other on a broader level.

I used to think teachers could be friends with their students, but then I realized I was confusing "friend" with "friendly." We can grow closer to students when we share a common interest or work on long-term projects, but in every interaction, we remain teacher/student, mentor/ mentee, not true friends, and this is wise.

As adults, age differences do not matter when designing new instructional programs, hiking mountain trails, or performing together in the same community orchestra. Adult friends have equal power to retain personal identity and shape the course of the friendship, including its dissolution, if necessary. School children, however, don't have that equal influence on growing relationships, and they are vulnerable: adults are in positions of authority, and this asserts greater influence on children than it does on other adults. Unless it's through Big Brother/Sister programs or something similar, it seems inappropriate for a 25-year-old to spend most of his days in the company of an unrelated 15-year-old in our society.

We look for balance between what to cultivate and what to limit in teacher-student relations. There are boundaries, yet we want to be inviting to students and make sure they know they are good company. For as long as the child is a minor, however, it's not the same as friendships we enjoy with adults. Teachers and students can share an equal interest in local sports teams, for example, trading team updates, retelling great moments in legendary games, and purchasing souvenirs for each other. These are acts of human connection, which is valuable to both parties. Students mature when adults extend these connections, and teachers enjoy the camaraderie for the team and seeing students as more than one more paper to grade.

Notice, though, that the teacher does not take the student out for coffee and vent about office politics. There are topics that are inappropriate for teachers to share with students, and such sharing can undermine learning relationships in the classroom, even when the teacher is already very familiar with the student and his family.

There are other dynamics at work, too. Clinical Social Worker, Michelle Selby, cautions that a teacher disclosing personal information with a student can be helpful when it is to help that student understand something, but never when it is for the purpose of adults filling their own needs, such as when seeking friendship or approval. Her husband, educator Monte Selby, adds, "A health teacher can help kids learn about human sexuality, but it is not appropriate for the same teacher to tell kids which student looks sexy or share intimate details of their own sexuality. Those efforts are attempts to fill adult needs, not support student learning."

While a friend might call us in the middle of the night when something upsets him or her, the teacher who receives such a call from a student remains the concerned mentor, calling the child's parents, health officials, a school counselor, or Child Protective Services after the call, if warranted. Our adult responsibility for the welfare of the child supersedes any element of friendship forged.

Some teachers dress and act like their students in an effort to ingratiate themselves with students. The opposite happens, however. Students prefer teachers to be adults, not overgrown versions of themselves. Students gravitate toward teachers who inspire them to become something more than they are today, not extensions of their current condition. Sure, teachers clown around from time to time, but the better teachers remain clearly adults, facilitating learning, offering insight, and representing larger society as students try on new vocabulary, behaviors, fashions, and politics, watching how we respond.

When we throw a party, we invite friends. When we struggle, friends comfort us. When we are insensitive, friends forgive us. Friends become friends over extended, shared experiences that are not found in 50-minute class periods five times a week. For a student to move from being one of our pupils to being a friend, we need time with one another beyond his school years. We can grow closer when coaching sports teams, directing marching bands, and working on school publications, and when sharing segments of our non-school lives, such as participating in the same church/synagogue/mosque, Scout troop, or running club. During these experiences, we genuinely enjoy each other's company, sometimes speak as peers about mutually knowledgeable topics, send cards/e-mails of healing when one of us is sick, and we cheer from the sidelines when one of us achieves something important. These are humane acts. Are they being friendly? Yes. Are they inappropriate? No. Do they constitute full friendship? No.

Teachers and students share small parts of life's journey with one another every day. If they find something in common, are thoughtful toward one another, and through extended time, develop trust beyond that of mere acquaintances, they can't help but become friendly with one another, and this is a good thing. As professionals, we still grade these students without bias, discipline them if they misbehave, and put them in positions of responsibility just as fairly as we ever did before. If they ask intimate questions, we let them know they crossed a line and let them apologize.

I am a better person for having been influenced by the strong character and insight of some of my students over the years. When they became adults, a few of them moved into my circle of good friends. With Facebook turning the word, "friend," into a superficial commodity these days, true friendship seems diminished and uncertain. In an increasingly insecure world, we can't afford a policy of, "Teachers may never be friendly with students," but we can help teachers and students recognize clear boundaries rightfully established in successful teaching-learning relationships.

We forget sometimes that, while different from an adult friendship, the teacher-student relationship is not a lesser connection. It is often more meaningful and special, with tremendous value to both parties. We try to live up to its promise for the short time we have with our students. A friend taught me this.

Providing Effective Learning Experiences

Making Sense:
More Than Making Meaning

You are required to attend an in-service training about teaching in the block-length class even though your school is not moving to a block schedule this year or in the near future. How attentive will you be to all the details about teaching in the block-length class? How long will you be able to remember the content if you do not reference it again almost immediately? Intellectually, you understand the material and maybe pick up a teaching tip or two, but most of the information quickly fades from your memory.

The instructional content we deliver in our classroom can make all the sense in the world, but students won't remember it unless it has meaning to them. In fact, David Sousa and Carol Ann Tomlinson, in their book, *Differentiation and the Brain: How Neuroscience Supports the Learner-Friendly Classroom* (2010), declare that nothing goes into long-term memory unless it makes sense and has meaning. Of the two, they say, meaning-making has much more impact on long-term memory than sense-making.

Yes, content must make sense to students in order for them to learn it. They must understand facts, labels, connections, subsets, algorithms, processes, stipulations, conclusions, causes, effects, principles, theories, rules, and logical reasoning. However, we can't assume learning occurred because students understood the content. We have to seek ways to make content meaningful, to ensure the content and skills we are teaching are relevant to their lives.

Mired in an overloaded curriculum and the factory model of schooling, we may not feel we have time to create meaningful experiences with content in every lesson, but it's worth making the attempt.

Make it last

In their book *Deeper Learning: 7 Powerful Strategies for In-Depth and Longer-Lasting Learning* (2008), Eric Jensen and LeAnn Nickelsen state, "You can't afford NOT to provide processing time in the classroom … too much too fast won't last." Those last six words are important to post at the top of our lesson plan books. Are we out to teach so students learn, or are we there just to present curriculum and document where students fall short?

Let's spend time designing learning experiences that create meaning for students. Here are some ways to create meaning in our lessons:

Connect new learning to previous learning. For example, discuss the role of the antagonist in a novel after discussing the role of the protagonist. Draw upon what students know about factorization when introducing prime versus composite numbers. Teach new key signatures in music by helping students compare them to already-learned key signatures.

Connect new learning to students' backgrounds. We know students have pets, so we draw upon that knowledge to talk about being responsible for another's well-being. We reflect on the issues surrounding local day labor gathering sites when discussing immigration laws and how local communities interact with state and federal agencies.

Model how the skill or concept is used. With demonstrations, think-alouds, self-talks, and modeling, students see the useful applications of what we're teaching. We demonstrate a lab procedure in the wrong sequence, and consequently, get an incorrect result. We go back, adjust the sequence, and are able to produce the correct result—all while stating aloud what we are thinking as we work.

Demonstrate how content or skills create leverage (gain us something) in other subjects. Here we weave relevancy and curriculum integration. This idea of leveraging is inspired by Doug Reeves' views on the appropriateness of curriculum standards in his 2010 book, *Transforming Professional Development into Student Results.*

In describing how teachers determine the major standards within a large array of standards, Reeves says that one of the deciding criteria is how the specific standard provides leverage for work in other subjects. For example, order of operations in mathematics is important for algebra class and beyond, so it should be in the nonnegotiable, super-important category in our planning.

To make specific topics meaningful to students, then, we have to show how they provide leverage for other tasks and thinking, such as demonstrating for students in science class how knowledge of electrical flow helps us figure out efficient circuit design or why a bulb fails to light. In PE, we can show students how knowledge of the interplay among metabolism, diet, sleep, and exercise helps us maintain a healthy weight.

Include a "So, why should we learn this?" section in every major lesson. Make it an official part of your lesson plan, so you attend to it regularly. Answer the question for yourself, then put it into words or demonstrations for your class so students capture it as well.

Try it right now. Why is it important to know and understand common structures for poetry? Types of government? Rational versus irrational numbers? The difference between masculine and feminine in Spanish? Electromagnetism? Dance in a physical education class?

Increase emotional connections. In all grade levels, but particularly in middle grades and high school, intense emotion increases engagement, and that engagement creates meaning for students. Elevate that meaning by raising the emotional intensity from time to time.

Students are humbled by a holocaust survivor sharing stories from Auschwitz, and they hang on every word. Students understand how important it is to disagree with someone without becoming divisive or physical by conducting formal debates, particularly when they argue for the proposition opposite their own beliefs. They protect local playgrounds from vandalism when they are the ones painting or building them through service-learning projects.

Create more access points in the mind. Increase the number of angles through which information is stored in the brain. With a math principle, for example, show visuals, discuss the concepts, practice with manipulatives, ask students to retell the concepts to others, and ask them to use art forms, engineering, architecture, and force and motion principles that apply to the concept.

If we could bake the principle into something we can eat, we could add smell and taste here. This is absurd, of course, but the idea is to increase the number of exposures and media used to interact with the content and skills. The more connections that are made, the more portions of the brain that "light up."

Prime the brain. Cris Tovani, Robert Marzano, John Hattie, and many others make compelling cases for teachers spending classroom time priming the mind for what it's seeking and about to experience.

Before a lab, we explain to the students (or help them discover for themselves) the purpose of the lab and the steps they will take to obtain that result, including any issues that might arise. Before beginning a lecture, we do the same thing: What specific content should students seek, what road map will the lecture follow, and where might there be "bumps" in understanding? Setting goals and revealing the itinerary go a long way to meaningful participation.

Separate and combine knowledge: analyze, synthesize. Erik Jensen and LeAnn Nickelsen remind us (*Deeper Learning: 7 Powerful Strategies for In-Depth and Longer Lasting Learning*, 2008) that specific knowledge becomes meaningful when we see the whole and its parts. Help students see how things fit together by breaking things apart, placing smaller concepts and facts in larger context, putting things together to create something new, and removing portions of the larger whole to see their effect on that whole.

For example, in English, explore how removal of one paragraph in an essay strengthens or weakens it. In history class, break down the provisions of the Treaty of Versailles from World War I into countries' goals, concessions, reparations, and ultimate effects. Ask students about the impact of each provision's inclusion and what might have happened had it been removed.

So what?

So what does this mean for you and your instruction? If it doesn't mean much, you'll move on, looking for an essay that catches your eye. By the time you finish reading this book, you will forget most of this essay's content. Everyone does this, including me, depending on the topic.

If your response to the "So what?" question changes your next lesson in some way, prompts you to analyze previous lessons in light of these ideas, or compels you to share an idea with a colleague, you might highlight a few points and rip out the pages for safe-keeping or record the ideas in the margin of your lesson plan book for later reference.

Whatever you choose, you carry the content forward because it matters; knowledge changes into something meaningful for you.

Metaphors Are Key
(Metaphor Intended)

> "Metaphor is often used as a teaching tool, or to convey difficult concepts .... Since metaphor allows for the substitution of ideas across differing areas of study, it is considered by some to be an interdisciplinary Rosetta stone."
>
> —from http://knowgramming.com/metaphor.htm

Metaphors are the workhorses of effective middle level lessons. Boil down everything you need to teach to its salient concepts, and you'll find metaphors to be a likely ally in your teaching efforts. Like the air molecules around us, metaphors are everywhere, flowing, usually unnoticed until they fail to make the point intended. When they work, students feel that intuitive "aha!" moment so many of us seek with our classes.

Did you catch the metaphors in the previous paragraph? Take a moment (another metaphor) today and listen to your students and colleagues converse. You'll hear metaphors such as:

- Let's frame today's conversation ...

- I'm a bit rusty on this ...

- It was anarchy in the cafeteria!

- There was an upturn in the economy.

- Breaking news ...

- Are you on the fence about it?

- If x = 2 and y = 4, what does 3x + 6y equal?

- Toss the idea around.

- Let's turn that vertical thermometer horizontally to create a number line for our integers.

- You need to have parallel structure in this sentence.

- I'm not using some cookie-cutter approach.

- Wouldn't it be great to harness the power of the sun?

- What's our benchmark for this standard?

- Can I grab two minutes of your time today?

- I was floored by his behavior.

- Google it.

- This fraction is only a tiny piece of the pizza compared to this one.

- Do you get the point of this?

We use metaphors in every lesson we teach, whether we realize it or not. One way to improve our teaching is to get strategic (a war metaphor) and consciously design metaphors. Many students are capable of understanding our subjects better if we give them metaphors to clarify and illuminate (another metaphor) the subject.

For example, some students grasp the concept of word roots if they see the idea of root portrayed through drawn "word trees" in which the root section of the picture lists the early origins of the word.

It's critical, however, that students have the personal background to understand the metaphors. Many adults understand the meaning of "We don't want another Bay of Pigs," when talking about a bloody, political conflict, but to our students, the reference conjures a rather silly mental picture.

"He flozzled his website." Is this a good or a bad thing? We don't know.

What if we changed it to "He flozzled his website, and the fallout was considerable"? We don't have any idea what "flozzled his website" means, but we realize it's probably something bad because we understand that "fallout" usually refers to dreadful things, such as the radioactive aftermath of a nuclear detonation. We can gather meaning for the unknown phrase "flozzled" because we understand the fallout metaphor.

Metaphors and their subcategory cousins like analogies, idioms, short stories, personification, and similes offer incredible insights to complex thinking. Consider teaching students common analogies such as:

- Antonyms
- Synonyms
- Part : Whole
- Whole : Part
- Tool : Its Action
- Tool User : Tool
- Tool : Object It's Used With
- Category : Example
- Effect : Cause
- Cause: Effect
- Action : Thing Acted Upon
- Action : Subject Performing the Action
- Object or Place : Its User
- Noun : Closely Related Adjective

Make it a daily habit to think in terms of analogies. For example, ask students for the category into which a particular topic fits; then ask for another item and its category. Ask students to take an idea or object through stages of increasing intensity; then compare it to another idea or object's similar progression. Ask students to consider an action and the thing acted upon; then generate a similar relationship with another action. For a fun competition promoting the learning of analogies, visit www.wordmasterschallenge.com.

Thinking metaphorically

Kelly Gallagher, secondary school teacher and author of *Deeper Reading* (2004), teaches students metaphors for their own sake, including the snow globe metaphor in which students identify elements or characteristics of a topic that are important enough to warrant inclusion in a pretend tourist's snow globe of the topic.

For example, in San Francisco, we might include the Golden Gate Bridge, Fisherman's Wharf, cable cars, and sourdough bread as objects for a tourist's snow globe. We then can ask students to create a new snow globe for San Francisco residents. This could include symbols of diverse populations, elements of the city's history, commerce, politics, art, and architecture.

Gallagher and others, including Kenneth Koch in his wonderful book *Wishes, Lies, and Dreams: Teaching Children to Write Poetry* (1999) suggest using mini-templates and sentence stems to help students get started thinking metaphorically. For example, we can use this cloze-type template:

_____ is (are) a _____ because

_____.

To really push students to think differently, the first blank should be filled with something intangible or not easily compared to other things, such as trust, a republic, a paradox, hope, a sequence, or an odyssey. The second blank is something tangible like a baseball, a canyon river, an iPod, or the Dewey decimal number on a library book's spine. The final blank is for the students' dexterous thinking. Here are a couple of examples:

- Improper numbers are ice cream cones with too many scoops of ice cream because both seem likely to topple over at any moment and both require quick action by the consumer to fix them.

- The antagonist of the novel is a brake pedal to the protagonist because he keeps slowing the progression of the protagonist toward his goals.

With all metaphors, of course, the deepest thinking and best learning come as students publicly defend their positions. This means they are required to cite sections of text or their learning that support the comparisons they draw. It's easy for middle school kids to say a literary character or an historic figure is like an onion, but the real learning happens when students must explain how the person has many layers, each one more interesting than the other.

Ask students to reinforce their metaphors with associated attributes and verbs. For example, if they say that debate opponents squared off about a controversial issue, they can continue the metaphor by describing who was in each corner of the controversy. They can describe a particular year in Congress as a three-ring circus with a particular political party as the ringmaster.

Keeping metaphors in mind

As we design our lessons, let's look for metaphors that help students learn. Research and years of practice show us that students best remember information if it is presented in a coherent structure the first time they experience it. Metaphors provide that structure. Graphic organizers are structural, spatial, and sequential metaphors that allow students to find meaning.

- A simple t-chart or Venn diagram is a metaphor for comparing and contrasting concepts.
- A timeline is a metaphor for presenting information in chronological order.
- A matrix allows students to picture in their minds (a metaphor) how to organize information, including what might be a subset

of something else, what might be redundant, what might run parallel, and what might lead to something else.

- As with most teaching practices, we must take the time to make the implicit explicit. This means we sensitize ourselves to the formal and informal metaphors we're using with students, and we make sure students understand their meanings. We're overt about it; we might do think–alouds (self-talks), student think–pair–shares, diagrams, and quick, frequent explanations of the metaphors. We can ask the class:

- What does it mean to triangulate something?

- If our thinking is parallel to someone else's thinking, what do we mean?

- The character said that life was like a carnival Tilt-a-Whirl. What did she mean by that?

- Kira just said she going to be toast tonight with these grades. Is this good or bad for her?

Remember, too, that middle level students are very concrete in their thinking. Make your metaphors vivid and tangible, if possible. I've taught the drafting portion of the writing process for years after first teaching students to sculpt with clay. While sculpting, they are required to describe the process using writing process concepts. Students sculpt, claiming: "This part needs more texture," "This needs to move up here," "This needs more support," "I'm wadding this up and starting over," "Can you look this over with me?"

Although we should keep using symbolic and abstract metaphors such as organizers and math signs, we need to also incorporate metaphors that use objects, movement, and students' bodies as much as possible. They hit home runs with young adolescents.

Try using a metaphor or two or five this week in your classes. As appropriate, teach metaphors and metaphorical thinking for their own sake; they're vital to success in every subject, not just language arts. Point out the metaphors used in everyday conversation with students and look for the metaphors in students' lives.

British author, G. K. Chesterton once claimed that, " … all slang is metaphor, and all metaphor is poetry." With the developmental nature of the humans they serve, schools are fertile ground for both metaphor and poetry in every subject and every action of the day. It takes practice, but both you and your students can get very good at metaphors, unlocking meaning in every discipline. The key fits, so let's turn it.

Creating Wonder Still Works

In case you haven't heard, this is the last year any school in the United States is allowed to grade students. Starting in the fall, all student achievement will be reported through extended narratives with accompanying student products analyzed against evaluative criteria established by the federal government. Canadian Parliament recently enacted the same legislation. Have you considered what changes you'll need to make in your classroom as a result of this new policy?

I'll bet every one of you reacted to that announcement. I might have gotten the same reaction by quietly stating that there's no more paper for the photocopier in the foreseeable future. Or maybe by yelling "Red Sox" or "Free Donuts in the Teacher's Lounge."

Just as writers must provide an opening hook to grab reader interest, teachers must reach their students before they can teach them. We are little more than the "Peanuts" cartoon teacher—Wah-wah, wah-wah-wah, wha-wha—when we give students the material and tell them to learn it because it's on a test. Learning lasts longer than next Tuesday's quiz when students are fully engaged in the process.

This isn't something that's just nice if it happens; it's vital to students' success. With an already overcrowded curriculum, however, and an all-hands-on-deck standardized test myopia, teachers are drifting away from curiosity-building because it takes time, and it's considered too much "fluff" for lessons with content-only rigor that are supposedly proven to create immediately improved test scores. Meaning and personal engagement are left for happier times.

Humans are naturally curious; they're ceaseless students, wired for pondering. There's a reason John Dewey, Jerome Bruner, Madeline Hunter, and many others who advocate self-discovery, meaningful learning, zones of proximal development, problem-based learning, and opening "hooks" are so popular: Students achieve better and more when they are invested in each subject they experience.

Let's have the courage and creativity to keep one of the most important aspects of our practice: providing a sense of wonder in the classroom. Ways to create wonder in our lessons are plentiful. You'll find one or more of the following strategies in every successful middle level classroom.

Use drama

- Dress up as an historical figure, a book's character, a math symbol, a scientific process, an art tool, or a piece of technology and ask students to interview you.
- Allow a student to explain something to the class using a hand puppet.
- Ask students to portray elements of a subject using drama, such as telling the story of a math or science process, an historical event, or the life of a particular punctuation mark.
- Create gentle confusion.
- Ask a student to conduct a meaningful conversation with you in front of the class without using a verb (an action word or any form of "to be" such as am, were, is).

- Teach the importance of pronouns by eliminating their antecedents. For example, "Give it to me" (without identifying "it"); "Did she like the gift you bought her?" (without identifying "her").

- Start an argument.

- Dare students to prove you wrong.

- Tell a student, "I disagree with you. Prove your point."

- Portray the devil's advocate side of an issue and ask students to respond.

Provide a sense of magic

- Encourage students to discover amazing patterns in numbers, such as the relationship between the middle number and the outside numbers when we multiply any two-digit number by 11 (Examples: 23 x 11 = 253, 51 x 11 = 561, 44 x 11 = 484).

- Place a Ping-Pong ball into the wide center of a funnel and blow forcefully from the opposite, narrow tube end of the funnel. As you blow, fast moving air along the funnel's wide, inner surface lowers the air pressure in the funnel and the Ping-Pong ball stays in the funnel no matter which way you bend your head as you blow the air—even bent over, looking down at the floor. For great science demonstrations that seem magical, check out great stuff at www.exploratorium.edu.

Create anticipation.

- Give students themes from an upcoming novel and ask them whether they agree with them.

- Give students statements of truth about an upcoming unit of study and ask them whether or not the statements are true and why.

- Give students a few pieces of the upcoming unit of study such as important vocabulary terms and concepts and ask them to predict what they'll be learning.

- Pose a problem to be solved.

- Ask students to determine the angle of trajectory for a rocket that you want to land at a particular location.

- Give students a set of materials and ask them to build the tallest free-standing structure they can within 10 minutes.

- Ask students to change the dynamics of a musical piece to appeal to a different audience.

Surprise them.

- Ask a colleague or parent volunteer to burst into your classroom at just the right moment and do something related to the day's topic. For example, someone could burst into the room as an early explorer and mandate strange new rituals everyone must now perform, such as Cortez might have done with the Aztecs.

- Pose a startling statement or question that gets students thinking about something in your presentation: "Students should be paid $100 per week for going to school." "As of today, you are all mushbidians from planet Zoliton." "This worked when I did it in zero-gravity." "Democracy isn't always the best policy—or is it?"

Show the larger context.

- Teach something complex that requires students to learn subsets of skills. For example, we might show students a video of an intense and well-done debate before teaching them debate technique.

- Show students a compelling PowerPoint presentation before asking them to create their own.

- Stimulate imagery.

- When teaching poetry, show particularly evocative moments from famous movies and ask students how the scene is poetic.

- When teaching about a system of government or a type of economy, conduct the class in the manner of that government or economy.

- Before teaching parts of speech or grammar, ask students to design a language from scratch. When they return with just an alphabet code, ask them how they will account for aspects like plurals, tense, gender, and numbers.

Foreshadow and create suspense.

- Make a provocative statement regarding the next day's learning: "Tomorrow, we find out how a desert lizard is the perfect metaphor for the civil rights movement," or "Tomorrow we find out how something the early Phoenicians did allows you to hold a school dance today."

- Announce to students on a Monday, "You will never be the same again," and ask them to look for the truth of this statement throughout the week.

Connect to the world.

- Show students at least three ways they'd use knowledge of slope and y-intercept (literary analysis, historical comparisons, the nitrogen cycle, conjunctions or anything else seemingly abstract and unrelated) in the real world.

- Bring in an expert in a field of study to demonstrate his work in front of the students, or alternatively, take a field trip to this person's work setting and watch him work or participate in his work. This personalizes the field for students.

Incorporate music.

- When teaching ratios and fractions, introduce some of your lessons with a look at musical time signatures, such as 2/4, 3/4, 4/4, and 6/8.

- Play music that creates a particular mood for the learning experience you want to provide.

Experience divergent thinking.

- Use Synectics (problem-solving process using metaphors): Ask students how punctuation is like music or how the battle just studied is similar to the Kingdom Protista.

- Ask provocative questions: "Why do we teach everyone in our society, not just those easiest to teach?" "History is said to be written by the victors. Is that happening today?" "What would Leonardo da Vinci think of an iPod?"

- Ask students to categorize items as you prepare to teach them about the Dewey decimal system or the Periodic Table of Elements.

Spark friendly competition.

- Compare your students' performance on a task with that of another class period (real or made-up) and gently prod them: "I think you can beat period 3's score."

- Announce to the class that you are the smartest person in the room. No one can find a mistake you've made because you haven't made any. Then pause and grin, daring anyone to try to out-think you. If someone finds a mistake, you have to shout his name at lunch in the cafeteria and explain how great he is. If you successfully defend yourself against accusations of a mistake, the accusing student must shout in the cafeteria how much he loves learning about your subject.

Appeal to ethics, morals, and fairness.

- Ask students to consider at what point national security supersedes our rights to privacy.

- Ask students to list the pros and cons of human genetic engineering.

Create prior knowledge.

- Let students play with an idea or object before reading or learning about it. For example, before reading the rules of football, have students play football.

- Before reading a new software manual, play with the software a bit.

- Before teaching students about a particular moment in history, give them the background of what was going on during that time.

- Provide visuals and manipulatives.

- When teaching students financial math, provide a tangible model such as real sales receipts, checkbooks, and bank statements.

- Use primary sources like copies of original documents, excerpts of statements recorded by the individuals involved, or videos of interviews with the author, scientist, or political figure you're studying.

Experiment and take risks.

- Put a slab of meat into a bowl of Coca-Cola and watch what happens to it over several days. Remind students that the stomach wall is much like this meat.

- Ask students to volunteer to do something a bit risky (yet appropriate) in front of the class, such as speaking extemporaneously, conducting an experiment, participating in a trust fall, or sharing a personal experience.

Use constructivism.

Through constructivist approaches, facilitate students' discovery of:

- The fact that we can't determine both an electron's exact location and momentum at the same moment.
- The relationship between biodiversity and the health of a biome.
- The role of primary, secondary, and tertiary colors and their effect on the viewer of paintings.
- The need for rules for verb conjugation.

Use narrative.

- Tell the story of an historical event or scientific discovery.
- Make up a fairytale about perimeter and area, rotation and revolution, or an adamant semi-colon.
- Share a personal experience regarding the subject you're teaching or ask a student to do so.

Make them laugh.

- Begin with a related joke: "What did the German cytologist say when the microscope fell on his foot? Ah! Mitosis ("My toes 'is'") broken!"
- Put some "bad" puns into the presentation: "This is just the tibia of the anatomy iceberg," "Do not tell an anatomical fibula," "Do I have to get sternum with you?" "You have some verb talking to me like that!" "Noun is the time to study a person, place, or thing,"

Create your wonder.

With all the emphasis on completing the curriculum and raising test scores, some of us hold court instead of really teaching. If we want students to do well, we have to teach effectively, and that means we grab students' attention and create a sense of wonder in the classroom.

Scientist Rachel Carson was right when she said, "If a child is to keep alive his inborn sense of wonder, he needs the companionship of at least one adult who can share it, rediscovering with him the joy, excitement, and mystery of the world we live in."

Share your passion for the subject; it's contagious to your students with whom you've built positive relationships. Socrates said that all thinking begins with wonder.

Beating a Path to the Brain

A F O N N I S S C A R C	Study and learn the individual letters in the box. Understand them. Find meaning in them. Move all of them to long-term memory.

A student might memorize these letters for a test later in the week. But understand them, find meaning in them, move them to long-term memory? Slim chance. Now look at the same set of letters this way: San Francisco. Those of us who are familiar with the city suddenly connect those letters to places we have seen or studied—Fisherman's Wharf, Alcatraz, the Exploratorium, or curvy Lombard Street. We might think of cable cars we rode or sourdough bread we ate. By chunking the individual pieces (letters) in a meaningful way, we make sense of the randomness and improve the chances of moving the information to long-term memory.

Chunking is one of many instructional strategies supported by recent research about the human brain. Our rapidly expanding knowledge of how humans learn offers exciting possibilities for teachers.

A few years ago, I made a presentation about the applications of brain research for middle level education to a group of Colorado teachers. After the session, the husband of one teacher came up to me. He explained that he was a trauma surgeon, had a child who suffered from brain damage, and was well versed in neuroscience. My heart started pounding, and I worried that I might have made a mistake in the presentation.

"Did I get the neuroscience wrong?" I asked him.

"No," he said. "You had it right. I want to tell you that those of us in the medical field are finding that the comments we made to patients about how the brain works just a few years ago are 180 degrees different from the truths we've found today. That's going to continue, too. If it's hard for us to keep up with the latest findings, then it has to be very difficult for teachers to keep up, given everything else they have to do."

We agreed that somehow teachers must stay informed about the new developments in brain research, whether at a professional conference, a school workshop, through a book discussion group, or by reading articles like this one.

Retaining the lesson

If I asked you what you learned yesterday, you might not be able to immediately recall the specifics. David Sousa, author of *How the Brain Learns* (2005), says that most people will forget 90% of what they heard in the past 24 hours unless they interact with the material. In her book, *Brain Matters* (2010), Patricia Wolfe explains that our brains begin discarding information within 18 seconds of receiving it unless we do something significant with the new data.

Now, it would be unreasonable to expect teachers to stop every 18 seconds in class, so their students could interact with a different set of facts. But, it is possible for us to make significant connections on a daily basis. For example, instead of lecturing for 30 minutes, then asking students to color a map or label a diagram, a teacher could stop halfway through the presentation and ask the students to use one of the 12 summarization techniques they previously rehearsed. Cindy and Harvey might choose a two-minute partner review in which Cindy first describes everything she learned in the previous quarter hour followed by Harvey describing everything he learned that Cindy didn't mention. Afterward, the teacher finishes the lesson. (By the way, of the many possible instructional presentations, lecturing—by itself—results in the lowest long-term retention rates.)

Another good way for students to interact with new information is to divide them into groups and ask them to design a flag with symbols that represent the significant points of the topic. For example, they might create a flag representing labor's interests during the meat-packing industry scandals of the 1920s, a flag representing the conjugations of regular verbs in French, a flag representing compound interest on a loan, or a flag representing the importance of stretching before and after exercise. On the back of each flag, students can write explanations for each component of the design.

Understanding how the brain moves information to memory is very useful for teachers. Researchers tell us that the ability to remember something accurately and thoroughly has more to do with how the information entered our minds than how we review it. The brain seeks wholeness. When we fail to adequately learn something the first time, our memories become piecemeal. The brain fills those holes with other information regardless of its accuracy, and worse, becomes convinced that whatever filled those holes is the original truth.

This confabulation happens every day in our classes. That's why we must be on the lookout for students' misconceptions and correct them as quickly as possible. Knowing this, I pay more attention to the front end of my lessons because I have found that it takes much more time and energy to undo bad instruction than to teach a concept correctly the first time. I use more frequent and formative assessments than summative assessments to evaluate student learning. I also try to be clear about my expectations. Instead of saying, "Read Chapter 17 and be prepared for a test on Thursday," I will say, "Let's take a look at the way this chapter is set up and discuss why we're reading it."

The Primacy-Recency Effect takes this idea to the next level. Sousa uses this phrase to describe the portion of a lesson that we remember best and least. In some middle school classrooms, teachers begin the period with announcements, attendance, and other clerical matters. They might end the period by letting students start on homework or clean up the classroom before the bell rings. But the middle of the period—when the least amount of material can move to long-term memory—is when they focus on the key parts of the lesson. What a waste of learning potential!

If we want to improve learning, we have to teach the big truths in the first 10 minutes of class and review them in the last 10 minutes. When students first enter our classrooms, they need to do something that reinforces the major points or skills of the lesson, not just exchange last night's homework. Changing our classroom sequences can be the difference between students remembering the principles of FDR's New Deal legislation or remembering that the Ecology Club will meet next Tuesday. (In block-length classes, we must complete more than one Primacy-Recency cycle during the extended period.)

Getting the brain's attention

The brain is basically a survival organ. It focuses first on feeding itself—getting enough nutrition and energy to work—then responds to any threats, such as extreme temperatures or emotional and physical danger. If its survival needs are met, the brain next focuses on what's most familiar or contextual. The pursuit of familiarity is so powerful that the brain will not move anything to long-term memory unless it is connected to something already there. Knowing this, smart math teachers will begin their lessons on percentages by tapping into students' prior experiences, perhaps focusing on the likelihood of rain in the weather forecast or discussing classroom survey results.

Explain differences first. Interestingly, we store information by similarities, but we retrieve it by differences. As middle school teachers, this means we should focus on similar topics several days or weeks apart to keep students from confusing the information the first time they experience it. If we have to teach similar topics simultaneously, we should explain the differences first to keep things clear.

Prime the brain. Continuing the hierarchy of focus, the brain next pays attention to what it has been primed to receive. So, if we ask students to watch a video and take notes, they will write everything or nothing but probably not the material we thought was most important. On the other hand, if we ask them to watch the video and record four ways Americans responded to the Soviet Union's launching of Sputnik, we can steer their brains toward the purpose of the lesson. Ask a naturalist to study an area of the forest for possible uses, and she will examine soil composition, tree cover, flora, fauna, climate, and the impact on animal habitats and surrounding ecosystems. Ask a housing development specialist to observe the same area, and he will focus on slopes in need of grading, heavy boulders that will need to be redistributed, the difficulty of connecting to nearby water systems, the cost of tree removal, and the neighbors' willingness to cooperate. Establishing the purpose of an assignment and activating personal background are critical if we want to create meaning and get good results.

Five or six interactions. Conventional wisdom says we need five or six different interactions with the material before we master it. Can we do this with every topic? No, but we can incorporate previous learning when teaching new units, thereby providing reinforcement and keeping those neural pathways open. We also can let students continue interacting with the information and growing new neural connections by using wait time in our classes. In other words, don't call on the first student who raises her hand. The moment we call on someone, all the other students relax and their brains shift to autopilot. Keep everyone in suspense and their neurons will continue firing. Better yet, keep those brains moving at warp speed by making a habit of asking students to comment on a classmate's response before you add commentary.

The brain is very elastic. It continues to grow dendrites with each new learning experience until the day we die. The more dendrites we grow the more neural pathways we have for future learning. In other words, the more we learn, the more we can learn.

If we want to help students learn well, we must immerse them in rich, diverse, and stimulating environments. Researchers tell us there are two stages in a person's life when the brain experiences phenomenal growth—from birth through age 2 and from ages 10 to 14. That's wonderful news for middle school teachers. It means we can profoundly influence students and shape their thinking, perhaps for a lifetime. So, let's use Socratic Seminars, inquiry methods, vivid simulations, authentic assessments, varied summarization techniques, block scheduling, and alternative instruction models that ignite innovation. Although new discoveries are made about the brain every year, one principle has remained constant: mindful teachers produce mindful learners.

Let Every Interaction Teach

The ultimate goals of education are tolerance, compassion, and courage. That's it. All those lesson plans, curriculum guides, supply orders, school board meetings, standardized assessments, papers to grade, parent phone calls, cafeteria duty periods, and field trips lead to just three outcomes: tolerance, compassion, and courage.

If this is really true, then a whole lot of effort should go into incorporating these concepts into our daily teaching. This is justification for more character education, right? Yes, but not in the way some schools approach it. Character education is not something done to students; it's done with students. If students experience compassion only as something that comes from outside them, the lesson isn't learned.

Although some schools swear by them, I'm not convinced that commercial character education programs with their posters, banners, daily announcements, and teacher-advisory materials make the dramatic differences in students' lives that they claim. At best, they offer educators a lexicon and a few ideas to incorporate with their own.

School-wide character education pep rallies are rarely as effective as we think they are, though time spent with some articulate and compelling motivational speakers such as Canada's Rick Hansen ("Man in Motion," who wheel-chaired around the world) is time well spent. Character education phrases repeated every school day during the morning announcements such as, "Make it a great day or not—the choice is yours," are corrupted by the monotonous cacophony of daily, first period wake-up mode, earning parody status with many students and teachers.

So how do we keep tolerance, compassion, and courage fresh and compelling for students? By living and affirming them daily. Occasional, blunt manipulation also works. Robert F. Kennedy was right:

> Each time a person stands for an ideal, or acts to improve the lot of others, or strikes out against injustice, he sends forth a tiny ripple of hope, and crossing each other from a million different centers of energy and daring, these ripples build a current that can sweep down the mightiest walls of oppression and resistance.

The essence of character

Let's remember the essence of each of these virtues as we teach them:

Tolerance. Tolerance refers to our respect for others' beliefs, nature, and behavior (adapted from the American Heritage Dictionary). Ignorance breeds suspicion, even to the point of racism. When students know each other, however, they are more tolerant of each other.

Teachers who provide experiences for students to share commonly held feelings inspire tolerance. Examples include teacher-advisory groups, physical projects such as painting the playground, cutting a trail, climbing a mountain, building an access ramp for students in wheelchairs, or putting on a class play.

Many icebreaker activities work as well: students interviewing each other and then introducing these classmates to the class; posting diet and exercise charts for students who agree to share one week's worth of information for the class to analyze in their unit on metabolism; individual students teaching small lessons within the larger unit to the whole class. Students also experience tolerance when we show them how they learn differently and that different ways of learning are not wrong or right, they just are.

Effective teachers substitute "readiness" whenever they use "ability" while promoting multiple approaches to problem solving. They teach students more than one way to present information, and they encourage differentiated personal responses to learning.

We advance both compassion and tolerance in students when we emphasize students' personal competence regarding their learning. If students feel competent, for example, they are not threatened by others' differences, or by life's problems. If they are feeling competent, they can extend themselves to others rather than conserve energy just to survive. If students feel incompetent, however, every problem seems too big to solve, and every person is too irritating to accept.

Personal competence opens the door to tolerance. In that vein, we make sure students experience success: we practice new behaviors in short chunks, provide frequent feedback, vary from whom the feedback comes, shorten assignments so students can get feedback more quickly, and we tier assignment challenges for developmental appropriateness.

Compassion. Compassion refers to how we help those who suffer, including our inclination to extend mercy to others. Compassion is modeled every time we listen to students sincerely—listening to understand, not just listening so we can ready our response.

We can also read stories of individuals and groups being merciful to others, even when there is no immediately visible, personal gain for the individual or group to be so. Great read-aloud and silent reading books that teach compassion and tolerance include Ron Jones' *The Acorn People* (1996), Nat Henthoff's *The Day They Came to Arrest the Book* (1983), Ben Mikelsen's *Touching Spirit Bear* (2005), Shel Silverstein's *The Giving Tree* (2004), Irene Hunt's *No Promises in the Wind* (2002), Melba Pattillo Beals' *Warriors Don't Cry* (2007), and Harper Lee's *To Kill a Mockingbird* (1960).

Compassion is also taught by taking the time after classroom occurrences of compassion to affirm the behavior of the individuals involved:

> "Mike and Kira, thanks for looking out for Ahmed on this project. His week-long absence really put him behind. Your extra help with him after you finished your work put him back on top. His parents thanked me for asking you to do this, but as you know, I never asked you to do it. You saw he was struggling and you helped. The world is a great place when people do what you did. Thanks again."

Compassion is taught every time we ask students to befriend someone who needs one, when students do service projects for the community, and when they write letters of encouragement to those suffering tragedy or loss.

Forgiving others their offenses is a compassionate act as well, so lessons in how to forgive have impact. Direct questioning also works: "What would be the most compassionate response to this person?" or "What would a compassionate person do in this situation?" If the word compassion seems to make your students uncomfortable, try substituting the word, "caring." The important thing is to use these questions and terms frequently and any time, not just in "character education" lessons. We can ask them when discussing daily topics with students: homework, current events, borrowing supplies, working in small groups, or a chronic behavior problem.

Courage. Affirming specific examples in class is a great way to teach courage. We can also read stories about individuals who stand up to others or successfully handle conflicts in their lives, not just those who survive adventures in the wilderness or battle monsters.

In addition to the books listed above, Sheila Gordon's *Waiting for the Rain* (1997) about two childhood friends—one white, one black—growing up during South Africa's apartheid, is a great choice. We can promote the idea that we don't learn to swim by staring at the water; we jump in and deal with what comes.

It takes courage to admit mistakes. We promote courage, then, when we ask students to confront their weaknesses constructively, admitting when they have erred and finding ways to make restitution or resolve problems. We have to model the process, however, because many middle school students think that making academic and personal mistakes makes you appear weak in the eyes of others. We have to prove throughout the year that recognizing and correcting mistakes is a sign of strength and future success.

To teach courage, we show students how it takes more courage to comment on the positive in someone instead of offering a put-down. It takes more mental skill to compliment than to complain. Promoting this means that we leave sarcasm and cynicism at the curb as we enter the school building each morning. We disagree with colleagues and students constructively. We invite critique of our teaching, including evaluations from administrators, parents, and the students themselves; and we hold ourselves accountable to their evaluations.

We do not hold students' current digressions against them or their generation as they experiment with society's expectations. We confront inappropriate behavior and attitudes immediately instead of ignoring them. For example, we openly question stereotypes in front of students. We might ask the student who summarizes a current event with the phrase, "It was an Islamic fundamentalist who blew up the car," with, "Why did you say it that way? Why did you or the news reporter use the person's religious affiliation to identify him, yet with other people, we don't do that? We don't say, 'It was an over-zealous Presbyterian that blew up the car,' so why should we do it here?"

We teach students that they will inevitably offend others at various points in their lives, but the courageous and mature thing is to be vigilant against it and perhaps even more difficult, be open to correction by those who care enough to help us.

Students will make a lot of mistakes that, on the surface, portend the end of civilization as we know it. Our students' current obsession with low-riding jeans is just one example. We cannot disparage society of tomorrow based on the actions of today's youth—tomorrow's leaders. Teachers who claim that kids today are poorly behaved compared to those of yesterday couldn't be more wrong. Check out the following quote from a speech by Hesiod in the 8th century B.C.:

> I see no hope for the future of our people if they are dependent on the frivolous youth of today, for certainly all youth are reckless beyond words. When I was a boy, we were taught to be discrete and respectful of elders, but the present youth are exceedingly wise and impatient of restraint.

One of the great things about courage is that it's contagious. Billy Graham once said, "When a brave man takes a stand, the spines of others are stiffened." He's right. If we act courageous and affirm the courageous efforts of our students, the whole class gets caught up in the spirit. Soon, the larger group is brave enough to tackle larger problems. I learned this myself with jarring reality when a high school gang member I once taught in middle school told me, "Gangs are only as strong as the community allows them to be." Wow, what can we accomplish when we are brave together?

Finding our bearings

Since the ancient Greeks, we have seen that it is the nature of the young adolescent to wander morally and to require adult interaction to find healthy compass bearings. We teach much more than the curriculum, and much of that is done in our daily interactions with students, not formal programs. It's scary to think our every move and word teaches or crushes those three touchstones: tolerance, compassion, and courage. Are we up to this great task?

Absolutely. Let's be brave five minutes longer and let every interaction, from loaning pencils to returning papers to full class discussions promote our profession's ultimate goals in the most formative years of human development, young adolescence. Provide ample opportunities in this school year to enable students to extend mercy, respect others, and dare greatly. It is the stuff of successful generations to come.

Notes on Note-Taking

Don't ask students to take notes during a lecture or first-learning experience. In most situations, it's not a good idea.

When we ask students to record meaningful notes while listening with full concentration to our lecture (or watching the lab demonstration or video, or paying attention to the docent on a field trip to the museum), we dilute both experiences.

While recording what a political candidate says in a speech, for example, the student misses the candidate's vocal inflections and body language that reveal his yet unspoken position on a controversial issue. While wrapped up in a compelling story from the teacher about the Cambrian explosion of new life forms over 500 million years ago, the student struggles to get it all down in a memorable way on paper, and by that point, the teacher has moved on to the next topic.

The brain operates by toggling back and forth between two or more foci, according to John Medina in *Brain Rules: 12 Principles for Surviving and Thriving at Work, Home, and School* (2009), not by paying full attention to multiple sources of input simultaneously. It turns out that multi-tasking is harder than we thought, even for today's supposedly multi-tasking generation.

It becomes particularly troubling for students who have any kind of auditory processing issue or learning disability. It's so overwhelming for these students, in fact, they resort to one of three responses: (1) Give up and accept a failing grade on the next day's quiz on this material; (2) Tune out and realize they'll have to learn it later on their own; or (3) Act up in class out of frustration. In short, they're drowning.

We can ease this burden for all students, not just the ones with learning challenges, by handling note-taking wisely.

Pencils down

First, we ask students to put their pens, pencils, and keyboards away while we are lecturing, demonstrating, showing a video, or making any other kind of presentation. We want their full attention. We want them to wrestle with the ideas, fully engaged in the effort to understand what's being presented, not in translating the material for later study.

Reading expository text is also a learning or presentation experience, so this means students read written text all the way through with their pens and pencils down. The first read-through is just to consider the ideas, maybe question them, but not to capture them.

There's an important element to this approach, however: Our presentation or written text must be broken into segments. We should present (or let students read) information for 10–15 minutes, then stop and ask students to process the information for 2–7 minutes. We continue to lecture or present for another 10–15 minutes, then stop and ask students to process again for another 2–7 minutes. We continue like this until the end of the period or the end of the presentation. This chunked approach allows students to fully engage in the presentation without having to process an overwhelming amount of material.

If the measure of our teaching success is the degree to which students learn the material, finishing the lecture within the class period pales in comparison to making sure students remember what they learn. This means we have to be strong enough in our teaching convictions to chunk our lectures and presentations and let students process the information for long-term memory several different times, even if this means we don't have time to finish the presentation.

Some students will feel anxious with this "pencils down and listen to the lecture" approach. They will be afraid that they will lose the information unless they write it down right away. This is understandable, so allow students to record 10–12 single words or phrases during each of those segments. These are words that caught their attention, concepts they thought were important, something they didn't understand, or something about which they have a comment. This list provides the reference points to which students can return during the processing period to record full, accurate notes for later study.

Processing learning

During those breaks between information segments and any time students take notes, there are many ways for students to process their learning. Here are some effective strategies:

Double-Entry Journals. Students record information, samples, charts, or tables on the left side of their paper or notebook and apply the knowledge on the right side through comparisons, practice exercises, mind maps, recoding of information, and other creative learning prompts.

Note Cards. Students record notes on index cards following a prescribed format such as labeling each card in the upper right-hand corner with its source and page, keeping the center of the card for information on just one topic within a larger topic, and labeling the upper left-hand corner for the topic's label.

Matrix. Students begin taking notes by first constructing a grid with squares in which they will record their notes. Across the top might be attributes in different categories but along the side might be different topics. For instance, we might list biomes along the vertical axis, but across the top might be: Primary Water Source, Sample Food Chain, Where Located, Typical Temperature Range, Three Typical Plants, 1 Unique Feature.

T-Chart. The teacher or student designates the topics of each column, and then the student fills them in. Suggested column topics include: fact/opinion, main idea/supporting details, before/after, cause/effect, similarities/differences, two different people/events/concepts being compared, fact/question, known/want to know, concept/myth associated with it, mistaken notion/correct interpretation.

Cornell Notes. This is a T-Chart with a summary underneath. Students record notes and other specifics on the right column of the T, and then encapsulate those notes on the left; or they create questions on the left that are answered by the material on the right. When folded along the T's vertical axis, this becomes a great study guide for flipping back and forth between question and correct response. Once the columns are filled, a line is drawn across the bottom and students summarize all the information above in two to five sentences.

Fishbone. Students record the main topic horizontally down the length of the paper, then provide lines shooting off that mid-line in a herringbone style on which they record subtopics of the main idea. Each of these can be further broken down into smaller herringbone lines shooting off those first lines.

Power Thinking. Students record notes on small slips of paper two or three inches in length. Main topics are labeled as Power 1 level. Anything that's a subtopic of the larger topic is labeled as Power 2. Anything that clarifies or supports Power 2 subtopics is considered Power 3. After recording notes on these slips, students then arrange them on their desks or tables with their fingers, placing everything within its proper hierarchy. (This idea is from *Differentiating Textbooks* (2003) by Char Forsten, Jim Grant, and Betty Hollas.)

Who, What, When, Where, Why, How, and What This Means to Me. Students set up a chart with these prompts prior to taking notes, then respond to each one of them as they process information. (This is based on an idea from Elaine Stephens and Jean Brown in *A Handbook of Content Literacy Strategies,* 2004.)

Note-taker's Critique. Provide students with examples of other students' notes on a topic. These can come from photocopying previous students' efforts in your class or by creating mock notes yourself. Make sure to have a variety of degrees of successful note-taking to share. Then ask students to critique the notes in light of what they've just learned: Are the notes accurate, comprehensive, and clear? If not, ask students to correct them so they meet the criteria you've outlined for successful notes.

Your Importance/Author Importance. The readers determine the importance of anything they read. To help students avoid focusing on the wrong thing, however, ask them first to read through text and record what they find important to themselves. You might even ask them to delineate these ideas in two columns: Things of Interest to Me and Things I Think Are Important. Then ask students to re-read the text, but this time they must focus on what they think the author thought was important and why they think as they do. This exercise, based on an idea from *Strategies that Work: Teaching Comprehension for Understanding and Engagement* (2007) by Stephanie Harvey and Anne Goudvis, helps students key in on salient concepts.

A great way for students to figure out what's truly important for them to record in their notes is for them to create a topic sentence and to identify the purpose for the study. For this section of this column, for example, my topic sentence would be "There are many ways for students to take notes." Anything they record in their notes would support that topic.

Notes that work

Great teachers never assume students are successful note-takers. They provide overt explanations and demonstrations of good note-taking throughout the year. They invite students to go back and revise their notes later in the day or week, heeding Bob Marzano, Debra Pickering, and Jane Pollock's message in *Classroom Instruction That Works: Research-Based Strategies for Increasing Student Achievement* (2004) that "Notes should be considered a work in progress" (p. 44).

We should consider students taking notes during class and while they study as something more than a classroom management strategy. It's an effective instructional practice if done correctly, and as students achieve academic success by using those notes, we should frequently remind them of the power of their note-taking. Many of them might even come to value the process and use it even when it's not required. Okay, maybe that's a stretch, but some will undoubtedly become "noted" scholars, a status eagerly sought. And the others? They remain noteworthy.

Homework: How We Assign It

I'm embarrassed to share this, but this actually happened in my classroom: A student came up to me during class and said that he didn't understand the topic I just taught. Admittedly, the lesson had not gone well, but I was tired and several students were waiting for my responses to their questions. In a less-than-inspired act, I tossed the student a figurative pacifier: "Do the homework assignment. It'll be made clear to you."

Wow, that was not the thing to do. I was trying to compensate for bad teaching through the homework assignment. The student shuffled back to his seat feeling just as much a failure as he was prior to going for help—maybe more so because my response removed all doubt that he was on his own.

Practice, practice, practice

Homework is never given to students so they can learn the material the first time around. Solid learning should be achieved before the first homework assignment. Homework is given in order for students to practice, reinforce, and extend what they already know.

Think about that for a minute. If we accept this premise, then we never give homework assignments unless we have evidence that students understand the material. Too often, however, teachers use vicarious assessments of one or two students to assess everyone in the class:

> Teacher: Before getting started on the homework today, let's see if you remember everything. Jerel, give an example of the commutative property, please.
>
> Jerel: 9 x 5 = 5 x 9.
>
> Teacher: Excellent. Wanda, how about an example of the distributive property?
>
> Wanda: 4(2 + 3) = (4 x 2) + (4 x 3) = 20.
>
> Teacher: Great! Okay, you all seem to have this, so everyone get busy with problems 1–30 on page 65.

Not so fast. We need physical evidence from every student, not just two students. We need to know that every student who practices the material understands the material correctly. Why? Because practice makes permanent, even though it may or may not make perfect.

If students practice content and skills incorrectly, it takes 10 times the emotional and intellectual energy to go back, undo that learning, and reteach it correctly. If students are struggling or have only learned partially, it's wiser to cancel or significantly alter the homework for that evening, reteach the information the next day, then let them do the assigned practice.

Monitor the whole class, including subsets of students within the room, and give different assignments to different subsets, if necessary. What is fair isn't always equal in instruction, and it's the same for homework assignments.

Advance knowledge

Homework should advance our subjects, not be just decorative or clerical. For example, asking students to get forms signed, cover their textbooks, or bring in a box of tissues for the classroom are appropriate requests, but they should never be a part of a homework grade.

Similar to this are art (or technology or performance) assignments that don't really advance students' learning of the intended topic. When my son Ryan was in middle school, his teacher asked students to make a diorama and a travel brochure about a book they were reading. It took him three weeks of cutting, gluing, coloring, and recutting and regluing to make a scene from the book and a travel brochure recommending readers "tour" the book.

When asked what the students were studying with this novel, his teacher said, "character development and literary devices." Nowhere in the diorama or on the brochure did students interact with their learning of character development and literary devices. It was an endurance test for both him and us, it bred resentment from the whole family, and it did not advance Ryan's learning about character development or literary devices.

By the students, for the students

If a student goes home and asks, "Mom, I'm supposed to do a report on phytoplankton. Can you tell me how to start?" we haven't prepared that student well enough.

Homework should be done by students, not students and their parents. If students can't do the assignment themselves, they're not ready to do it. We occasionally have busy days in which we didn't prepare students for the assignment properly and they need parental assistance, but it shouldn't be the norm.

Get up and move

Young adolescents need daily exercise for their minds to function, so assign physical exercise or sports as homework in content subjects. And, if hours of homework are cutting into students' exercise time after school hours, change the homework assignments so they don't.

Seriously, we should be assigning homework like "Play basketball for 45 minutes," "Walk two miles," "Toss a Frisbee with a friend for an hour," and "Do 10 push-ups." These activities will do more for student learning than a lot of the assignments we currently give. We can still give those more sedate assignments, but monitor students' load so they can still get moving after school hours.

How much is too much?

It's simplistic, but reasonable: Add a zero to the grade level for the number of minutes of homework assigned per night: 6th grade = 60 minutes, 7th grade = 70 minutes, 8th grade = 80. Be clear, though, that this is all subjects combined! Research indicates that after 50–100 minutes, depending on the student, doing homework has diminishing returns and can actually harm the school's mission to teach students. Of course, other research indicates that doing anything other than reading for enjoyment after school hours is a waste of time (see Alfie Kohn). The point here is to be very judicious with your assignments: Will practice after school hours of this meaningful work improve long-term retention of its content?

Exception, not rule

"No homework tonight" should be the default choice, not, "There is homework tonight." Reading Alfie Kohn's work got me thinking about this. Across America, Kohn says, teachers are on automatic pilot and assign homework because they think that's what teachers do. Some homework has merit, but a whole lot of it really doesn't advance our cause.

Some of us claim that students must have daily practice with our topics, or they will fall behind. Research and anecdotal evidence don't support that. The mind, including our subconscious, needs time away from studying to assimilate the learning and come back to it later with a fresh outlook. Connections are still made. Students will flourish by taking a day or two away from them on regular basis.

Pull them in

The homework we assign needs to be compelling. As Kohn points out, people learn better when they practice things they like to study or do; they don't learn much when practicing things they resent. So, instead of asking students to define the vocabulary terms, ask them to consider the worth (utility, beauty) of each word and hold a Word Bazaar in which they barter for words to use. Instead of answering comprehension questions about a history topic, ask students to read the material then write a rationale or speech as to why the topic should or should not be taught in schools, citing at least four key aspects of what they read in the textbook.

No busywork

Let's end the use of homework passes. Instead, don't assign anything that's "skip-able." If it is skip-able, it is busywork. Homework should matter. Not doing it should result in something noticeably less in the student. If we want to reward students in some way, we can use Homework Deadline Extension certificates on which we've checked a box allowing a particular assignment to be turned in one, two, or three days late, depending on the level of the reward.

Make a choice

Occasionally allow students to determine how best to practice the day's learning. Giving the options creates that important ownership young adolescents crave; it also can teach self-advocacy. Given a choice of practice activities for homework, we can help them figure out which one will have the greatest impact on their long-term retention of the skills and content. This is especially effective if we take a few moments the next day and facilitate students' reflections on the effectiveness of their choices.

Accountability

Everyone should turn in a paper, even if they didn't do the assignment. I found this one in Neila Connors' wonderful book *Homework: A New Direction* (1991). This way no one knows who did and did not turn in papers as students file by the turn-in basket. Students who didn't do the homework assignment write the following on the paper they submit: name, date, name of assignment, why he or she did not do it, parents' names and daytime phone numbers.

During the day, we call the parents and read directly from the student's paper about why she didn't have her assignment. It might be for very legitimate reasons, of course, but now we have a clear record that we can all readily access and compare to see if there's a pattern that needs addressing. It's particularly effective, too, if the student makes the phone call and reads her reasoning to her parents.

Give it a break

It's time to stop giving homework over the weekend and over long holidays. Yes, the verdict is in: homework done over winter or spring vacation usually doesn't result in learning. It imbues the vacation atmosphere with grim menace, sparking angry survival modes in both parents and children whose health is better achieved by enjoying each other's company and taking respite from the daily grind.

We get more out of students during the school week when students have constructive relationships with family members and others over the weekend. We can still assign homework Friday afternoon, but it's not due until Tuesday or Wednesday.

How'd they do?

Finally, whatever we do, we must provide feedback on homework assignments. This is so central to homework's impact on student learning, it makes assigning anything without providing feedback close to a complete waste of time. Robert Marzano and others have the research citations on this, but the fact remains that if students receive feedback from themselves, their classmates, their teachers, or someone else, they learn dramatically more from the homework experience. So, in the same planning breath we use to design our homework assignments, we need to ask ourselves, "… and how will students receive descriptive feedback on this?"

What would our lives as teachers be like if we didn't assign homework? How would we teach differently so students were sure to learn the material while in class, and over the course of a week? Are we relying too much on our homework assignments to do our teaching for us?

In the yearnings of the student within each of us, there's some truth waiting to be recognized. It may be time to listen to it and do the ethical thing: make homework worth doing and mark it appropriately.

Differentiation

Differentiating for Tweens

Effective instruction for 12-year-olds looks different from effective instruction for 8-year-olds or 17-year-olds. Combine the developmental needs of typical tweens and the wildly varying needs of individuals within this age group, and you can see that flourishing as a middle-grades teacher requires special skills.

It's not as overwhelming as it sounds, however. There are some commonsense basics that serve students well. The five strategies described here revolve around the principles of differentiated instruction, which does not always involve individualized instruction. Teachers who differentiate instruction simply do what's fair and developmentally appropriate for students when the "regular" instruction doesn't meet their needs.

Strategy 1: Teach to developmental needs

Reports from the Carnegie Corporation (Jackson & Davis, 2000) and the National Middle School Association (2003), as well as the expertise of veteran middle school teachers, point to seven conditions that young adolescents crave: competence and achievement; opportunities for self-definition; creative expression; physical activity; positive social interactions with adults and peers; structure and clear limits; and meaningful participation in family, school, and community. No matter how creatively we teach—and no matter how earnestly we engage in differentiated instruction, authentic assessment, and character education—the effects will be significantly muted if we don't create an environment that responds to students' developmental needs. Different students will require different degrees of attention regarding each of these factors.

Take tweens' need for physical movement. It's not enough for tweens to move between classes every 50 minutes (or every 80 minutes on a block schedule). Effective tween instruction incorporates movement every 10 to 15 minutes. So we ask all students to get up and walk across the room to turn in their papers, not just have one student collect the papers while the rest of them sit passively. We let students process information physically from time to time: for example, by using the ceiling as a massive, organizer matrix and asking students to hold cards with information for each matrix cell and stand under the proper location as indicated on the ceiling. We use flexible grouping, which allows students to move about the room to work with different partners.

Every topic in the curriculum can be turned into a physical experience, even if it's very abstract. We can do this for some or all of our students as needed. We can use simulations, manipulatives, body statues (frozen tableau), and finger plays to portray irony, metabolism, chromatic scale, republics, qualitative analysis, grammar, and multiplying binomials (Glynn, 2001; Wormeli, 2005). These aren't "fluff" activities; they result in real learning for this age group.

To address students' need for self-definition, we give them choices in school projects. We help students identify consequences for the academic and personal decisions they make. We also teach students about their own learning styles. We put students in positions of responsibility in our schools and communities that allow them to make positive contributions and earn recognition for doing so. We provide clear rules and enforce them calmly—even if it's the umpteenth time that day that we've needed to enforce the same rule—to help students learn to function as members of a civilized society.

Integrating developmental needs into tweens' learning is nonnegotiable. It's not something teachers do only if we have time in the schedule; it's vital to tween success. As teachers of this age group, we need to apply our adolescent development expertise in every interaction. If we don't, the lesson will fall flat and even worse, students will wither.

Strategy 2: Treat academic struggle as strength

Young adolescents readily identify differences and similarities among themselves, and in their efforts to belong to particular groups, they can be judgmental about classmates' learning styles or progress (Jackson & Davis, 2000). At this junction, then, it's important to show students that not everyone starts at the same point along the learning continuum or learns in the same way. Some classmates learn content by drawing it, others by writing about it, and still others by discussing it—and even the best students are beginners in some things.

Unfortunately, students in nondifferentiated classes often view cultural and academic differences as signs of weakness and inferiority. Good students in these classes often try to protect their reputations as being the kids who always get the problems right or finish first. They rarely take chances and stretch themselves for fear of faltering in front of others. This approach to learning rarely leads to success in high school and beyond.

Educators of tweens need to make academic struggle virtuous. So we model asking difficult questions to which we don't know the answers, and we publicly demonstrate our journey to answer those questions. We affirm positive risk taking in homework as well as the knowledge gained through science experiments that fail. We push students to explore their undeveloped skills without fear of grade repercussions, and we frequently help students see the growth they've made over time.

In one of my classes, Jared was presenting an oral report on Aristotle's rhetorical triangle (ethos, pathos, logos), and he was floundering. Embarrassed because he kept forgetting his memorized speech, he begged me to let him take an F and sit down. Instead, I asked Jared to take a few deep breaths and try again. He did, but again, he bombed. I explained that an oral report is not just about delivering information; it's also about taking risks and developing confidence. "We're all beginners at one point, Jared," I explained: This is your time to be a beginner. The worst that can happen is that you learn from the experience and have to do it again. That's not too bad.

After his classmates offered encouraging comments, Jared tried a third time and got a little farther before stopping his speech. I suggested that he repeat the presentation in short segments, resting between each one. He tried it, and it worked. After Jared finished, he moved to take his seat, but I stopped him and asked him to repeat the entire presentation, this time without rests.

As his classmates grinned and nodded, Jared returned to the front of the room. This time, he made it through his presentation without a mistake. His classmates applauded. Jared bowed, smiled, and took his seat. His eyes watered a bit when he looked at me. Adrenalin can do that to a guy, but I hoped it was more. Everyone learned a lot about tenacity that day, and Jared took his first steps toward greater confidence (Wormeli, 1999).

Strategy 3: Provide multiple pathways to standards

Differentiation requires us to invite individual students to acquire, process, and demonstrate knowledge in ways different from the majority of the class if that's what they need to become proficient. When we embrace this approach, we give more than one example and suggest more than one strategy. We teach students eight different ways to take notes, not just one, and then help them decide when to use each technique. We let students use wide- or college-ruled paper, and we guide them in choosing multiple single-subject folders or one large binder for all subjects—whichever works best for them.

We don't limit students' exposure to sophisticated thinking because they have not yet mastered the basics. Tweens are capable of understanding how to solve for a variable or graph an inequality even if they struggle with the negative/positive signs when multiplying integers. We can teach a global lesson on a sophisticated concept for 15 minutes, and then allow students to process the information in groups tiered for different levels of readiness—or we can present an anchor activity for the whole class to do while we pull out subgroups for mini-lessons on the basics or on advanced material. Our goal is to respond to the unique students in front of us as we make learning coherent for all.

In the area of assessment, we should never let the test format get in the way of a student's ability to reveal what he or she knows and is able to do. For example, if an assessment on Ben Mikaelsen's novel *Touching Spirit Bear* (Harper Trophy, 2002) required students to create a poster showing the development of characters in the story, it would necessarily assess artistic skill in addition to assessing the students' understanding of the novel. Students with poor artistic skills would be unable to reveal the full extent of what they know. Consequently, we allow students to select alternative assessments through which they can more accurately portray their mastery.

In differentiated classes, grading focuses on clear and consistent evidence of mastery, not on the medium through which the student demonstrates that mastery. For example, we may give students five different choices for showing what they know about the rise of democracy: writing a report, designing a Web site, building a library display, transcribing a "live" interview with a historical figure, or creating a series of podcasts simulating a discussion between John Locke and Thomas Jefferson about where governments get their authority. We can grade all the projects using a common scoring rubric that contains the universal standards for which we're holding students accountable.

Of course, if the test format is the assessment, we don't allow students to opt for something else. For example, when we ask students to write a well-crafted persuasive essay, they can't instead choose to write a persuasive dialogue or create a poster. Even then, however, we can differentiate the pace of instruction and be flexible about the time required for student mastery. Just as we would never demand that all humans be able to recite the alphabet fluently on the first Monday after their 3rd birthday, it goes against all we know about teaching tweens to mandate that all students master slope and y-intercept during the first week of October in grade 7.

Thus, we allow tweens to redo work and assessments until they master the content, and we give them full credit for doing so. Our job is to teach students the material, not to document how they've failed. We never want to succumb to what middle-grades expert Nancy Doda calls the "learn or I will hurt you" mentality by demanding that all students learn at the same pace and in the same manner as their classmates and giving them only one chance to succeed.

Strategy 4: Give formative feedback

Tweens don't always know when they don't know, and they don't always know when they do. One of the most helpful strategies we can employ is to provide frequent formative feedback. Tween learning tends to be more multilayered and episodic than linear; continual assessment and feedback correct misconceptions before they take root. Tweens learn more when teachers take off the evaluation hat and hold up a mirror to students, helping them compare what they did with what they were supposed to have done.

Because learning and motivation can be fragile at this age, we have to find ways to provide that feedback promptly. We do this by giving students short assignments—such as one-page writings instead of multipage reports—that we can evaluate and return in a timely manner. When we formally assess student writing, we focus on just one or two areas so that students can assimilate our feedback.

To get a quick read on students' understanding of a particular lesson, we can use exit card activities, which are quick products created by students in response to prompts. For example, at the end of a U.S. history lesson, we might ask, "Using what we've learned today, make a Venn diagram that compares and contrasts World Wars I and II." The 3-2-1 exit card format can yield rich information (Wormeli, 2005). Here are two examples:

3—Identify three characteristic ways Renaissance art differs from medieval art.

2—List two important scientific debates that occurred during the Renaissance.

1—Provide one good reason why rebirth is an appropriate term to describe the Renaissance.

3—Identify at least three differences between acids and bases.

2—List one use of an acid and one use of a base.

1—State one reason why knowledge of acids and bases is important to citizens in our community.

Strategy 5: Dare to be unconventional

Curriculum theorists have often referred to early adolescence as the age of romanticism: Tweens are interested in that which is novel, compels them, and appeals to their curiosity about the world (Pinar, Reynolds, Slattery, & Taubman, 2000). To successfully teach tweens, we have to be willing to transcend convention once in a while. It's not a lark; it's essential.

Being unconventional means we occasionally teach math algorithms by giving students the answers to problems and asking them how those answers were derived. We improve student word savvy by asking students to conduct an intelligent conversation without using verbs.

(They can't; they sound like Tarzan.) We ask students to teach some lessons, with the principal or a parent as coteacher. Students can make a video for 4th graders on the three branches of government, convey Aristotle's rhetorical triangle by juggling tennis balls, or correspond with adult astronomers about their study of the planets. They can create literary magazines of science, math, or health writing that will end up in local dentist offices and Jiffy Lube shops. They can learn about the Renaissance through a "Meeting of Minds" debate in which they portray Machiavelli, da Vinci, Erasmus, Luther, Calvin, and Henry VIII. The power of such lessons lies in their substance and novelty, and young adolescents are acutely attuned to these qualities.

Ninety percent of what we do with young adolescents is quiet, behind-the-scenes facilitation. Ten percent, however, is an inspired dog and pony show without apologies. At this "I dare you to show me something I don't know" and "Shake me out of my self-absorption" age, being unconventional is key.

Thus, when my students were confusing the concepts of adjective and adverb, I did the most professional thing I could think of: I donned tights, shorts, a cape, and a mask, and became Adverb Man. I moved through the hallways handing out index cards with adverbs written on them. "You need to move quickly," I said, handing a student late to class a card on which the word quickly was written. "You need to move now," I said to another, handing him a card with the adverb on it. Once in a while, I'd raise my voice, Superman-style, and declare, "Remember, good citizens of Earth, what Adverb Man always says: 'Up, up, and modify adverbs, verbs, and adjectives!'" The next day, one of the girls on our middle school team came walking down the hallway to my classroom dressed as Pronoun Girl. One of her classmates preceded her—he was dressed as Antecedent Boy. Both wore yellow masks and had long beach towels tucked into the backs of their shirt collars as capes. Pronoun Girl had taped pronouns across her shirt that corresponded with the nouns taped across Antecedent Boy's shirt. It was better than Schoolhouse

Rock. And the best part? There wasn't any grade lower than a B+ on the adverbs test that Friday (Wormeli, 2001).

Navigating the tween river

Of all the states of matter in the known universe, tweens most closely resemble liquid. Students at this age have a defined volume, but not a defined shape. They are ever ready to flow, and they are rarely compressible. Although they can spill, freeze, and boil, they can also lift others, do impressive work, take the shape of their environment, and carry multiple ideas within themselves. Some teachers argue that dark matter is a better analogy—but those are teachers trying to keep order during the last period on a Friday.

Imagine directing the course of a river that flows through a narrow, ever-changing channel toward a greater purpose yet to be discovered, and you have the basics of teaching tweens. To chart this river's course, we must be experts in the craft of guiding young, fluid adolescents in their pressure-filled lives, and we must adjust our methods according to the flow, volume, and substrate within each student. It's a challenging river to navigate, but worth the journey.

The Day I Was Caught Plagiarizing

Young adolescents are still learning what is moral and how to act responsibly. I decided to help them along.

One day, I shared a part of an education magazine column with my 7th grade students. I told them that I wrote it and was seeking their critique before submitting it for publishing. In reality, the material I shared was an excerpt from a book written by someone else. I was hiding the book behind a notebook from which I read.

A parent coconspirator was in the classroom for the period, pretending to observe the lesson. While I read the piece that I claimed as my own, the parent acted increasingly uncomfortable. Finally, she interrupted me and said that she just couldn't let me go on. She had read the exact ideas that I claimed as my own in another book. I assured her that she was confused, and I continued.

She interrupted me again, this time angrily. She said she was not confused and named the book from which I was reading, having earlier received the information from me in our preclass set-up. At this point, I let myself appear more anxious about her words. Her concern grew, and she persisted in her comments until I finally admitted that I hadn't written the material. Acting ashamed, I revealed the book to the class. The kids' mouths opened, some in confused grins, some greatly concerned, not knowing what to believe.

The parent let me have it then. She reminded me that I was in a position of trust as a teacher—how dare I break that trust! She said that I was being a terrible role model and that my students would never again trust my writings or teaching. She declared that this was a breach of professional conduct and that my principal would be informed. Throughout all of this, I countered her points with the excuses that students often make when caught plagiarizing: It's only a small part. The rest of the writing is original; what does it matter that this one part was written by someone else? I've never done it before, and I'm not ever going to do it again, so it's not that bad.

The students' faces dissolved into disbelief, some into anger. Students vicariously experienced the uncomfortable feeling of being trapped in a lie and having one's reputation impugned. At the height of the emotional tension between the parent and me, I paused and asked the students, "Have you had enough?" With a smile and a thank-you to the parent assistant, I asked how many folks would like to learn five ways not to plagiarize material; then I went to the chalkboard.

Students breathed a sigh of relief. Notebooks flew onto desktops, and pens raced across paper to get down everything I taught for the rest of class; they hung on every word. Students wanted to do anything to avoid the "yucky" feelings associated with plagiarism that they had experienced moments ago. I taught them ways to cite sources, how to paraphrase another's words, and how many words from an original source we could use before we were lifting too much. We discussed the legal ramifications of plagiarism. Later, we applauded the acting talent of our parent assistant.

One student in the room that day reflected on this lesson at the end of the year:

I know I'll never forget when my teacher got "caught" plagiarizing. The sensations were simply too real.... Although my teacher is extremely moral, it was frightening how close to home it struck. The moment when my teacher admitted it, the room fell silent. It was awful. All my life, teachers have preached about plagiarism, and it never really sank in. But when you actually experience it, it's a whole different story.

To this day, students visit me from high school and college and say, "I was tempted to plagiarize this one little bit on one of my papers, but I didn't because I remembered how mad I was at you." That's a teacher touchdown.

References

Glynn, C. (2001). Learning on their feet. Shoreham, VT: Discover Writing Press.

Jackson, A., & Davis, G. (2000). Turning points 2000: Educating adolescents in the 21st century. New York: Carnegie Corporation.

National Middle School Association. (2003). This we believe: Successful schools for young adolescents. Westerville, OH: Author.

Pinar, W. F., Reynolds, W. M., Slattery, P., & Taubman, P. M. (2000). Understanding curriculum. New York: Peter Lang Publishing.

Wormeli, R. (1999). The test of accountability in middle school. Middle Ground, 3(7), 17–18, 53.

Wormeli, R. (2001). Meet me in the middle. Portland, ME: Stenhouse Publishers.

Wormeli, R. (2005). Summarization in any subject: 50 techniques to improve student learning. Alexandria, VA: ASCD.

Endnote

This article was originally published in 2006 in Educational Leadership, *63(7), 14–19. Printed with permission from Association for Supervision and Curriculum Development.*

Differentiated Instruction: Setting the Pedagogy Straight

The most common sentiment among readers of books on differentiated instruction (DI) is that DI is just good teaching. It's whatever conscientious teachers do to increase students' learning over that which otherwise could be achieved by a one size-fits-all approach. Simultaneously, DI builds learner dexterity and self-advocacy so students can handle anything that is not differentiated for them.

If it's so constructive, why would anyone declare differentiated instruction a corruption of curriculum and instruction, as education author and consultant Mike Schmoker did in his September 29, 2010,

Education Week article, "When Do Pedagogic Fads Trump Priorities?" Schmoker's declaration, combined with University of Virginia professor Daniel Willingham's denouncements of learning styles as unsubstantiated by research and hurtful to students' learning, leaves educators in flux: Do we differentiate instruction, assessment, and curriculum, or not?

Not just a gentle ripple across a sleepy mountain pond, the statements of these respected thinkers created white-capped, crisscrossing currents that capsized more than one school's differentiation efforts. Although questioning conventional techniques is a hallmark of professional practice and necessary for school vitality, this round of questioning created misinterpretations and misguided responses. More than a year later, confusion lingers, and some teachers have used the suspicions raised by these authors to justify unresponsive teaching practices and to declare students' classroom failures as the fallout from diluted curriculum and overhyped fads.

Setting the record straight

Let's correct these misrepresentations and put educators' minds at ease: Differentiated instruction is highly effective practice. Students learn more with it than without it. To knowingly omit differentiated instruction from our classroom instruction is a willful act of educational malpractice. We should worry when a colleague or our own child's teacher expresses pride in not differentiating.

Consider the following examples of differentiation instruction and where you would find fault with the teaching:

- Mrs. Hunt provides three examples of a math algorithm successfully applied because her student, Eric, doesn't understand it after just two.

- Gabriella redoes an assignment after receiving corrective feedback from her teacher.

- Mr. Grebing draws upon his knowledge of Kira's background in baseball to construct an analogy that helps her understand the world of geometric planes.

- Uri is encouraged to use one of three other methods to learn his content vocabulary after experiencing frustration using flash cards alone.

- Nicole demonstrates close to 100% mastery of the unit goals on the pretest, so Mr. Lounsbury truncates the first few days of learning for her and provides a satellite study instead that allows her to take the topic much deeper than that planned for the rest of the class.

- Because of a learning disability, RJ uses a sliding aperture made of cardstock interlocking Ls to focus his eyes on just one portion of the busy text and not be distracted by the rest of the page.

- After a lecture, six students still don't see the relationships among different elements in the topic, so Mrs. Hollas pulls them to a conference table and helps them create a hierarchal graphic organizer that enables them to see how some elements are subsets of others.

- Gregorio isn't engaged in a topic that normally excites him. Mrs. Silver sits beside him and asks quietly if something is bothering him this day.

- Matt, an English-as-a-second-language student, is falling behind, and it's due to his lack of familiarity with academic language. Mrs. Nickelsen incorporates additional academic vocabulary-building activities into the unit, she highlights key words on task direction sheets, and she confirms directions individually with Matt several times a week.

Most of us find little to fault in these scenarios. As ethical teachers, we would never leave students to ignorance, or let their immaturity serve as full measure of their potential. Instead, we assess students as they learn, then we respond to the insights generated by that data, and we adjust instruction accordingly. If differentiation seems like common sense, it is.

So why would Schmoker attack DI? Perhaps it was a reaction to concerned colleagues who expressed distorted interpretations of differentiation, such as an overreliance on learning styles or multiple intelligence theory as sole differentiation delivery methods. Maybe he didn't have time to do a thorough exploration of differentiated practices and he overreached in his generalization. Whatever the case, as a result, we're left with confusion in the profession and, for the students of teachers who embraced Schmoker's arguments, frustration.

In the 2010 article, Schmoker writes, "In a series of e-mails, I explained...that there was no research or strong evidence to support its widespread adoption. I asked, with increasing importunity, for any such evidence. Only after multiple requests did I finally receive an answer: There was no solid research or school evidence." He states, "We now have evidence that the investment in DI ... was never fully warranted. It is on no list, short or long, of the most effective educational actions or interventions."

Differentiated instruction is too large a collection of principles and strategies to serve as a proper, narrowed focus for scholarly research. Asking for the research on DI is similar to asking for the research on good teaching. Where do we begin to answer such a question?

Because more than one strategy at a time is incorporated into most differentiated approaches, we adjust instruction frequently in response to changing student needs, and because life throws many unanticipated curveballs into the messy business of learning, it's hard to protect the integrity of the experimental design and declare correlation or causation when looking at DI's impact.

We can do it over time, of course, and with a great array of observations, but it's hard to draw the conclusion: Was Melanie's lack of performance due to her parents' separation? A new baby brother? The teacher's use of manipulatives? Choice of novel? Poverty? Lack of a rich literacy environment at home? Bullying? Too few practice sessions? Too many tests on the same day? Teacher use of a confusing metaphor during the instruction? No visuals during the lesson? No breakfast that day? Illness earlier in the unit? Substitute teacher didn't teach the right lesson earlier that week? Something else?

To get closer to the truth when critiquing DI, we need to see research about its component elements, such as:

- Tiering for readiness
- Flexible grouping
- Scaffolding
- Adjusting the pacing of delivery or support so content is more meaningful and easily retained in long-term memory
- Using respectful tasks
- Adjusting the amount of practice for different students according to what is needed
- Rephrasing an example so it makes better sense to a student
- Using descriptive feedback to revise students' skills and knowledge
- Compacting curriculum so advanced students don't stagnate
- Providing nutritious breakfasts to those who do not have them
- Building prior knowledge where this is none so information "sticks" in the mind
- Coming to know our students well so we know what buttons to push so they learn more effectively

- Designing lessons to increase what students capture the first time the topic is taught rather than relying on hours of remediation to fix misconceptions and build missing foundations.

As a frequent reader of Schmoker's other works, I know he sees the instructional value of these elements. Few would doubt their veracity. Here's the thing: These are all elements of differentiation.

As Diane Heacox wisely reminds us, differentiated instruction is a mindset, not a set of recipes to follow. It's responsive teaching: We respond to what we perceive students need in order to learn, and if that differs from child to child, we adjust instruction accordingly, rather than leaving them floundering. Is it really acceptable to say to 11-year-old Jeremy, "You didn't learn it the way I taught it, and that's just tough. Get used to it, kid." This is unconscionable.

Looking at the whole

Schmoker writes, "[D]ifferentiated instruction...claims that students learn best when...grouped by ability, as well as by their personal interests and 'learning styles.'"

Although I part ways with my differentiation colleagues with the word "ability" because "readiness" is more accurate and useful, I agree that these references are found in the DI literature. In the field, however, that last designation is more commonly referred to as "learner profiles" not "learning styles." A learner profile is a set of observations about a student that includes any factor that impacts his learning. Figure 1 on the next page is a partial list of what might be included, and included only if the factor affects students' learning in a regular classroom.

Figure 1: *Sample Factors to Include in Learning Profiles*

Family dynamics	Transiency rate
Social-economic status	Individualized EP
English language learner status	Learning disabilities
Gifted/advanced	Physical health
Emotional health	Speech and language Issues
Behavior/discipline concern	Nationality (if influential)
Diet (if influential)	Religious affiliation (if influential)
Technology access/comfort	Multiple intelligences
Personal background/experiences	Leadership qualities
Ethics	Collaborative nature
Personal interests: sports, music, books, hobbies, movies	Weekly schedule
Home responsibilities	Politics
Down's syndrome	Behavior/discipline
Tourette's syndrome	Asperger's syndrome
Hearing or visual challenges	Auditory processing issues

Learning styles can be included on this list to the degree that we find them a justified consideration: Do boys learn differently than girls? Do some students need time to reflect quietly before diving into a task? Does this child need to fiddle with something in his hands to keep his attention on the speaker at the front of the room? Does that student need to use a laptop or does he like to record information using paper and pencil?

I agree with Schmoker, Willingham, Hattie, and others that we do not have as much research on learning styles as we need to make all the claims our profession makes about them, but Schmoker is guilty of creating an inappropriate synecdoche of learning styles, using a small portion of something to indicate the larger whole. Worse, he judges the whole based on the limitations of one of its smaller pieces. This is neither accurate nor helpful.

Schmoker writes, "I saw frustrated teachers trying to provide materials that matched each student's or group's presumed ability level, interest, preferred 'modality' and learning style. The attempt often devolved into a frantically assembled collection of worksheets, coloring exercises, and specious 'kinesthetic' activities."

He writes later, "With so many groups to teach, instructors found it almost impossible to provide sustained, properly executed lessons for every child or group—and in a single class period. It profoundly impeded the teacher's ability to incorporate those protean, decades-old elements of a good lesson that have a titanic impact on learning, even in mixed-ability classrooms."

If this chaos is happening, it is a corruption of DI. No one is asking teachers to differentiate 24-7. That's physically impossible. We do it as we can and as warranted, and that's it. As the factory models they are today, schools were not meant to teach all students, only the ones who get it first. DI was invented to mitigate the negative aspects of the curriculum-by-age conveyor belt. We don't have time to teach well in a

50-minute period even when we don't differentiate, so we might as well do the best we can when students fail to thrive or need something more advanced. Those "protean, decades-old elements of a good lesson" are well-defined in the differentiation canon.

When we graduate and go into the working world, we have a skill set that matches a job's skill needs. We gravitate (self-differentiate) toward those jobs we're good at doing. We don't have to be good at everything everyone else in the company is good at doing at the exact same time and to the same degree of proficiency.

In school, however, we have to be good at everything everyone else is good at doing, all at the same time and to the same degree of proficiency. No wonder we adjust things occasionally, or often, for students for whom the regular, one-size-fits-all classroom doesn't work. We teach so students learn whenever and however it occurs, and that may take different paths for different students. We don't just present curriculum and document each child's rise and fall with it.

No room for fluff

Schmoker writes, "And [DI] dumbed down instruction: In English, 'creative' students made things or drew pictures; 'analytical' students got to read and write."

Again, nothing could be farther from the truth. This isn't even close to differentiation ideology. With these comments, Schmoker lets his fiery contrarianism get away from him, relying on the reports of disgruntled others, superficial understanding, and personal observations of a minority of teachers implementing differentiation badly. I want to pull him to one side and tell him, "Dude, do your homework."

Differentiated instruction is far more demanding on students than undifferentiated approaches. It provides the proper challenge at the proper time in the learning, and it always pushes students to transcend current status. There's no room for "foo-foo-fluff'" activities such as drawing and coloring a character from a novel when the student is supposed to learn how to analyze literary devices. We don't ask a student to do an oral presentation on argon when he can't balance chemical equations; we teach him to balance equations. We might change the path he takes to get there, but the ultimate goal is never diluted—he will balance chemical equations.

If watering down is happening in the name of differentiation, blame the teacher trainers for teaching inaccurate ideology and practices, or administrators for letting it happen in their buildings, but don't impugn the whole of differentiation.

Finally, Schmoker lists the three big elements needed to teach students well:

1. "...[C]oherent, content-rich guaranteed curriculum—that is, a curriculum which ensures that the actual intellectual skills and subject matter of a course don't depend on which teacher a student happens to get,"

2. "...[S]tudents read, write, and discuss, in the analytic and argumentative modes, for hundreds of hours per school year, across the curriculum.

3. "... [C]lear, curriculum-based objectives and assessment, followed by multiple cycles of instruction, guided practice, checks for understanding (the soul of a good lesson), and ongoing adjustments to instruction."

Differentiated instruction elevates each of these aspects, it doesn't diminish them. The third description, in fact, is one of the biggest tenets of DI. What does Schmoker think, "... cycles of instruction, guided practice, checks for understanding ... and ongoing adjustments to instruction" mean? They call for us to be reiterative in students' learning and to differentiate instruction as necessary so all students, not just the easiest ones to teach, learn that content-rich curriculum.

In his March 2009 article for *Phi Delta Kappan*, "What Money Can't Buy," Schmoker calls for teachers to check for understanding repeatedly as well. Why check for understanding? So we can adjust (differentiate) instruction as needed. With these declarations alone, Schmoker nullifies his entire anti-differentiation premise.

Consider the four non-negotiables of differentiated instruction as identified by Carol Ann Tomlinson, one of the original targets of Schmoker's commentary, in her response to Schmoker published in *Ed Week* (Available at www.differentiationcentral.com):

> (1) a learning environment that provides high challenge and support; (2) quality curriculum that emphasizes deep understanding of content and ensures that both teachers and students recognize what is essential for students to know, understand, and do; (3) formative assessment that allows teachers to know where students are relative to essential outcomes; and (4) adapting instruction, using the formative-assessment data, to ensure maximum success of each learner.

'Look familiar? It's exactly what Schmoker is calling for us to do. Tomlinson continues,

> There is obviously no research to support a frantically assembled collection of worksheets and coloring exercises. By contrast, abundant empirical research and research from neuroscience support the assertion that students learn when work is appropriately challenging for them, and conversely, do not learn when work is consistently too easy or too hard; in other words, student readiness matters. Research also shows that students learn better when they find work personally relevant and engaging; in other words, student interest matters. The third element of the model, learning profile, represents research evidence on how gender, culture, intelligence preference, and learning style may impact learning. While some experts question the concept of learning style, other skilled researchers who have recently studied available data on the topic conclude that the jury is still out on its validity. Many experts caution, as do we, that using instruments lacking in validity and reliability to categorize individuals as having a particular learning style is unwarranted.

> (To reference that research, visit www.differentiationcentral.com)

Readers are invited to read John Hattie's *Visible Learning* (2009) that Schmoker uses to justify his anti-differentiation stance. Hattie synthesizes over 800 meta-analyses of education studies, and many of them point to responsive teaching practices to increase students' learning.

All about options

To his credit, Daniel Willingham, author of *Why Don't Students Like School* (2009), and one of Schmoker's go-to researchers for proof that differentiation doesn't work, has posted videos declaring that the lack of research on learning styles, not differentiation, is the concern. In fact, he says that we should differentiate according to students' personality, motivation, and interests, and that students are not interchangeable among their classes, adding, "I wouldn't want a child of mine in a class where a teacher didn't at least try to do it [referring to differentiation]."

Willingham and Tomlinson are correct. Most students can learn by hearing, seeing, and doing. It helps in some situations to hear something spoken aloud, to see content laid out in a drawing or photo, or to see the motion of multiple parts working together to perform a function via computer animation, but almost all students can learn well in each of these ways, and even better if they are combined. Just because someone enjoys listening to information doesn't mean we teach her how to build an engine by oral description alone. We show her how it works, and we ask her to take apart an engine and put it back together, and then do it multiple times, throwing in a curveball once in a while so she can think flexibly about it.

If we use a baseball scoring analogy with a student learning statistics, he recognizes the clear application of the school topic and remembers the concepts better as a result. That's successful differentiation and good teaching. This does not mean, however, that we must use baseball every time we teach this child, that all baseball players learn best through baseball analogies, or that they cannot learn well through many of the same strategies employed with the rest of the class. It means only that we know our students well, and we successfully use that information to plan lessons to provide what each student needs to be successful.

As Tomlinson wrote in her June 2010 blog on the ASCD Edge website (www.ascd.org) in response to Daniel Willingham, "The goal should not be to pigeonhole students, but rather to provide options for learning and to help students become increasingly aware of what supports their learning at a given time."

Differentiated instruction has become prevalent because it works, not because it is an overhyped, shaky theory. Most critics of DI cite the lack of research in learning styles as proof of its misplaced orthodoxy, but that is reckless because it distorts the truth, and educators with little time to analyze the data and conversations are misled. It's similar to pronouncing SmartBoards as an instructional failure because some teachers use them as drying racks for t-shirts after the class tie-dye activity. We see the silliness right away.

Learning styles are neither the definition nor the primary component of differentiated instruction. As with any practice, they can be distorted and misapplied in any school building by any number of educators. Declaring differentiation wrong due to "iffy" evidence on learning styles is ignorance, not epiphany. I genuinely enjoy Schmoker's writings and many contributions to our profession, but he missed the boat on this one. It's time for him to set the pedagogy straight so our students can get back to learning successfully.

Tiering: Adusting the Level of Challenge

Each of us has classes with students who are a little more or a little less advanced than their classmates. We struggle to tailor activities to these students' developmental level while keeping them focused on the standards for our subjects. There's no room for "filler" activities that do not provide substantive learning, however, and it's disrespectful to ask them to do puzzles, read a book, or work with a struggling classmate while we think of something different for them to do.

In these situations, we can adjust the challenge of an assignment or assessment to meet their needs. Notice that we're changing the nature of the task, not the workload. We don't give them more or less work, and we don't tell some students to finish in two days what other students are given a week to complete. Instead, we change the sophistication level of the prompt and/or the student's response to it.

For example, imagine you are teaching students about the phases of the moon. For students who master the information quickly, we can ask them to correlate moon phases with tide cycles, investigate how people first determined that the moon doesn't actually change shape, create a display indicating the difference between solar and lunar eclipses, or explain how the moon phases would be different if the earth didn't tilt off its vertical axis.

For students who are struggling with the moon phases, we can dip string into paraffin to make a layer, as when making candles, to vividly portray waxing. We can turn off the lights and manipulate Styrofoam balls and a flashlight to simulate various stages of lunar illumination. We can point out how the phases would be different if the moon were consistently in the same plane as the sun and earth, and we can create a story that serves as a quick mnemonic to memorize the phase sequence. Would some of these advanced and struggling student approaches serve all students, not just those identified? Sure. The point is to plan enough options so we can be flexible while teaching.

On mastery

One of the first concerns middle school teachers express when tiering lessons and assignments is whether it is fair to tier some lessons but not others. The best response is to focus on what we're trying to teach. Many writers and researchers define tiering as adjusting the task's readiness level, interest, or student's learning profile to maximize learning; however, the last two are lateral moves, not vertical. Here, we define tiering as: changing the level of complexity or required readiness of a task or unit of study in order to meet the developmental needs of the students involved. This is similar to Carol Ann Tomlinson's concept of "ratcheting."

Defining mastery is important when tiering. For each assessment, for instance, are we going for concept attainment or automaticity? Teachers with a working definition of mastery can apply it when determining what they'll accept as evidence of mastery. Here's one I've been using for years that works well:

Students have mastered content when they demonstrate a thorough understanding as evidenced by doing something substantive with the content beyond merely echoing it. Anyone can repeat information; it's the masterful student who can break content into its component pieces, explain it and alternative perspectives regarding it cogently to others, and use it purposefully in new situations.

For more insight, examine the definitions of mastery provided by some of the big thinkers in education, such as Jean Piaget, Howard Gardner, Madeline Hunter, Grant Wiggins, Jay McTighe, and Jerome Bruner.

Tiering assignments

Now, let's walk through how to tier an assignment for varied readiness levels. For example, if we want students to graph the inequality, $6x + 3y < 2$, we isolate the y to one side of the equation, plug in for x in order to get a corresponding y, create an x/y chart in order to get a few ordered pairs, then we graph the solution on a 4-quadrant graph.

$6x + 3y < 2$
$3y < -6x + 2$
$y < -2x + \frac{2}{3}$

x	y
0	$\frac{2}{3}$
3	$-5\frac{2}{3}$

When it comes time to tier this lesson for different readiness levels, it might look like this:

For early readiness students:

- Limit the number of variables for which student must account to one. ($y > 2$)

- Limit the inequality symbols to "greater than" or "less than," not "greater than or equal to" or "less than or equal to."

- Provide an already-set-up 4-quadrant graph on which to graph the inequality.

- Suggest some values for x such that when solving for y, its value is not a fraction.

For advanced readiness students:

- Require students to generate the 4-quadrant graph themselves.

- Increase the parameters for graphing with equations such as $-1 < y < 6$.

- Ask students what happens on the graph when a variable is given in absolute value, such as $/y/ > 1$.

- Ask students to graph two inequalities and shade or color only the solution set (where the shaded areas overlap).

How did we arrive at these leveled tasks?

We list every skill or bit of information a student must use in order to meet the needs of the task successfully. Most of what we teach has subsets of skills and content that we can break down for students and explore at length. For instance, among the many skills needed in the math problem above, students need to know how to isolate a variable, deal with integers, set up a 4-quadrant graph, and establish an x/y chart.

We tier tasks by designing the full-proficiency version first, then we design the more advanced level of proficiency, followed by the remedial or early-readiness level, as necessary. This keeps us from watering down our expectations or drifting too far from essential understandings we're trying to teach.

We respond to the unique characteristics of the students in front of us. We don't always have high, medium, and low tiers. We may have four advanced groups, one on grade level, and none below grade level. For other units, we might have three below grade level and one that is close to collegiate level.

We don't tier every aspect of every lesson. We focus on one small element of the lesson, not the whole unit; to do so would be too cumbersome.

Choose from your running list of great ways to increase the challenge of assignments. Students can:

- Manipulate information rather than echoing it

- Extend the concept to other areas

- Increase the number of variables that must be considered

- Work with advanced resources

- Add an unexpected element to the process or product

- Work independently

- Reframe a topic under a new theme

- Share the back-story to a concept: how it was developed

- Identify misconceptions or prejudice within something

- Negotiate the evaluative criteria

- Deal with ambiguity and multiple meanings or steps

- Make authentic applications to the real world

- Argue against something taken for granted or commonly accepted

- Synthesize two or more unrelated concepts or objects to create something new

- Critique something against a set of standards

- Work with the ethical side of the subject

- Work with abstract concepts and models

- Respond to more open-ended situations

- Identify big picture patterns or connections

- Defend their work

Tiering comes in many formats. Some of the more popular ones include:

Learning Contracts: Students enter into independent study with an agreed-upon set of tasks supporting adjusted goals.

Learning Menus: Similar to learning contracts, students are given choices of tasks to complete in a unit or for an assessment. They are required to do the "entrée" tasks, may select from two "side dish" tasks, and may choose to do one of the "dessert" tasks for enrichment. (See Carol Ann Tomlinson's book, *Fulfilling the Promise of a Differentiated Classroom* (2003).

Cubing: Students receive foam or poster board cubes with a different task written on each face; each task has a different complexity level than the others. Given a topic, students: Describe it, Compare it, Associate it, Analyze it, Apply it, Argue for it or against it.

Summarization Pyramid: Create a pyramid of horizontal lines, then ask students at different readiness levels to respond to tiered prompts as they interact with the topic. Great prompts for each line include synonym, analogy, question, three attributes, alternative title, causes, effects, reasons, arguments, ingredients, opinion, larger category, formula/ sequence, insight, tools, misinterpretation, sample, people, future of the topic

RAFT: Students choose from a short menu of options for each aspect of the assignment—Role, Audience, Format, and Topic—to design their own prompt. The "T" can also stand for Time Period, such as pre-Civil War, 2025, or ancient Greece, and the topic is the same for all students.

Change the Verb: Raise or lower the challenge level by changing the verb in your prompt. Consider using:

Analyze…	Construct…
Revise…	Rank…
Decide between…	Argue against…
Why did…	Argue for…
Defend…	Contrast…
Devise…	Develop…
Identify…	Plan…

Classify...	Critique...
Define...	Rank...
Compose...	Organize...
Interpret...	Interview...
Expand...	Predict...
Develop...	Categorize...
Suppose...	Invent...
Imagine...	Recommend...

Tic-Tac-Toe Boards: Students must choose two from one category and one from another, do three in a row, or choose one from each of three categories to complete the task.

Keeping students above water

When we tier lessons and assessments, our students succeed. When we fail to adjust challenge levels for students who vary in readiness, students sink. We're there to do what it takes to help our students make sense of their learning and find meaning in it, and that means doing different things for different students some or a lot of the time.

Adjusting assignments to meet the needs of students reminds me of the story shared by Patti Kinney about a woman trying to feed medicine by the spoonful to her sick dog week after week. It's a wrestling match. One night the dog knocks the spoon, the medicine, and the medicine bottle to the floor and then races over and licks the medicine off the floor. The woman is exasperated, realizing she could have succeeded all these years just by pouring the medicine into a bowl and letting the dog lap it up. When she told her veterinarian about her discovery, he responded, "Well, there you go. It's not the content, it's the presentation."

Flexible Grouping
in the Classroom

Remember the Fibonacci sequence? It's a series of numbers in which each subsequent number is the sum of the previous two: 0, 1, 1, 2, 3, 5, 8, 13, 21, 34, 55, 89, and so on. One of the most fundamental concepts in mathematics, it is the basis for the Golden Ratio in architecture and nature, some financial markets, and is seen in the works of great composers such as Debussy and Bartok and in the novels of Dan Brown, Philip K. Dick, and Matt Reilly, among others.

Some students will be astounded to find so many Fibonacci numbers and their applications in their everyday world after just one introductory lesson from you. They will marvel at what was there all along, wondering why they had not seen them before. Other students, however, will not "tune in" so quickly and will need to study many Nautilus sea shells and pine cones before they see the sequence.

The differences between these two groups of students are manyfold: familiarity with the topic and reference points, neural development, language bias, and personal investment in school. Nevertheless, both groups of students are in your 47-minute, fifth period class, and worthy of developmentally appropriate instruction. What's a middle grades teacher to do?

Effective teachers know that one group size rarely fits all, so they use flexible grouping based on informed decisions. To guide their decisions about grouping, they can ask themselves the following questions:

- Is this the only way to organize students for this learning? Do I always teach this way, and if so, why?

- Where in the lesson could I create opportunities for students to work in small groups?

- Would this part of the lesson be more effective as an independent or small-group activity?

- Why do I have the whole class involved in the same activity at this point in the lesson?

- Will I be able to meet the needs of all students with this grouping?

- I've been using a lot of [insert type of grouping here—whole class, small group, or independent work] lately. Which type of grouping should I add to the mix?

If it's time for some flexible grouping in our lessons, we can group according to many different factors and structures, including whole class or half class, teams, small groups, partners, triads, quads, one-on-one mentoring with an adult or peer, learning centers, online wiki groups, readiness, interest, and learner profile.

Let's define those last three, in particular.

Readiness refers to how ready students are for more complexity in their lessons. As students develop proficiency, we move them into more challenging tasks, which may mean moving into differently focused or structured groups. Students struggling to read text appropriate for third graders shouldn't be asked to learn content by reading text written for eighth graders; students move on to negative exponents only after they understand exponents and reciprocals.

However, more complexity doesn't mean more workload. We change the nature of the task, not the quantity of the task. We don't give advanced students two labs to do, for instance, if the rest of the class is only doing one. Instead, we ask the advanced group to investigate something more complex than the rest of the class is investigating.

Interest refers to how we can help students learn the material in meaningful ways.

Learner profile refers to any factor that affects a student's learning: family situation, learning preferences, specific talents, cultural background, languages spoken in the home, economic stability or instability, access to technology, repeating or skipping a grade level, reading proficiency, and so on.

Making sense

As we consider grouping students, two important cognitive science principles come to mind: 1) students learn best when information makes sense and is meaningful, and 2) there are two clear steps to every learning experience: accessing the information and processing the information. While these two principles intersect, when we consider flexible grouping, it's important that we consider them separately.

For example, in the initial "making sense" portion of a lesson, we often present information through lecture, demonstrations, videos, and assigned practice. Some students respond better to lecture than do others; some need to think individually before responding to the larger group; and some need to talk about a topic in order to understand it. Most students can learn through all three strategies but may achieve success sooner via one or more of them. We might form groups to meet these and other learning differences as students first begin to learn content.

To help students process the information into long-term memory, we may have to structure the groups differently—perhaps by interest, such as favorite sport, music group, or author. Students connect with and process the content when we help them see how it manifests in their lives: "I need to learn to read because I need to be able to read video game instruction manuals, posts on my social networking site, World of Warcraft magazines, and the rotating message signs on the front of city buses that I ride to and from school."

Offering different analogies and cultural references based on students' personal lives helps them remember the material and apply it in useful situations.

The research sections of the Association for Middle Level Education website (www.amle.org) are full of presentations and citations about homogeneous versus heterogeneous grouping, as are the sites for other professional education organizations. In reviewing these sites and reflecting on current classroom practices, we find the wisest course is to keep classroom groups' membership dynamic, not static. We prefer semipermeable membranes. This means that we rarely maintain the same small group for a whole grading period, let alone a whole year. We're not afraid of temporary homogeneous grouping.

Being flexible

We are vigilant in our formative assessments, too. If we discover that a student's assignment to one group is not working for him or the group, we give the student or group the tools to make it work or we move the student to another group. Kay Burke's *What to Do with the Kid Who…: Developing Cooperation, Self-Discipline, and Responsibility in the Classroom* (2008)) has helpful advice regarding these tools.

We are usually thoughtful about students' group assignments, but sometimes we miss something or a variable doesn't turn up in the student's performance until he's with the group. Revising our decisions in light of the new evidence is better than adhering stubbornly to the original groupings.

If a student believes she has been placed in a group beyond her competence level and asks to be removed, we investigate to determine if we made a mistake in the group assignment or if the student just needs a vote of confidence or an additional tool to tackle the more complex tasks. If, upon investigation, the student's needs are better served by moving her to a slower paced, less-complex-task group, we move her.

Interestingly, she won't balk at the re-assignment nor will she feel like she is a slow learner, going to the "dummy" group. Students crave competence, and when they don't experience it, they shut down, looking for ways to escape. This need to escape is most commonly expressed in middle school with requests to get a drink of water, use the bathroom, or run an errand.

If a teacher has a classroom culture in which a subgroup within the class is considered the "dummy" group, it's time to suspend the curriculum and address the issue. Every person in the classroom, even the 4.0 students, should experience what it's like to be a complete beginner at something at least once a marking period. If students are not able to develop coping strategies for complex, difficult tasks in middle school when stakes are not so high, they won't develop the temperament and neural pathways for handling such demands in high school, college, and the working world where the stakes are much higher. For more on this, see my "Failure Preferred, Actually" column later in this book.

We also want to make sure students do not see differences in learning rate and style as weakness. Instead, students should recognize that all of us learn at different rates and in different ways, despite the fact that most schools are not designed to respond well to those who deviate—higher, lower, laterally—from the exact norm.

Grouping for goals

Whatever we do, all groups must be doing respectful tasks—tasks that are developmentally appropriate, not busywork. For example, we don't tell students who can't identify historical themes in the Constitution to simply draw pictures of what is meant by each of the first 10 Amendments. Instead, we give them the tools to perceive those historical themes. Some of these tools are more concrete, while others are more abstract, but all of them focus on intended curriculum goals.

Even schools with predominantly one culture—social, national, economic, academic—are still abundantly diverse within those cultures.

Some of those students need quiet reflection while others need interaction with others; some need more practice time than others; some can see the math applications in music and some will need specific analogies to make those connections clear. With these students, flexible grouping to maximize instruction is too important to receive only occasional attention. Instead, it's part of our weekly modus operandi.

Just like the Fibonacci sequence, regrouping for flexible purposes weaves through much of our lives. And just like those numbers, each new learning is the sum of the previous learnings; those pairings and repairings matter. Orchestrated by informed, purposeful teachers, these groupings afford opportunities for student learning not to be missed.

Gifted in the Middle School

You know the student I'm talking about. He's the one who doesn't get it. Everyone else moves ahead, but this guy isn't a quick learner, and he's left in the dust yet again. He jokes that he couldn't answer the last three questions—the easy ones—because he was thinking about last night's basketball game. But deep inside he imagines what others think of him: dumb as dirt. For a moment his eye catches yours. He knows that you see through his facade of bravado. He looks away quickly and your teacher heart breaks for him. What does he need that you aren't yet able to give?

Now look at your gifted students. Are their needs being met? Do their faces conjure the same emotional response as the struggling student's? For years, it was easy for me to make every student who wasn't academically strong into a personal cause. Society wasn't fair to these children, and I was going to do whatever it took to give them an equal chance, the respect they deserved, and the tools for success. It was a noble fight for the underdog.

My gifted students, I thought, would learn in spite of what I did. They didn't need me; they'd get it on their own. Their situation didn't warrant the same level of personal calling or professional expertise. Boy, was I wrong.

The diverse gifted

Gifted students deserve just as much conviction and personal investment as students with severe learning disabilities. Gifted students are deeply challenging, and it's just as sorrowful when their needs go unmet. I've had the opportunity over the past two and a half decades to teach regular education students, gifted students, and students with learning disabilities. And while I, like other teachers, have specific strategies I use for struggling students and average students, I also have strategies specifically for gifted students, whether they are in self-contained classrooms or learning alongside their peers in regular classrooms.

For example, differentiated instruction is vital. There is more diversity in gifted classes than in regular education classes. Check out the students in a seventh grade class I once taught:

- Two students couldn't write on grade level, yet they were taking high school mathematics courses.
- At least six students in the class were writing on a level comparable to high school seniors.
- Some students could speak in three languages fluently and some hadn't mastered one.
- A few were almost musical prodigies, and others couldn't carry a tune.
- Some were still playing with action figures and watching Cartoon Network for hours each day and others were writing Congress and programming in java and C++.

If anything, their diverse profiles and readiness levels were more extreme than regular education students, pulling more on my teacher expertise, not less.

As we design our daily lessons, we can pull from a menu of learning experiences we've developed that enable students to achieve 100% mastery on every assessment. We rank those learning experiences in order of complexity. If an intended activity is too simple or too complex for a student, we put it back into the menu of options and pull out something of a different complexity.

We can meet gifted students' needs by extending the breadth or depth of study, the pacing of the study, or its complexity, not its workload. For example, we don't give gifted students more work than regular education students. If I want to teach plot profiles in a novel social studies unit, my gifted students might be assigned to do comparative plot profiles among several previously read novels, rewrite a story to reflect a different plot profile, or examine the patterns of plot profiles for a particular genre.

Sometimes our gifted students finish their work ahead of other students. Should we allow them to do puzzles or read a book while they wait for classmates to finish? Is it fair to ask them to help a struggling classmate?

No. Some students get to the end of what I know about a topic. They grasp a procedure, apply it correctly several times, and seem ready to move on to the next topic, but do they have the conceptual understanding? Not always.

Beyond the what

David Sousa, in his book *How the Gifted Brain Learns* (2003), says that many gifted students coast along, learning procedure after procedure in rapid succession only to be thwarted on standardized tests or complex tasks because they never spent time developing and analyzing the concepts behind those procedures. We can guide these students to investigate, on their own, in greater depth—to understand the "why" and "how," not just the "what to do." We become the facilitators and the learners as the gifted students share their investigations with us and spend time exploring.

It's important for teachers of gifted students to use the textbook as a resource, not the curriculum. Students' inquiries and levels of readiness will transcend most textbooks. They thrive on primary sources and their own opportunities to distill what's salient. Subjecting them exclusively to somebody else's interpretation will not meet their needs.

Gifted students tend to seek greater autonomy in their studies. They want choices in assignments and projects. They want to pursue non-traditional methods of demonstrating mastery, such as creating a website on a topic rather than an essay; conducting a panel discussion among experts instead of presenting an oral report; or conducting inquiry labs instead of verification labs.

Instead of asking them to describe the effect of railroad expansion in the 1800s, we can ask them to rank five government policies of the time period in order of importance to the railroad and explain how those rankings would differ from the rankings of the same policies by Presidents Lincoln or Hayes. We invite tangential thinking and look for multi-dimensional comprehension from the students.

Behind the label

Some of my gifted students are stuck on their label. When they don't understand something immediately, they question whether they are as smart as they thought. They are fragile, afraid of doing anything that might threaten their status. These gifted students rarely take on challenging or creative assignments for fear they will struggle—which to them is a sign of weakness.

We must show all of our students, gifted or not, that academic struggle is a virtue, not a weakness. That means we have to struggle to learn something in front of them and show them that people who struggle academically are still respected by others. Unfortunately, many students identified as gifted associate their personal value only in regards to their gifted label. They may spend a large portion of their school day trying to justify the label instead of taking chances, pushing themselves academically or artistically in ways that might change that status. We need to make sure they are invited to do this and they have a safe place to do it.

These are the years in which their brains are "hardwired" for how to handle defeat and disappointment. Let's get them ready to take advantage of every brick wall they hit by decreasing our praise for their products and increasing our praise for their decisions during the learning process.

Food for thought

Three quick concerns about our response to gifted or accelerated students:

First, gifted students need extended time with one another. Part of every day needs to be spent in the company of other gifted students. For many of them, it's the only time they feel comfortable and the time they really progress academically. It's not elitist to say they should spend time with their "own kind." Rather it's a way to respond to their specific needs just as we respond to the needs of students with severe learning difficulties.

Pullout programs in which students meet once a week for an hour don't have the positive effect we think they do, according to Sousa. Time and funding to such programs would be better spent providing training and resources for teachers to differentiate instruction for their gifted students in the regular education classroom.

Second, remember that giftedness and learning disabilities are not opposites. Many of my moderately and profoundly gifted students have learning disabilities such as dyslexia, ADD, Tourette's syndrome, and Asperger's syndrome. Learning disabilities are not equal to "dumb"; they are simply a different way of processing and connecting to the world. "LD" can also mean "learns differently."

Finally, remember that we need to rally increased complexities and depth for advanced students around the same standard, not a different standard. If they already know a set of science facts, for example, we don't make them go learn a set of science facts from another domain. Instead, we facilitate more advanced, novel, or extended applications of the original set of facts. Kelly knows the sequence of the planets already, ask her to learn how gravity, rotation, and revolution play roles in keeping them in that sequence, or ask them how planetary sequence affects each planet's atmosphere, the number of moons a planet can have, or the make-up of each planet's core.

Exchanging gifts

In the end, Howard Gardner was right. It's not how smart our students are, it's how they are smart. We all have gifts, some more visible than others, and some to a greater extent.

Students with demonstrably extreme intelligence levels are unique, and they require different approaches and as much devotion and energy as students with other labels. If we leave them to their own devices, without clear direction and compassion from knowledgeable adults in their lives, they fail to thrive.

Let's do more than measure and celebrate their gifts—let's offer them ours.

Emancipating the English Language Learner

As you cooraptoriliate these words, make sure you flimp the scoglottora in proper schimliturn. You will only understand this column if hickitow glisps in baggaduanation. Use your joomering and begin.

Huh?

Look, everyone else reading this article has begun his or her work, why haven't you? Seriously, use your joomering and get started.

What exactly do you want me to do?

Hmm. Maybe you're not ready for the level of comprehension this book requires of its readers. We might have a remedial book for you, perhaps something from Charlotte's Web?

No, I really want to know. I can do whatever you ask, but I don't know what it is. I'm actually a good reader and thinker, but I don't use your words or have experience with your culture. Do not think of me as unintelligent!

Maybe I could find something from the basic teacher texts for you if I only had the time. Just sit here a moment while I explain this information to the other readers and let them move ahead. I know this means you'll be further behind than you already are, but it's all I can offer right now.

Wow. Just a couple of moments of walking in an English language learner's shoes and a few things are abundantly clear:

- Well-intentioned yet uninformed teachers can offend English language learners (ELLs) if they are not careful.

- Some ELL students don't receive appropriate instruction for their intellectual level.

- We feel a lot of anxiety when we don't know the language or culture of the country in which we are living—so much so that some of us stop trying. It takes a tremendous amount of energy and patience every day to remain attentive and engaged when you're learning a language, and some days ELL students are so emotionally drained they can't muster either one.

We need to be mindful of the emotions at play when asking students to do all this thinking aloud in a language and culture foreign to their own. Students are stressed not only about learning a new academic concept, but also about having to adjust to different cultural expectations in which they may not succeed.

Debra Coggins and her coauthors explain in *English Language Learners in the Mathematics Classroom* (2007):

> For students from cultures in which students are expected to wait to be asked before speaking, and where students are not expected to ask questions of elders, it is very important for the teacher to explicitly set the expectation for students to ask questions and express their opinions in the ... classroom. Otherwise, classroom discourse becomes an exercise in trying to participate in a game where only others know the unwritten rules.

Simple strategies

If we embrace the promise of America from its earliest roots, we realize that with the noted exception of native peoples, we are a nation of immigrants. What can those of us not trained in working with English language learners do in our regular classrooms to help them succeed?

Twenty minutes of empathetic reflection on the needs of ELL students yields some common sense responses that truly help them learn (Note: These are similar to the ones listed earlier in this book in the article on students transitioning to middle school):

1. Speak slowly and clearly.

2. Repeat important words and information several times.

3. Extend time for responding to prompts as necessary.

4. Avoid using idioms and colloquialisms until students are more advanced with our culture; if we use them, we take the time to explain them.

5. Gesture and point to what we are referring.

6. Ask students to read text more than once.

7. Label objects and concepts in the classroom frequently.

8. Provide a lot of specific models, including hands-on experiences.

9. Use visuals during instruction: pictures, illustrations, graphs, pictographs, as well as real objects.

10. Frequently demonstrate what we mean, not just describe it.

11. Make ELL students feel as though they belong and have a role to play in classroom learning. One way to do this is to find something in the student's background that connects to the topic we're studying.

12. Use thinking aloud or self-talk to model the sequence of doing the task.

13. Use cooperative learning groups; let ELL students work with English-proficient partners.

14. Let students draw responses occasionally instead of writing them; use more than one format for assessing students if the general approach won't allow ELL students to accurately portray what they know.

15. Find ways to enable ELL students to demonstrate their intellectual skills and maintain dignity.

16. Give students quick feedback on their word use: An ELL says in halting English, "This correct paper?" and we say in affirmation, "Yes, that is the correct paper. Thank you."

17. Spend time before lessons on important topics to build a personal background in English language learners so they have an equal chance to attach new learning to what's already in their minds. This is good for all students, not just ELLs, of course. If we're about to teach students about magnetic fields, for example, we can let them play with magnets, lightly pouring iron shavings near their poles to watch their pattern of dispersal or gathering.

18. Stay focused on how ELL students are doing toward reaching their learning goals, not how they're doing in relation to other students. This is huge. We remove all hope when we ceaselessly cajole ELL students into proficiency by comparing them to language-proficient students.

19. Recognize the difference between conversational language and academic language and that students need help with both; learning one does not mean you've learned the other.

20. Take the time to learn about English language learners' home countries. This engenders good will and allows you to make connections in the curriculum.

In addition, in *English Language Learners in the Mathematics Classroom*, the authors remind us to

- Invite ELL students to learn and explore ideas in their own languages first, then translate them to English.

- Provide ELL students with response stems, such as, "One thing that I learned was …."

- Ask students to restate classmates' comments as they begin their own comments.

- Relate concepts in story format before specific instruction.

Stephen Cary, author of *Working with English Language Learners: Answers to Teachers' Top Ten Questions* (2007) favors authentic talk over compliance talk. "Authentic talk" refers to real conversations about real topics to satisfy real needs, even when this includes the incorporation of local colloquialisms, phrasings, and terms. Consider the value of this dialogue:

- Where can I buy soccer cleats? Mine are too old. I can't turn fast in them. I'm the sweep this weekend.
- Wow, I hate playing sweep. I'm a mid-fielder.
- I can't play mid-field very well. It's too tiring. You have to be everywhere.
- Yeah, but you can get the other team off sides.
- Sometimes, but I don't think about that a lot. So, the cleats?
- Oh yeah. Over at Fair Oaks Mall, there's a sports store near the soft pretzel shop.

Students need plenty of experiences with real conversations.

Something else to consider

Some people—educators included—equate low language proficiency with diminished mental function. Because teachers are so accustomed to using verbal and written responses as students' manifestation of internal thought, they think ELL students are not capable of abstract or sophisticated thinking because their words are not abstract or sophisticated. As a result, they don't ask ELL students to make comparisons, analyze data, connect ideas, synthesize concepts, or evaluate performances. By not pushing their ELL students this way, teachers allow these students to fall further behind.

Add to this the reality that our society tends to be insensitive to those who do not speak our language well or who do not have our same cultural references.

Many English language learners who are employed in service positions such as custodian, stock clerk, construction worker, and housekeeper have extraordinary depth, complexity, and rich educational backgrounds but are doing these jobs because their lack of language skills prevents them from working in other positions.

One year, I taught a student whose family escaped from brutality in former Romania. The student's parents had been math professors at prestigious universities in Romania. Here in the United States, however, the student's father was cleaning offices in the building next to my school and the mother was teaching English at the local library.

Even ELL students who are not from such academically advanced families think in wonderfully imaginative ways, often beyond what can be expressed in English.

To not include metaphors and analogies in ELL students' learning experiences due to language struggles is like assuming they don't know how to feed themselves because they don't eat the same food we do. It's pompous, and it denies ELL students their basic instruction. We can't save advanced thinking only for advanced language proficiency students.

Freeing learners to learn

At this point in the 21st century, it is no longer acceptable to consider ELL students as someone else's problem or beyond our instruction. They are just as much a part of the modern teacher's daily commitment as taking attendance and making sure students have their supplies.

We have effective tools for the regular education teacher to help ELL students find every success in our schools. It's time to free them from what lack of language proficiency would impose.

Teaching Vocabulary: Work Smarter, Not Harder

No matter how you frame it, words are power. Students are looking for that power, so let's give it to them: the power to think critically, to learn for themselves, and to achieve their goals. Let's teach them vocabulary terms, and let's do it well.

Effective vocabulary instruction in middle school has 10 principles.

1. **Spend time reading.**

    Vocabulary development is directly proportional to time spent reading. You want to increase students' vocabulary? Increase the time spent reading. "Today we're going to learn vocabulary, students, so please take out your novels/newspapers/magazines/blog-postings/scripts/satires/game manuals and read for 30 minutes." Seriously, we do a world of good for vocabulary development by getting students to read for extended periods of time. This doesn't mean we don't ever do specific word study, but it does mean we increase the time spent reading.

2. **Teach words for their own sake, in addition to the terms associated with units of study.**

    Students can paraphrase, draw analogies, identify metaphors, and think deeply about topics when they have large vocabularies. Try to keep the number of new vocabulary terms not associated with any specific unit of study to 10 or fewer words per week, but doing just one word per day is fine, too.

If we do 20 words a week for 36 school weeks, that's 720 words per year, but students will remember only a small portion of them in June. If we do 10 words a week (or less), that's 360 words per year, and students will remember all of them. The testimony to our teaching is what students carry forward after their time with us, not the amount of curriculum we presented. Here, less is more.

3. **Build integration, repetition, and meaningful use into vocabulary instruction.**

Janet Allen reports in her helpful book *Words, Words, Words* (1999) that research identifies these three avenues to effective vocabulary instruction. Build them into your vocabulary approach weekly.

Use the words in more than one application or context, provide repeated exposure (If it's in sight, it's in mind, so put in sight anything you want in mind), and facilitate students' use of the word in meaningful ways: in conversations, writing, and thinking.

Another way of looking at this is to normalize a new word's use. Work it into your lessons without calling attention to it: "I was at a play last night and the patron next to me kept coughing into his hand. Based on yesterday's health lesson, what part of his body should he have used instead?" (answer: the bend of his elbow) Smile and act surprised when a student calls out, "Hey, patron is one of our vocabulary words!"

4. **Do not make the first night's vocabulary assignment looking up the definitions in the dictionary and using them properly in a sentence.**

You're not helping anybody with this assignment. Students will most often record the shortest definition, and they rarely make the effort to consider whether the definition makes sense.

To save all of us time and hassle, please give students the definitions you want them to associate with the words and ask them to interact with the words in a substantive manner. As for writing sentences using the words, this should be assigned only after several successful interactions with the words and after students have proved their full understanding of the terms. In other words, this should be one of the later assignments in your vocabulary unit, not among the first.

5. **Don't rely purely on defining the words or asking students to figure out a word using context clues.**

   Each of these strategies by themselves has little to no effect on learning. Using the two together actually has some impact, but most often we have to incorporate additional strategies to learn the terms well.

6. **Help students relate words to their world.**

   Most students begin to capture a vocabulary term if they can reconfigure or reimagine the word's meaning to fit their own reality. So find ways to do this. For example, some students learn vocabulary by drawing webs, symbols, or flow charts. Some students understand imperialism, westward expansion, and hegemony better if put in terms of local gangs' turf wars. The connections among parabolas, gravity, inertia, and Newton's Laws are suddenly meaningful when students analyze YouTube clips of skateboarders competing on multiple half pipes.

7. **Start teaching students Latin and Greek prefixes and word roots.**

   If I were ruler of the education universe, I would mandate courses in Latin for every student in middle school. A background in Latin opens many doors, building the autonomy students seek. With clear knowledge of prefixes and roots at the very least, students can make sense of text, summarize, and think critically. Consider, for example, the many words with cardi, astr, ped/pod, bi, poly, mis, and un in their construction, instantly deciphered by students as having to do with heart, star, foot, two, many, incorrect, and not. So equipped, adolescents can learn on their own.

8. **Teach students a lexicon for studying vocabulary.**

   Among the most useful words to teach students as they study vocabulary terms are root, stem, prefix, suffix, affix, acronym, coin, colloquial, connotation, denotation, malapropism, onomatopoeia, palindrome, simile, spoonerism, metaphor, personification, Portmanteau word, figurative, syllable, and common parts of speech: noun, pronoun, adjective, adverb, conjunction, preposition, interjection, gerund, and verb. Vocabulary learning excels with a working language for word study.

9. **Spend considerable time helping students with subtle difference analysis (SDA).**

   In SDA, help students identify words/concepts that are close in meaning, but not an exact match with one another. Identify how they are similar and what makes them "just off" the match. Example pairs include outstanding/exemplary, confined/restricted, elaborate/complex, intelligent/smart, child/offspring, and house/home.

   Isolating the subtle differences helps students learn both vocabulary terms and it helps them think critically about topics—noting nuanced differences, breaking concepts down into their component pieces, and providing evidence for their claims. Many students in middle and high school are just now seeing the gray areas of worlds they once considered black and white; it's a part of maturation. We can provide great assistance with subtle difference analysis.

10. **Express great enthusiasm for words and their wise use.**

    If we find redundant phrasing frustrating yet sometimes entertaining, for example, and we share that pet peeve with students, they'll find multiple examples of redundancy in print and others' conversations and share them with you: She said, "2 a.m. in the morning!" They wrote, "advance forward" instead of just, "advance." He said, "baby puppy," but puppies are babies already. If you share your love of spoonerisms and malapropisms, students will flood your desk with them. If you show how helpful it was to learn a new word, they'll want the same mini-epiphany you've experienced.

No Wonder English Is Hard to Learn
(Source Unknown)

The bandage was wound around the wound.

The farm was used to produce produce.

The dump was so full that it had to refuse more refuse.

We must polish the Polish furniture.

He could lead if he would get the lead out.

The soldier decided to desert his dessert in the desert.

Since there is no time like the present, he thought it was time to present the present.

A bass was painted on the head of the bass drum.

I did not object to the object.

The insurance was invalid for the invalid.

They were too close to the door to close it.

The buck does funny things when the does are present.

A seamstress and a sewer fell down into a sewer line.

To help with planting, the farmer taught his sow to sow.

The wind was too strong to wind the sail.

After a number of injections my jaw got number.

Upon seeing the tear in the painting I shed a tear.

I had to subject the subject to a series of tests.

The Native American took a bow after tying a bow in the string of his bow.

Reading Between the Lines

My captain does not answer, his lips are pale and still,
My father does not feel my arm; he has no pulse or will,
The ship is anchored safe and sound, its voyage closed and done,
From fearful trip the victor ship comes in with object won;
Exult, O shores, and ring O bells!
But I, with mournful tread,
Walk the deck my Captain lies,
Fallen cold and dead

        —from "O Captain! My Captain!" by Walt Whitman

Walt Whitman's poem is worth teaching to every middle school student because of its stirring imagery and exemplary poetic structures. For years, I thought this poem was about a captain who steers his ship into a safe harbor after some harrowing experiences at sea, only to die from injuries suffered during the journey. My perspective changed when one of my high school teachers provided some historical context. Whitman was a medic during the Civil War, and he considered Abraham Lincoln a hero, almost an angel of our wounded country. The poem is Whitman's dirge for the president, written in anguish after Lincoln's assassination in 1865. Oddly, the night before the assassination, Whitman dreamed of a tall ship coming into port under full sail. Now when I read his poem, the symbolism shows me that language can reveal as much about history or other subjects as it does literary devices. However, it took a skilled teacher to understand that I needed background information and experience interpreting poetry before I could make such connections.

Helping children to understand what they read might be the single most important skill a teacher can impart—at any grade level and in any subject. Reading comprehension is the key that unlocks every door in school and most of the doors after school. I know that providing meaning and context consumes valuable class time, but if we don't teach reading comprehension initially, we will have to invest more time and resources later filling the gaps. Take it from someone who has taught science, history, math, English, physical education, and health. All of us are reading teachers.

Researchers analyzing the math scores on the National Assessment of Educational Progress (NAEP) found that about half of the errors occurred because of problems with reading. In other words, students made mistakes not because they couldn't do the math, but because they couldn't understand the directions, identify the important information in the word problem, or recognize the vocabulary terms. If we think about how critical it is for students to grasp subject terminology, recognize the syntax and structures of equations and problems, and interpret directions, we realize the necessity of focusing on reading in every course we teach.

In middle schools, reading comprehension has far more to do with a student's personal background than his or her decoding skills. We've all had students who could read fluently in class yet couldn't answer basic questions about the material or remember any of the concepts the next day. Emphasizing vocabulary words isn't enough. Sometimes teachers think that if they define the hardest words in their courses, students will understand the text. Yet, researchers who study the human brain have found that moving information to long-term memory storage requires both meaning and comprehension. If we want students to remember what we teach them, we have to provide background knowledge where none exists.

This takes careful planning. Before asking students to read President Woodrow Wilson's speech on the Fourteen Points, for example, we might show them a movie about World War I, listen to a recorded copy of Wilson's speech, or discuss the historical context by referring to a map of the world at that period in history. Before assigning the textbook chapter on muscle development, we might show students how to do some stretching exercises and describe the results of improper techniques. In each situation, background information can prepare students for what they will see in print.

Sometimes we encourage students to underline or highlight important information in articles and books. This can be an effective technique, but many young adolescents don't know how to identify the main idea in a paragraph or how to sift the key facts from a string of unfamiliar sections.

One way to help students make sense of information they are reading is to point out the different structures found in texts, such as:

Enumeration—Focuses on listing facts, characteristics, or features. Signal words include *to begin with, secondly, then, most important, in fact, for example, several, numerous, first, next, finally, also, for instance, and in addition.*

> Example: The giant squid lives in many places, including New Zealand. It can reach a length of 60 feet, but some scientists believe it can grow as large as 70 feet. Its beak is shaped like a parrot's and its eyeball is the size of a hubcap. To date, the only evidence we have of the giant squid's existence comes from nonliving samples, including carcasses that have washed ashore or wound up in the stomachs of sperm whales. In addition, explorers have found sucker marks on the skin of sperm whales, indicating some kind of struggle with the giant squid below the ocean's surface.

Time Order—This involves putting facts, events, and concepts into sequence using time references to order them. Signal words include *on* (date), *now, before, since, when, not long after,* and *gradually.*

> Example: Since the days of Jules Verne and his book, *Twenty-Thousand Leagues Under the Sea*, humans have been fascinated by the giant squid. Dr. Clyde Roper, a teuthologist at the Smithsonian Institution in Washington, D.C., has long been interested in finding

the giant squid. In 1996 and 1997, he launched a full-scale expedition to Kaikoura Canyon, an underwater canyon off the coast of New Zealand. During the trip, he carne within 100 feet of the giant squid many times, but was unable to videotape it. Today, he's getting ready for another trip to find the elusive sea creature.

Comparison/Contrast—Explains similarities and differences. Signal words include *however, as well as, not only, but, while, unless, yet, on the other hand, either/or, although, similarly,* and *unlike.*

> Example: A giant squid is usually very gentle and passive. A Humboldt squid, on the other hand, is very aggressive. Its feeding frenzies are worse than a shark's. A Humboldt squid can strip off an animal's flesh in seconds, similar to the destructive power of a piranha. Although both types of squid have two tentacles and eight arms, they use them to catch food in different ways.

Cause/Effect—Shows how something happens through the impact of something else. Signal words include *because, therefore, as a result, so that, accordingly, thus, consequently; this led to,* and *nevertheless.*

> Example: Because sunlight cannot penetrate the ocean's depths, most of the area is completely dark. As a result, many of the ocean's bottomdwelling creatures have eyes that don't work properly, or they have no eyes at all.

Problem/Solution—Explains how a difficult situation, dilemma, or conflict developed and what was done to resolve it. Signal words are the same as Cause and Effect above.

> Example: In the deepest parts of the ocean where the giant squid lives, the water pressure of 800 pounds per square inch is so strong that it would crush most animals. To compensate, the creatures that live at these depths don't have air sacs that can implode at extreme pressures. Humans traveling to the bottom of the ocean must take precautions as well. Because of the extreme conditions, submarines must use very thick glass and metal and slowly take on pressurized water as they descend.

We can show students how to analyze text structures through graphics they can use for note-taking and test preparation. For example, a Venn diagram of interlocking circles is useful for listing similarities and differences (compare/contrast), a timeline can help with text in chronological order, and a web with one center circle surrounded by smaller circles of information is good for enumeration.

The ability to summarize expository text is a critical skill for middle school students, and there are many good methods for showing them how. In the PQRST method, students Preview the text to identify its main parts, develop Questions they want answered, Read the material, and State the central idea or theme. Finally, they Test themselves by answering questions (or they Teach the material to someone else).

My colleague, Susan Hynes, shared another good summary method at a faculty meeting last school year. Here's the one-sentence sequence: Something (independent variable), happened (change in independent variable), and (effect on the dependent variable), and then (conclusion).

> An example is: The torrential rain fell, causing the rich soil to wash away from the hillsides, which prevented certain trees from growing on the hillside.

You also can use this method with fiction writing: Somebody (characters), wanted (plot/ motivation), but (conflict), so (resolution).

Other reading comprehension techniques worth incorporating in all classes:

- SQ3R: Survey, Question, Read, Recite, Review. In the first step, students read the headings of each section and the first sentence of each paragraph, look at the graphics, and read the chapter summary. Then they turn the headings into questions. For example, "Freedmen's Bureau Makes an Impact" becomes "What was the Freedmen's Bureau and how did it affect the South?" In the first of the three Rs, students read to answer their questions and write the information in note form under each question. Next, students cover their answers and read the questions, reciting the answers from memory. To review, students write a summary of what they learned, based on the answers to their questions.

- The Cornell note-taking system is effective with all students, but especially those who have trouble organizing material and focusing. Two of my favorite websites for explaining and demonstrating the method are operated by Dartmouth (www.dartmouth.edu/admin/ acskills/no_framesllsg/cornell.html) and Heartland Community College in Illinois (www.hcc.cc.il.us/divisions/ascitutor/index.htm). For the latter, click on "Study Skills Resources" at the top.

In elementary school, students primarily read narrative texts—the information comes in story form. Although the story form is still important in middle schools, expository text takes precedence. To help students learn how to analyze and comprehend expository text—a skill essential for success in high school, college, and careers—we must build the foundation in every class every year of middle school.

Mark Twain was right when he said that the man who does not read good books has no advantage over the man who can't read. Our students need reading instruction and inspiration throughout their middle school years.

Writing in the Content Areas

After hearing a guest speaker describe the giant squid as not sinking or floating but "hovering" comfortably a mile below the ocean's surface, one of my seventh graders wondered how this could happen. I told her that the squid maintained neutral buoyancy in water.

"What is neutral buoyancy?" Amy persisted.

"The squid can float completely still, not floating to the surface or sinking to the bottom, with little or no movement of their arms," I replied. When she asked for further clarification, I directed her to a website I knew of and asked her to write about what she found there. I wasn't trying to deflect Amy's inquiry, and she didn't groan that this was science class, not English class. I often asked my students to write and she understood the process could deepen her knowledge about a topic.

"It's all because of the stuff that's in kitchen floor cleaner," Amy wrote in her learning log later that day. "The giant squid is full of ammonia, I mean, ammonium ions. I'm not sure what ions are, but the website said they were lighter than water. I guess if you have just the right amount of these ammonium ions, it could keep you from sinking. I wonder if a giant squid sometimes gets too many ammonium ions and floats to the surface. Where do the ions come from?"

Amy didn't get all the facts right (ammonia is different from ammonium ions) but she had a general understanding of neutral buoyancy. I reviewed her learning log and corrected a few misconceptions. I also knew she would learn more about the topic in eighth grade.

I taught English for the past several years, but I previously taught math, science, history, and physical education. In each subject, writing helped my students learn content and self-expression, whether they were describing an improper algorithm, analyzing their lab results, or explaining the benefits of cardiovascular exercise.

As standards-based education becomes the norm in most states, teachers of every discipline are being asked to incorporate writing into their regular assignments and assessments. It's a worthy goal, but not always easy to accomplish if your training as a writing instructor and your own experience as a writer are limited. To start, try working with an English teacher on your team or grade level. Create a lesson together. Better yet, take the state standards for each of your subject areas and look for natural connections between them.

Building writing into every subject

There are four components to a writer-friendly classroom. The first is time, which refers both to the duration and frequency of writing. For most people, their best thinking comes after 15 or 20 minutes of writing. You might not be able to provide that much time in a typical 55-minute class. Extended block schedule classes are better for this. But you probably can devote at least 5 or 10 minutes for brainstorming, categorizing, or explaining ideas on a regular basis. When students write routinely in your class, they become more analytical and comfortable exploring issues in greater depth.

The second important component is choice. When I ask students to create a diary entry from a person in the Reconstruction era, I let them choose to write from different perspectives. The students get the same benefit from the assignment whether they portray a freed slave, a colonel in the Confederate Army, a homeless eight-year-old boy sleeping under a bench at a train depot, a Union solider returning to his job in the city, or the mother of four sons killed in the Civil War. I can assess their comprehension of the content by requiring them to include reflections on particular events in their diaries.

The third component of a writer-friendly classroom is structure. All of us can remember assignments in which our first response was, "I don't know how to start." We needed help taking the first step. Good writing seldom stems from a teacher saying to students: "Write something."

You can provide direction in many ways, but encourage higher-level thinking by requiring your students to do more than report information. Sometimes all it takes is a strong verb in the writing prompt. Instead of telling them to "Explain photosynthesis," for example, how about asking them to "Compare photosynthesis to a computer?" Instead of, "Tell the story of the Lusitania's sinking," how about "Argue against the government's theory for how the Lusitania sank"?

We also need to teach students the writing structures that occur within our subject specialties. For example, science journals tend to use passages of facts that are observable or provable: "The anole crawled to the left side of the container and returned to the original green color. Its chest rose and fell in rapid succession." The situation or problem is fully described without interpretation until the end of the section. In contrast, history textbooks often report events chronologically, frequently adding commentary along the way.

Response is the fourth component of a writer-friendly classroom. Writers need an audience (readers) for their work. Nothing motivates students more than knowing their work will be received by a real person. That person shouldn't always be you, the teacher. Find opportunities for other teenagers, parents, and professionals in the community to read and respond to students' writing.

The writing process

We can't just assume that if we give data to students, they will be able to turn out a product based on it. I've known many teachers who announce a writing assignment on Monday, tell students that it's due on Friday, and never say another word about it other than to remind students about the deadline. As teachers, we have a responsibility to use writing as an instructional tool, providing opportunities for students to craft sentences while they're interpreting the philosophical teachings of Socrates or making sense of algebra.

The full process looks like this:

- Teacher provides a pre-writing exercise— something that sets context or stimulates thought.

- Students brainstorm, discuss, or map ideas.

- Students write an initial draft according to the chosen format.

- Students revise drafts after conferring with others and obtaining more information, if necessary.

- Students edit their final drafts.

- Students write their final versions.

- Students share their writing in some way.

The pre-writing experience might consist of a reading from homework, a two-minute video clip, or a class discussion. An initial brainstorming session usually lasts from two to ten minutes before we ask students to begin writing. Drafting can take 10 to 20 minutes, or it can be completed overnight or later in the week.

Revising refers to adding, deleting, and moving around ideas, sentences, and paragraphs, changing the tone, addressing a different audience, or making any number of changes that will improve the writing. Editing is when students deal with issues such as noun-verb agreement, punctuation, and organization.

Don't focus too much on grammar and mechanics before this stage. When the goal is clarifying students' thinking, we want to concentrate on the ideas and connections they are making, not whether they have placed periods at the end of each sentence. Remember that every student won't need to go through every step of the writing process. Vary the requirements according to each student's skills and your own objectives.

Specific ideas for selected subjects

Math—Almost any topic or skill in math can be linked to a writing assignment. You can ask students to compare three-dimensional shapes, explain two ways to solve a problem, or analyze trends in the stock market. Encourage your students to draft a proposal to the city council for a new bridge and explain why the recommended structure represents the sturdiest and most cost efficient option. How about a speech advocating the value of math in today's society or a "Dear Abby" column for math-phobic students?

Art—Students can write autobiographies to go with portraits, explain what art can tell us about a particular time period, or develop synthesis writings, such as "What does blue sound like?"

Science—This area has many natural uses for writing, from lab reports to poetry. Ask your students to examine a common scientific misconception, explain how it was perpetuated, and consider how it could be corrected. Ask them to write a science fiction story that includes key facts about a topic, critique an experimental design, or research and write a journalistic account of a scientific discovery that changed the world.

Social studies—In addition to the ideas already mentioned, consider asking students to write a conversation between two famous people, using vocabulary from the era; analyze a political cartoon; prepare notes for a debate; or create a pledge, anthem, or constitution for a new country.

Like those neutrally buoyant giant squid, when we write about topics, we become immersed in them. We are ready to explore and move deeper than we ever thought possible. So, take the plunge. Use writing as an instructional tool that can open new routes to success with your students.

Mirror and Sieve: Summarization as a Powerful Learning Strategy

Assignment: "Read and summarize the chapter."

Wow, wait one minute! I can't summarize right now because I have to copy these 15 pages from the dictionary, sort my pencils, think about food, stare at my shoe, and IM 40 friends. Yeah, that's it. I'm busy. I'll read and summarize tomorrow.

For many students, summarization is a fuzzy process: They don't know what content is important and what's not. They aren't sure about the main idea of the paragraph or its supporting details. "How do I restate the sentence in a new way when the author already said it as clear as anyone can? How do I summarize an experience?"

Lack of clarity and specific methods give any strategy a bad reputation. It doesn't have to be like this. Summarization can be a compelling learning strategy for middle school students if they understand the process and know how to use a variety of summarization techniques.

Learn as they go

Summarizing is restating the essence of text or an experience in as few words as possible, or in a new, efficient manner. Students can summarize through writing, but they can also summarize orally, dramatically, artistically, visually, physically, musically, as well as in groups and individually.

We remember best what we experience at the beginning and end of a lesson. It's important to structure lessons to provide those important summarization experiences.

- We can summarize to assess students prior to presenting the lesson and then use students' responses to guide our instruction. Pre-unit summarizations also prepare students for what they will learn.

- We can summarize during a unit to help students monitor their own comprehension and to provide us with feedback about how well students understand the lesson.

And, of course, we use summarization after a learning experience to help students process what they have learned and move the material into their long-term memory.

Summarizing is not magic. Harry Potter can summarize his potions text without his wand. Students simply have to be tenacious, they have to practice, they have to learn multiple methods of summarizing, and they must be inclined to revise their thinking as perspective and information warrant.

The basics of summarization

Let's get specific: Teachers can use specific practices to help students learn to summarize successfully, to know what portions of the text or elements of the experience are important to highlight.

Create students' personal background with the material prior to summarizing. It will shape what they think is salient. The student with a passion for baseball who has played the game for years is going to write a very different summary of the World Series than a kid who's never worn a baseball glove or watched a game.

A student who understands the dynamics of a musical piece (forte, allegro, legato, piano) will write a better summary of a concerto's three distinct movements than a student with no knowledge of the terms.

Students who have little or no background in the content prior to summarizing may struggle. The key is to provide background where there was none. Explain the geography of World War I before reading about specific battle campaigns. Teach students about the role of verbs in our everyday communications before teaching tenses or conjugations. Let students mix and match pigments before teaching them the color wheel. Very little goes into long-term memory unless it's attached to something already in storage.

Prime the brain so it will pay attention and determine what's meaningful in text or experience, as Pat Wolfe reminds us in *Brain Matters: Translating Research into Classroom Practice* (2001). Asking students to read Chapter 14 of their history text book and summarize the important information is like asking students to watch a 50-minute video on solar systems and "take notes." They'd write everything or nothing, but either way it would be overwhelming and very little of it would go to long-term memory. Instead, we ask students to "Watch this video and focus on the role of gravity in keeping planets in orbit." We are priming the brain for what's to come and summarizing what we want students to look for.

One way to prime the brain is to explain how the text or experience is structured. Our ability to retrieve information for a test or application down the road, in fact, has mostly to do with how it was structured when it first entered our minds. So go ahead and teach students how the chapter is set up: chronologically, compare/contrast, cause/effect, problem/solution, enumeration.

Show students how paragraphs are structured, including stronger evidence at the beginning and end, general claims followed by evidence, and how to determine a topic sentence. Teach them that topic sentences have two parts: the subject and the author's claim about it. Give students repeated practice in determining the topic sentences for a variety of paragraphs—it's the essence of summarizing.

Teach students to use analogies. Determining how a concept or event is analogous to something else clarifies and illuminates the ideas.

It's one reason we use so many allegorical descriptions when teaching. Making analogies between a political belief, math concept, paragraph structure, scientific principle, or historical event and a common everyday activity can transform learning.

Chunk text and experience. It's easier and more effective for summarizing. As experts in content, we can pre-read a section of text and determine the best way to segment the material for summarization by first-time readers. When we break longer experiences into segments, we're not diluting the text's message; we're presenting it in a way that promotes student learning.

Chunk lectures. Lecturing is one place we see the power of summarization. While straight lecturing does not typically promote information moving to long-term memory, chunked lectures do the opposite. Chunking lectures means we lecture for approximately 15 minutes and then pause and initiate a brief (1to 10 minutes) summarization or processing activity around the information just presented. Then, we continue our lecture. We leave time for summarization at the end of the lecture as well, but it is less powerful if we have not included some summarization throughout the lesson.

Note: Summarizing does not mean calling on individual students to respond to our quick review questions. The students who are activating their neural pathways are learning, so keep all students activating those pathways, not a select four or five.

Avoid opinions. Summaries are not commentaries. They are clear and undistorted gists of the reading, lecture, or experience. If it helps students to bypass their personal opinions or judgments, ask them to preface summaries with the phrase "According to the author [or speaker or experience leader]." This way, students stay focused on what was truly in the text or experience. They can form their personal interpretations and reactions to the information separately. This is an analytical practice that serves budding scholars well.

Teach students to judge length. When we're done deleting, selecting, and combining salient information to include in our summary, only 10 to 26 percent of the original material should be used. If more than 26 percent of the text is selected for inclusion in the summary, we've not encapsulated enough. If this proportion is difficult to achieve, it may be a sign that summarizing is not the proper way to handle the text or experience. Summarizing is only one of hundreds of ways to interact with material.

Teach students to evaluate their summaries. Six critical questions include:

- Does the summary convey the information accurately?
- Does it convey all of the important elements? Does it convey too much or too little?
- Are the ideas in the right sequence?
- Did I leave out my opinion and report an undistorted essence of the original content?
- Did I use my own words and style?
- Would someone else using this summary gain all the information they needed to know to understand the subject?

Give students time to read the text at least twice. Great summarizers often read passages at least twice: the first time to get the general overview and the second time to determine what is salient. We can determine the important material only when we have clear purpose and a general overview of what's coming.

Teach students to paraphrase. Young adolescents find paraphrasing difficult because their exposure to more advanced language usage is still limited. We can be sensitive, then, to students who get nervous trying to paraphrase without plagiarizing. After all, they reason, the author already said it well, how can I say it differently?

To improve their paraphrasing skills, do the following:

- Increase their vocabulary and their use of it. Make vocabulary terms and their synonyms part of everyday language in the classroom. Find ways for them to make word substitutions and play with language to fit their needs.

- Offer multiple examples of successful paraphrasing and let them copy the structure of those paraphrasings in their own work. Don't worry, they'll outgrow their models.

- Show how easy it is to paraphrase something incorrectly, and why making such errors is frustrating for everyone involved. Ongoing evaluation of paraphrasing will help students critique their own work while it's in progress, not just after it's done.

Teach students to listen and read actively. One of the most effective responses for listeners is "So what you're saying is...." This forces us to summarize the message with the clear intent of getting it right. Students can use the same openers with text: "So what the author is saying is...."

Information archeologists

Students not only need to know facts, but they must be skilled information archeologists as well. They must dig for information, make sense of it, and attach meaning to it. One of the greatest gifts we can teach students, then, is how to identify salient information, no matter what subject we teach or how it's presented, as well as how to structure that information for meaning and successful application.

Summarization isn't an add-on to an already bursting curriculum, nor is it something limited to writing. Summarization enables free exploration of ideas as well as their blunt analysis. Both a mirror and a sieve, it's in a powerful position to impact middle school success.

Innovative Summarization Strategies

3-2-1: The teacher identifies the catagories for each number and the students responses on half sheet of paper. For example: 3 concepts you learned today, 2 ways today's topic is analogous to a favorite sport, and 1 question you still have.

Body Sculpture: Small groups of students discuss the topic's salient attributes, then form a frozen tableau using every group member's body to symbolically portray the topic.

Charades: The traditional party game is a highly effective way for students to portray what they consider important in the text or experience.

Concrete Spellings Acronyms: Ask students to spell their vocabulary terms in a manner that expresses their meaning. Example: "Waxing" is written with each letter getting larger than the previous letter, "waning" is written with each letter getting smaller than the previous letter.

Exclusion Brainstorming: List five words from the lesson, one of which doesn't belong. Students must identify the one word that doesn't fit and explain why. Example: Suspensions—clear, no dissolving, settles upon standing, larger than molecules ("clear" would be circled because suspensions are not clear).

Partners A and B: After 15 minutes of lecturing, have students stand with a partner. Partner A relates everything he remembers from the previous 15 minutes while Partner B listens. After one minute, switch roles. Partner B must relate everything he remembers while Partner A listens—but Partner B cannot mention anything already mentioned by Partner A.

Point of View: Students retell an event from another point of view. The point of view doesn't have to be that of a person. How about talking about December 7th, 1941 from the USS Arizona's point of view? ...Explaining long division from the divisor's point of view?

Save the Last Word for Me: After reading text and identifying three or four lines from the text that cause personal reactions, students gather in small groups. The first person shares one of his chosen lines without commentary. Each member of the group reacts to the line before the originator shares how he reacted. Then the next person poses a line, and everyone reacts before he shares his reaction. Continue around the group in this manner.

Additional Teaching Techniques

Sponges and Warm-ups

Using only base numbers with exponents, generate five equations that all equal 24.

Give evidence to support or refute "capitalist" as an appropriate description of the main character.

Categorize the 26 elements in three ways with no one category consisting of fewer than three elements.

Students should never have free time in a regular classroom. Our time with students is too short to waste a moment. Sponge activities and warm-ups are great ways to maximize learning and keep students engaged in those inevitable in between and "down" times, such as before the bell rings; when teachers are distributing papers or supplies; or when students are cleaning up, moving from one place to another, waiting for classmates to finish, or waiting in line.

Sponge activities "soak up" dead or transition time with something substantive and related to the day's lessons. They are not, however, "fluff" activities with little or no educational merit. Singing summer camp songs is not a useful sponge activity for an eighth grade science class, but singing those songs with their lyrics rewritten to express phase changes in matter (liquefaction, fusion, freezing, solidification, vaporization, condensation, sublimation, deposition) is. Okay, maybe rap songs would work better than camp songs.

Warm-up activities can be done to review material or prime the brain for new learning when students first enter the room, but they can also be done in the middle of class to get students' minds ready for what is to come.

Rev up the brain

Sponges and warm-ups can be done orally, individually, in groups, through writing, artistically, physically, and musically. They literally keep students' brains active and growing the dendrites necessary for learning.

Sponges and warm-ups vary in complexity. While teachers in primary grades might ask students to find 10 things in the room that begin with "R," middle grades teachers might ask students to find two aspects of our modem culture that can be traced back to our country's early belief in Manifest Destiny. While the formats may vary, their focus is always on relevant and substantive content:

- Explain to your partner why integers are also rational.

- Using your hands and arms, demonstrate the difference between diffusion and endocytosis (pinocytosis and phagocytosis) in a cell.

- With a partner, identify three arguments against what I just taught you.

One way to create effective sponges and warm-ups is to break down the day's topic into its basic components or subsets of skills. For example, if we're teaching students to add fractions with different denominators, great sponges and warm-ups would include:

- If someone were stuck finding the lowest common multiple between two numbers, what two pieces of advice would you give him or her?

- Draw a quick mind map or flow chart of the steps needed to reduce a fraction to lowest terms.

- Translate three mixed numbers into improper fractions.

Of course, it's always a bit more enjoyable if we put a fun or interesting twist into the mix:

- Arrange the following fractions in order: 3/10, 3/5, 1/2, 2/9, 1, 12/20 (Teacher note: Two of these fractions are equal to each other. Students will have to decide how to represent this.)

- What's a quick way to tell whether or not 88,050 is divisible by 6, and is it?

- Kendall poured 1/2 of a gallon of hot salsa into Gerard's 2/3 of a gallon of lime Jell-O solution and mixed it up. Then she poured all of the spicy mixture into our class's drinking cups. If every cup holds 6 fluid ounces, then how many cups did she use?

Plan sponge and warm-ups in advance and have them ready to use whenever there's time to fill in the class. Write them into your plan books rather than leaving them to chance, although some of our best ideas strike as we are teaching, not while planning. Be open to those sudden epiphanies!

Start collecting

Collect warm-ups and sponge ideas wherever you go. You'll gravitate toward a few dozen that really work for your subject and teaching style, but it's always good to add to the repertoire. Remember to look at sponges and warm-ups used in other subjects, too. Many of them are adaptable to more than one subject: We can write an ode to the Monroe Doctrine, but we can also write an ode to graphing inequalities and to the almighty verb.

Try the *In-Out Game*. Students determine the classification a teacher's statements exemplify, then confirm their hypothesis by offering elements "in the club" and elements "out of the club." They don't identify the club (classification); they just give items in and out of it. If the students' suggestions fit the pattern, the teacher invites them to be a part of the club. The game continues until everyone is a member—everyone "gets it."

Here's an example: "She is in the club, but the class is not. They are in the club, but the penguins are not. You are in the club, but the donuts are not. Give me something in and out of the club." A student guesses correctly that the club is for personal pronouns, so she says, we are in the club, but moon rocks are not." To make it a bit more complex, announce the club's elements and non-elements in unusual ways that must also be exemplified by the students, such as making all the items in and out of the club alliterative or related in some way. This can be as obvious or as complex as you want it to be. It's a great choice when meeting diverse readiness levels in the class.

More great sponge and warm-up ideas:

- Ask students to respond to concepts posted on newsprint posters around the room. They write their reactions on the posters themselves.

- Collect feedback from students about a recent test, unit, lesson, or experience.

- Announce to the class: "As you put away materials, be thinking about..."

- As you pass back papers the day before a test, state the first question on the next day's test and ask what a good answer would be.

- In the lull after a test, ask students to identify content/skills that weren't on the test, or ask students to come up with a great additional question for the test and to call on someone to answer it.

- In the Manner of the Word: One student leaves the room. The rest of the class determines an adverb. The other student returns and tries to guess the adverb by asking students to perform pretend tasks "in the manner of the word." Good tasks are ones that have multiple steps such as ordering a pizza, changing a tire, changing a diaper, making a pizza, building a campfire.

- Ask students to come up with alternative titles to a book or event, or, "If (insert a real person under study) were to write a book, what would its title be?"

- Who they would cast in the role of _____ in this book...

- Ask students to generate as many words as they can think of that mean the opposite of _____ .

- Give students an answer for which they have to generate a dozen or more sincere questions.

- Ask students to form "statues" with three to five classmates' bodies that symbolically portray a concept being studied.

- Ask students to rewrite one verse of a popular song to express the content they are studying.

- Play charades or Pictionary with content-related words.

- Ask the class to divide into two or more groups and line up according to a given criteria. They must try to be first, but they must also be accurate. Examples include lining up according to structures, relationships/analogies, sequences, increasing/decreasing values, time order, categories with examples, and critical attributes.

- Play summary ball. Students stand up and toss around a beach ball. Each time students get the ball, they must share something they've learned about the day's topic within three seconds or sit down. Any soft object appropriate for tossing in a classroom will work.

Remember that some of the best sponges and warm-ups are based on specific skills within a larger topic: great opening lines, a piece of evidence, or one claim in a thematic essay; samples of well-crafted and not-so-well-crafted hypotheses in the scientific method; patterns in verb conjugations; opportunities to state multiple rises-over-runs before determining slope of a line; finding latitudes of multiple locations around the Earth before adding longitudes. Sure, we can add flavor to some of these ("Give me a great opening line to this thematic essay if Captain Jack Sparrow [Johnny Depp in the Disney movie Pirates of the Caribbean] were writing it."), but they always come back to meaty content and skills.

No learning wasted

The NAACP is right: A mind is a terrible thing to waste. Let's do everything in our power to avoid wasting our students' minds with "time suckage" in school—a term coined by a colleague of mine at Rachel Carson Middle School, Rachel Moritz. It refers to anything in teaching and learning that results in us spinning our wheels with no real or positive outcome for all the work put into it. Examples include homework assignments or lessons that do not result in learning, meetings that go nowhere, extended paperwork that does nothing to help a difficult situation, programs that no one attends, in-services on skills we've already mastered, and standardized testing with no diagnostic or educational merit.

I hereby challenge all elementary, middle school, and high school teachers to go fight time suckage at every turn. Leave no classroom moment unclaimed. Students need us to crusade for what can be in education, not just what is. Let's live up to the promise by using all the time given to us. We can start by incorporating compelling and content-specific sponges and warm-ups in every lesson.

Bringing Life to Class Discussions

"Bueller? Bueller?"

Look in on class discussions today and what you'll see (I hope) is a far cry from the classroom of gaping-mouthed, drooling, blank-faced students in the John Hughes 1986 film *Ferris Bueller's Day Off.*

One great way to get students to think critically and move information into long-term memory is through dynamic class discussions. Socrates recognized that the brain was innately social and that oral interaction was one of the most effective strategies to help people understand their own and others' thinking. Today, class discussion is one of the most effective strategies we can use in our classrooms. However, ensuring these discussions are effective requires clear principles and strategies.

Whoever asks the questions does the learning. If I ask a student about a topic and listen to his answer, especially if I'm interested in the topic and the student, I'm learning a lot, but the rest of the class is sitting passively. Do you see something wrong with this picture? I am the teacher; I already know the material. My goal is for students to learn it. Students, therefore, need to be asking the questions, not me.

Compelling questioning

Education expert and author Betty Hollas says that teachers ask 80 questions for every 2 questions students ask in a typical classroom. Inquiry experts, cognitive science, and personal experience tell us that students learn the most when they ask the questions themselves. This means great teachers make sure students ask more questions than they do. To do this, we have to make question-asking compelling and habitual.

The habitual aspect is easy. As many days as possible, ask students to brainstorm questions, queries, and investigative starting points for as many topics as time allows:

- Create 10 good questions to which "colloquialism" is a good answer.
- What are all the possible things we'd want to know about cuneiform writing?
- What do you wonder about your future?
- What questions might a visitor from another planet ask after observing our election process?

- Pretend you're a radicand (the number under the radical sign in a square root). What would concern you as this math algorithm progresses?

- Create all the "Why …?" questions you can about light and the way it behaves.

- Skim the whole chapter and list at least eight questions the chapter seems to answer.

Making question-asking compelling is another issue, however. Here we're trying to make students so curious that they form their own questions: "Why does it do that?" "What will the effect be?" "What are the exceptions to this rule?" "Why do you believe that?" "How is this false?" "Where's my mistake?" and, "What would happen if …?"

We can create curiosity by presenting students with puzzling phenomena, surprising facts, challenges to accepted opinions, appeals to imagination, playful situations with manipulatives, connections among seemingly disparate concepts, moral dilemmas, and personal dramas when facing struggle.

Redirect one student to another and to another.

Instead of responding to students' contributions in class, get your students to talk to each other. For example, if one student answers your question, don't be the one to declare the response valid or not valid, or to ask follow-up questions. This makes you the "pivot man" in the learning—all learning goes through you.

As an alternative, ask a second student to give evidence to support or refute what the first student said; then ask a third student to critique the second student's evidence. Go back to the student who first responded to the question, and ask her to respond to what these other two students said. This creates a triad, thereby tripling the positive anxiety in the classroom. A little positive anxiety is actually healthy. We want students so concerned that they will be called upon to say something intelligent that they remain on their toes mentally. To be effective, however, we have to do this redirection a lot because students have to know it's going to happen.

By the way, the long-held advice from veteran teachers still serves here: When leading class discussions and asking questions of students, always state the question to the class before calling upon a specific student to respond. This invites percolation, which builds those neural pathways. When we call on one student to respond, the rest of the brains in the class go into rest mode … unless, of course, we have that pushy habit of calling on other students to debate the first student's comments, as described above.

Don't forget all the research on "wait time," too. Typically, teachers in the United States wait between 0.2 and 2.0 seconds for students to consider their answer and respond, but research shows that waiting 10 seconds or more leads to more depth, thinking, and investment in the conversation. It takes practice, but it's worth promoting this expectant silence so students know you're counting on them to come up with a quality response, not just any response.

Negate students who convey incorrect information in class discussions, but help them retain dignity while being corrected. Sometimes students say the wrong thing, and we don't want the rest of the class to think it's correct. We need to correct the false information, but we don't want students to feel so rejected by our negation of their comments that they shut down, fearful of contributing anything more to the conversation. There are several ways to handle this constructively and keep students contributing:

1. Act interested in understanding the students' comments, even when you're not. A great way to do this is to ask students to tell you more about their statement or idea. By explaining their point further, they eventually discover the fallacy of their thinking, which is much more effective than when we point out the fallacies to them.

2. Share empathy. Tell students that you used to think this way (even if you didn't) but that you changed your mind once you read and considered the information at the bottom of page 165 (the page intended for last night's reading, which this student failed to do). You might frame it as, "I understand how you could conclude … but let's see if the text information changes your thinking."

3. Alter the current reality. When a student responds to a question with an incorrect answer, change your question so the student's response is the correct answer. We can go on from here and re-ask the intended question with someone else. We can also re-ask the question of the earlier student after a period of clarifying conversation in the class.

4. Do not accept "I don't know" as an answer. Turn it around quickly and say, "If you did know, what would you have said?" I learned this from a teacher in Naples, ME, many years ago, and it has served me and my students well. Very often, they answer fully, and what they say is actually on target. They just didn't trust themselves. This strategy is safe for the hesitant student because it's just a conjecture that will be considered but not judged. Try it on colleagues at committee meetings, too; it works just as well.

5. Allow the student more time or to ask for assistance: "Would you like to text a friend (if texting is allowed in your school) or ask for assistance from somebody in the room?"

6. Affirm the portions that are correct and disregard the other elements.

Incorporate question-asking structures and models.

This is a call for frequent opportunities for peer critique, think-pair-share, paired verbal fluency (partners relating what they've learned and asking each other questions about it), and defense of claims and personal opinions. Four structures that work particularly well are the inquiry method, Socratic Seminars, formal debates, and deductive/inductive reasoning. There are dozens, if not hundreds, of good books and websites that provide the specifics about incorporating these strategies.

Be the model.

We can be models of personal inquiry by demonstrating successful class discussion techniques every day. As we do, we're mindful of the social dynamics involved. By making participation safe and enticing, we invite students to progress. What goes unlearned and unachieved because we didn't teach students how to question their world?

Using Drama to Teach in the Content Areas

Player King:	Tis deeply sworn. Sweet, leave me here awhile; my spirits grow dull, and fain I would beguile the tedious day with sleep. (Sleeps)
Player Queen:	Sleep rock thy brain, and never come mischance between us twain! (Exit)
Hamlet:	Madam, how like you *this* play?
Queen Gertrude:	The lady protests too much, methinks.
Hamlet:	O, but she'll keep her word.
King Claudius:	Have you heard the argument? Is there no offence in't?
Hamlet:	No, no, they do but jest, poison in jest; no offence i' the world.

King Claudius:	What do you call the play?
Hamlet:	The Mouse-trap. Marry, how? Tropically.
	This play is the image of a murder done in Vienna: Gonzago is the duke's name; his wife, Baptista: you shall see anon; 'tis a knavish piece of work: but what o'that? Your majesty and we that have free souls, it touches us not: let the galled jade wince, our withers are unwrung.

—Act 3, Scene 2, *Hamlet*, William Shakespeare

What a compelling scene! These lines create riveting images of Hamlet's brutal insinuations as they strike the heart of King Claudius, whose careful demeanor unravels more quickly with each passing line. We almost feel sorry for the king, his guilt betraying him, and Hamlet's trap so thorough in its snare.

Wait a minute. Some of us who haven't seen or taught *Hamlet* have no idea what's going on in this scene. Its content and emotional intensity elude us. We're lost, and reading the lines only confuses us further.

Shakespeare never intended for his plays to be read silently. They were to be acted aloud, staged in such a manner as to reveal plot and characters by visual, auditory, kinesthetic, and contextual means. Shakespeare's story and commentary on humanity are not revealed unless they are portrayed dramatically, and to be most effective, portrayed by students themselves. The same active illumination and subsequent long-term retention can be achieved in any subject by using drama as the medium.

Students are naturally dramatic. Listen to their stories told in the hallways or check out their daily peaks and valleys of social risk-taking—the drama is there. It goes farther than that, though. Their minds process the world as narration, not exposition. Stories are better understood and retained longer for their compelling and organized nature. Add to this the physical relaxation and enjoyment we all feel when a presenter tells a story to explain a concept, and we have enough evidence to pursue drama in the content areas.

All about presentation

Drama in the content areas can take many forms. Imagine one student named "Peri" walking around a large rectangle of student desks calling to the beautiful "Area" who's on the inside. Area spreads her arms out, claiming that all of the inside area is hers. Peri calls to her, wanting to "meter" ("meet her"). This silly demonstration of Peri on the outside trying to meter (perimeter) helps students visualize the difference between area and perimeter.

How about commercials for various types of government, systems of the body, periods of history, or types of figurative language? For example, "Have you had your daily dose of Multivitamin Metaphor yet? It's alliterative and much more direct than Simile Chewables that leave that 'like or as' aftertaste. Multivitamin Metaphors: The Pillars of Healthy Living."

Imagine the role-playing opportunities as students learn about constellations, ecosystems, or historical reenactments. We are no longer passive observers when we have to fight for our rights in a simulated Continental Congress.

We can't help but say something when our own civil rights are trampled upon during our unit on the Civil Rights movement. We chant, "Rise over Run" with the armed forces while they climb a slope toward a y-intercept. We marvel at the analogies made between romantic teenagers and the behavior of particular atoms when in the presence of one another. The importance of verbs reaches new heights when we try to hold intelligent conversations with students without either of us using verbs.

We can use pantomime to isolate a variable in math equations or science experiments and to differentiate between transitive and intransitive verbs. Students can write a dialog between scalene, equilateral, and isosceles triangles who are arguing the merits of different-length sides. In each task, students discuss the critical attributes of the concepts involved, and then they dramatically present them for a specific audience.

This is the stuff of long-term memory. Those of us who cringe because we can't imagine how to do it ourselves need to simply give the assignment and get out of the students' way.

Process of illumination

Living graphic organizers are another way to use drama in the content areas. Make them big. Use the whole room or a larger area beyond your classroom's walls, if necessary.

- Place a huge Venn diagram on the ceiling and have students stand in the appropriate sections underneath it, according to information they hold on notecards.

- In her book *Learning on Their Feet: A Sourcebook for Kinesthetic Learning Across the Curriculum K–8* (2001), Carol Glynn describes a way for students to create a sieve of Eratosthenes by portraying numbers in a matrix, then sitting down according to mounting criteria as prime numbers are left standing.

- Once a student has literally walked through a gigantic version of the energy transfer cycle of the human heart, Hannibal's journey, or the FOIL method of multiplying binomials, all the information they have about those topics back at their desks has meaning; with meaning, content moves to long-term memory.

Education liberation

Drama doesn't just illuminate, it liberates. Give an adolescent a puppet and have him stand behind a façade and use the puppet to explain a concept. He'll be comfortable speaking because he's not speaking, the puppet is.

Reading about something and answering questions doesn't put us in the front row. Dramatic content does. Consider your discipline's subtopics and how they might be portrayed dramatically as monolog, dialog, skits, interviews, or game shows.

Check out Jeff Wilhelm's idea, "To Tell the Truth," from his book, *You Gotta BE the Book: Teaching Engaged and Reflective Reading with Adolescents* (2007) in which four students portray a literary character or historical figure, mathematician, or scientist, and classmates ask questions of each one, determining which one answered the most realistically for the person portrayed.

Remember Steve Allen's "Meeting of Minds," a PBS television show in the 1970s? I was a middle school student during that time, and I still remember watching Theodore Roosevelt take on Cleopatra about some of her leadership policies. My students have done a meeting of minds for the past several years, and their understanding of complexities of both people and times has deepened significantly. Animals can debate people's encroachment on habitats, or ancient civilizations can be brought through a United Nations Time Portal to debate modern world issues like whether or not planet Earth should have one language or many, or whether or not rap music lyrics should be censored.

Designing dramatic experiences for content learning can be daunting at first, but it gets easier each time we do it. Here's the basic sequence:

1. If you can, teach participants basic acting tips about voice and body language, as well as how to take risks in front of others. Get ideas from your school's drama teacher if you're stuck.

2. List the essential and enduring knowledge of your topic. These are those critical attributes that students must portray.

3. Determine an angle on the topic with compelling drama or conflict around which the drama can take place. Will the atoms make a successful covalent bond given the presence of other atoms?

4. Create names (if necessary) and the basic storyline.

5. Let students design the experience as part of their learning, if you'd like.

6. Review the directions and/or script, checking for clear and accurate portrayal of content and effectiveness in teaching the material.

Drama puts folks into the scene, transcending the text, eliciting insight beyond what they could get by simply reading or watching. "I get it now" is a common student response after portraying content dramatically.

A whole new world

Dramatic portrayal of facts and concepts motivates reluctant learners, especially those who still process information in a concrete way or those who require physical movement every 10 minutes to relieve growth plate stress on the ends of their bones. When we portray someone, a process, or a concept, we get inside the subject. We speak with confidence about it, and our analysis of it is mature and accurate.

We can do big simulations from highly recommended companies like TEACHINTERACT, but we can also do smaller strategies like holding debates among parts of speech or producing CDs burned with pictures from the Great Depression with our students' voiceovers reading from imagined journals of those portrayed in the pictures.

Hamlet realized drama's power when he said, "The play's the thing wherein we'll catch the conscience of the king." Let's enable drama to be the thing wherein we'll catch the conscience of the student. Look to the front of the room and watch molecules dance farther apart as matter changes state. You can almost see their brains growing. It's a great day for teaching.

Say "Yes" to Lectures

The teacher opens an umbrella over his head while standing in the middle of the classroom. He appears not to recognize how unusual this is. Concerned about the teacher's mental health, students lean forward as he begins to speak:

> "By all that's righteous and worthy, I beseech all of you to gather close and be compelled by the amazing story I weave for you this morning. Yes, there will be conflict as you focus all your intellect on trying to find fault with my rhetoric. I shall plant at least one falsehood to see who among you is truly wizened; a prize to generate great envy to the one who finds it first. These three tools shall guide our passage. "

The teacher gestures to three objects displayed in the front of the room: a stuffed seagull, a mathematical compass, and an orange. The teacher continues. "Be the first to anticipate how each will be used, metaphorically or not. Pens, pencils, and iPads down and off. Eyes looking into our civilization's past." Do I have your attention?

This teacher's introduction to an instructional lecture is engaging, which is important to the effectiveness of the lecture. But, teachers must do more than entertain students with drama and a sense of the unknown; they must help students process and retain the content.

Lecturing is one of the most popular teaching techniques in secondary school classrooms, but straight lecture for an entire class period is not an effective way to help students process information into long-term memory. There's more to the learning experience than listening to content. In fact, less than 10% of the meaning we receive from lectures comes from the words themselves. The vast majority (90%) of the message comes from how we perceive the speaker's physical movements, vocal inflections, and facial expressions during the lecture. Students need these extras to understand the message.

Lectures can hold students' attention if the presenter uses adequate forethought and has a skillful delivery.

Lecture structure

The best lecturers are storytellers at heart, and just as stories have plots, lectures have road maps with points of interest and enticements to keep the audience listening. To plot our instructional lectures, we consider where on our lecture's path we will reveal the following six elements:

1. Hooks to create curiosity. These should be at the beginning and throughout the lecture.

2. Goals and outcomes. Begin with the stem "As a result of this lecture experience, students will know and be able to do the following…"

3. Major concepts. Most effective lectures have no more than five major concepts.

4. Supporting details for the major concepts.

5. Ways for students to access information. How will students grasp the information and make sense of it? Consider the words you say, sequence of information, graphic representations of ideas and other visuals for clarification and emphasis, student-teacher interactions to clarify thinking, and formative assessments to give you and students feedback on the message conveyance.

6. Ways for students to process information. How will students recode information for themselves in a meaningful way? Consider analogies/metaphors, anecdotes/asides that personalize the story for students, summarization techniques, personal relevance, connections to other units of study and other classes, and the importance of providing enough background knowledge prior to the lecture so students have something on which to hook the new learning.

Additional elements to consider

Invite contrarianism. Invite students to identify incorrect information and arguable ideas in your lecture. Arguing with and correcting adults' mistakes are very compelling activities for middle grades students.

Present in fives or fewer. Cognitive scientists remind us that most students typically are able to memorize no more than five unrelated items in a given learning (see Pat Wolfe's 2010 book, *Brain Matters*.) Let's rally around this five or fewer concept when we lecture. This is an example of keeping it simple:

> Two of the most frequent mistakes students make with this application are (1) downloading an incompatible version with the device they're using, and (2) forgetting that what they see in the small screen is only 1/50th of the whole landscape available for use.

Use novelty. Novelties, props, and the unexpected keep students engaged. To create a sense of curiosity, ask someone to burst into your room with information or objects related to the lecture's content or incorporate optical illusions or a simple magic trick in the presentation.

Make it relevant. Punctuate lectures with the names of students' favorite locations, music groups, websites, and movies in purposeful ways. "Consider the shape of the parking spaces at the mall. Are they slanted or straight, and does one of these create more available spaces on finite pavement than the other?"

Use props. Hold an unusual prop in your hand or Velcro it to your shoulder for the first portion of the lecture, eventually incorporating it into the presentation. Portray yourself as an historic figure, well-known celebrity, inanimate object, or general concept as you present the information: "As a semi-colon, I'm lonely. Nobody understands me, and I'm never used. I can be a lot of help, however, especially when a period at the end of the sentence is too strong a sentiment."

Limit Note-Taking. We diminish both meaningful note-taking and personal engagement when we require students to take notes during our lecture. It's physically impossible to get the full message of a lecture via its combination of words, facial expressions, body movements, nuances, and vocal inflections while also transcribing personal interpretations in an organized manner for future recall. Instead, stop every 10 to 15 minutes and lead students in a 2- to 6-minute processing of what they just experienced through note taking, summarization, or some other technique useful to them. If a student is panicked by not being able to take notes during the lecture, allow him to record no more than 10 words in a bulleted list during the lecture period, each of which can be developed with details during processing breaks.

Co-Lecture. Consider co-lecturing with a student, parent, teacher, librarian/media specialist, subject expert, or administrator. Two voices are more interesting than the singular voice students hear every day. Co-lecture as a tag team. One speaker has the floor for a short time, tags the other, and moves to the sidelines until tagged to return to the front of the class. Or, one person can lecture while the other records the important information on the board in front of the class. Or, the speakers can engage in quick back-and-forth interactions to keep things lively.

Prime students. Prior to a lecture, prime students' brains for what's to come. Priming includes two elements: Explain what students will learn from the lecture and then provide students with a road map of what they will experience:

"As a result of today's lecture, you will understand (1) how Pythagoras arrived at his theorem, (2) how the theorem works, and (3) how to identify Pythagorean Triples. First, we will work with tangrams and graph paper, then we'll analyze three successfully determined hypotenuses and sides in right triangles, followed by sample practice problems. After critiquing each other's practice, we'll chase down those triples."

Foreshadow. Foreshadowing what's to come not only creates anticipation (another healthy legacy from Madeline Hunter), but it also provides logical connections for the brain. Both are helpful to students' long-term retention of knowledge.

Use humor. We all enjoy humor while we are learning. We relax, become more attentive, and as a result, our brains process incoming information better. Collect and insert into your lectures humorous comics, cartoons, photos, quotes, anecdotes, online (appropriate) videos, and clever turns of a phrase. Students will remember the entire lecture, not just the funny aside or visual. Avoid any humor that does not relate to the topic or something familiar to students, and avoid humor that is directed at any one student or subgroup of society.

Memorize the first ten minutes. The first ten minutes of your lecture are critical. Memorize this portion of the presentation. Don't read from a script or PowerPoint—you'll kill your credibility with students, and it's hard to recover from that death. And, fight the urge to read PowerPoint slides word for word. Design your slides as launching points, clarifying graphics, information to be applied, and provocateurs, not mini-versions of articles to be read.

Interact with your audience. Increase audience interaction to maintain engagement. Create suspense when using a narrative model, incorporate individuals and small groups in demonstrations or role-playing at the front of the room, and ask students to respond to statements or questions by raising hands, clicking buttons in audience response systems, or leaning left or right according to levels of agreement.

End it right. Conclusions are really important, so let's make them count. They need to reveal a powerful punch, a provocative idea, or a closed loop. Yes, we revisit important information in a conclusion, but we also incorporate an apt metaphor, quick anecdote, or graphic that weaves everything together for the audience in a memorable way. Don't default conclusions to the school bell. Plan them ahead of time.

Our lectures can be boggy tar pits that mire students in feeble learning, or they can be catapults that push students into higher orbits. The difference is the degree to which we are able to engage our students.

Making Field Trips Matter

This conversation took place during a field trip on which I served as a parent chaperone a few years ago. It was for my daughter's 6th grade class.

> "Okay, everyone," the parent chaperone said as she guided her group of five sixth grade students through the Smithsonian Air and Space Museum Annex located outside of Washington, D.C. "Look sharp. We're trying to find an old fighter plane with a cartoon shark's mouth on the front cowling. It's #3 on the list." She waved the scavenger hunt sheet the sixth grade team had given to every student and chaperone.

> "Hey, #7 asks what time Charles Lindbergh's watch stopped," said 12-year-old Rishi. "I see his flight suit in that glass case over there. It might have it."

> "Good thinking, Rishi," the parent said. "Let's check it out on the way to the fighter planes."

> T. J. called out, "Look over there. That plane is painted like a yellow cab. Number 13 asks us to find the plane that looks like

a taxi. That has to be it." His classmates quickly raced to the display panel near the guardrail and recorded the name of the plane in the blank next to #13.

"You guys are doing really well," their chaperone beamed. "We're going to be finished with the entire scavenger hunt in 15 minutes."

Several students nodded in excitement. However, one turned to the parent and asked, "But we don't have to be back to the buses for another two hours. What are we supposed to do until then?"

Everyone looked toward the parent. She paused, eyeing the classroom teachers gathered together drinking coffee in the museum snack bar. "Uh … I'm not sure," she said slowly, then brightened and looked at her charges. "But I know we can think of something to fill the time. If you see something interesting let us know."

When asked later about the purpose of this field trip, the sixth grade team leader said it supported the new science curriculum on which students would be tested. When asked to identify the science concepts and facts students were supposed to learn on the trip, the team leader was silent.

The silence spoke volumes.

The point is?

Unfortunately, trips like these are more common than some of us realize. It's time to make middle school field trips matter. The trips should support the school's twin missions of teaching the curriculum and facilitating student growth.

Maryland's Montgomery County Public Schools direct that field trips should be considered "… a living laboratory in which learning is acquired through active hands-on experience with the rich resources of the local community." They add that field trip research proves that field trips "increase student knowledge and understanding of a subject… add realism to the topic of study … [and] provide an opportunity to develop and enhance a student's socialization and citizenship skills" [www.mcps.k12.md.us/curriculum/socialstd/FT/Field_Trip_start.html).

A quick scavenger hunt at a museum dedicated to flight history does not result in any kind of learning that makes the trip worthy of scarce school resources. Where was the focus on gravity, thrust, propulsion, Bernoulli's principle, air pressure, air as mass, curvature of the wing, and the myriad compelling flight-related science principles likely to be found in our science curriculum and on state exams?

How might the middle school team leaders have pumped up the relevance of the Air and Space Museum trip and engaged students in meaningful ways? Here are a few ideas:

- Set up times for each student group to be with a docent or interpreter for the major exhibits. This would give students the backstory they needed to appreciate what they were seeing.

- Ask students to research historical figures whose work was on display at the museum. This would personalize the experience for students when they viewed the exhibits.

- Invite a member of NASA, an official from nearby Dulles Airport, or someone from the Airline Pilots Association to join the students and explain some of the basic flight principles involved in getting planes, rockets, and helicopters off the ground.

- Ask students to watch one of the more scientific or historical IMAX films and process its content afterwards.

- Ask students to use the principles learned during the trip to create their own flying machines.

- Guide students in their observation of flight history; ask them to extrapolate about the future of manned flight.

- Guide students as they note parallels among the evolution of flight, technology, and our society.

- Guide students as they explore flight evolution's impact on commerce, government, communication, and diplomacy.

Field trip timing is important, too. The science field trip to the museum was conducted on the Friday afternoon before the school district's extended winter holiday. Why did the teachers schedule the trip for a day when a number of students were already going to be out of school? The team leader said that it was a day on which students were very excitable and wouldn't be paying attention to anything anyway. Since they wouldn't get much done in school, they decided to do this trip instead.

If a field trip is "skippable" by some students without major impact on their education, we need to reconsider its appropriateness. We should schedule field trips on days when we can maximize the number of student participants and when students are very attentive. It is a waste of school time, money, and personnel to conduct a field trip on a day when students are likely to be absent or their minds are pulled in other directions. If you need substantive, compelling, last-day-before-the-holiday activities, consider exploring and extending content knowledge by:

- Debating interesting topics
- Conducting poetry slams
- Watching student presentations
- Filming a video
- Doing simulations
- Doing service learning projects
- Designing websites
- Putting on performances for other classes or grade levels.

Some teachers and schools are so focused on state exams that they don't allow students to participate in outdoor field trips like ropes courses in the few months prior to the exam. "We don't have one day to waste," they claim.

I disagree. In fact, outdoor education problem-solving experiences will do more for students and their test scores than cramming in 10 more pages of their test-preparation workbooks would ever do. Inhaling great volumes of fresh, non-institutional air; frequently working bones, muscles, and joints; getting oxygen and nutrients to the brain; learning to think flexibly; laughing; analyzing problems then negotiating with others on how to solve them; and summoning the courage to take risks and later being affirmed for doing so all have a positive impact on academic performance. Students return from these experiences more relaxed, open, thoughtful, and focused.

The angst-ridden days of test preparation are the precise time such trips are needed.

A matter of purpose

As you plan field trips for this year, consider whether the experiences provide

- Ample hands-on activities
- Meaningful interaction with content
- Vivid, real experiences
- Opportunities for students to grow or learn in some significant way.

The trips should be strongly connected to the school's mission, and they should be done a day on which most students will be present and attentive to the content of the experience. They should be conducted only if students have been prepared for the experience: they've studied the topic, they've been given the backstory for what they will see or hear, they appreciate what they are about to experience, they understand their purpose in going. If these attributes are missing from your field trip, don't go. You serve your students more effectively by continuing your lessons in the classroom.

Great field trip experiences for middle school students include, but are not limited to

- Journeys to interview or hear someone of historical significance
- Museums and galleries in which students get serious background and interaction opportunities with experts or docents
- Outdoor education programs in which students engage in nature study and interaction in meaningful ways—often with an interpreter or geologist or naturalist
- Off-campus simulations such as Civil War re-enactments and cultural performances
- Shadowing experiences with professionals
- Service learning opportunities
- Behind-the-scenes tours
- Work with primary research sources
- Major events in the community.

If there is no budget for off-campus experiences, consider using virtual field trips. Most large museums, for example, have a significant portion of their artifacts scanned in three-dimensional images, ready for you to download for your students. Some research scientists and archeologists allow classes to connect with them while they are in the field conducting research. Do an Internet search on "virtual field trips" to get a sense of what's out there, ready to be projected on the classroom screen.

Every day counts

Schools are significant and serious institutions of learning focused on academics and student growth. We are charged with teaching diverse and changing individuals a massive curriculum that rarely fits within the school calendar. We can't afford to waste one day that does not advance our cause. Field trips can have dramatic impact on student learning. We should take advantage of that fact and provide substantive trips that matter, conducted on days that will likely lead to real learning.

Remember: Rote Memorization Works

Imagine 40 pages filled with 10-point font, single-spaced text. Reciting these lines dramatically (once memorized) takes 2.5 hours of nonstop talking and inflecting. In your mind's eye, see those endless, tiny lines. Did I mention you have two weeks to memorize them before performing them without error to five history classes and gathered dignitaries at one of your university's theaters? There, you have one sequence of my life at Virginia Tech in 1980.

I was a part of the Wordweaver's Performance Ensemble, and we did this sort of thing regularly. To succeed, we learned how to memorize text and ideas quickly and accurately. Today, I pass along those same memorization techniques plus a few new ones to my students. Many students report that those strategies were among the more useful things they learned in my class. (And here I thought it was my great lectures on the giant squid or how to write a paragraph that they liked best.)

Louis Pasteur was right: "Chance favors the prepared mind," and sometimes that preparation requires students to memorize content. Let's be clear: We should never settle for students merely parroting back to us what they've memorized as a demonstration of mastery. In *Poor Richard's*

Almanac, Ben Franklin wrote, "Tim was so learned, that he could name a horse in nine languages; so ignorant, that he bought a cow to ride on." A memorized Periodic Table of Elements is useless unless we understand the reasons for clustering the elements in families as they are in the table, and we can use that knowledge in scientific applications.

While we will leave what constitutes mastery for another column, we can declare here that memorizing information is a useful stepping stone to learning, and if we don't teach students how to memorize, we make learning more challenging than it needs to be. Let's liberate students and teach them basic memorization techniques.

Check these out

The remainder of this piece describes some of the more successful rote memorization techniques I've taught students over the years. Some of these come from performance directors, fellow actors, and me; others come from my high school Spanish teachers at Langley High School (Thanks to Sra. Chinn and Sra. Pontari) in McLean, Virginia, back in the 1970s. What you're doing is making sure students have the tools for learning the curriculum, which is always helpful. In the end, using these techniques actually moves your students closer to achievement than they would have moved without them.

Some of the techniques are peculiar, but they work, so don't be too quick to dismiss them. Remember, too, that doing just one of these rarely works; it's doing four or five in tandem that's most effective.

1. Practice reciting the information while looking at your eyes in a mirror. Looking at just your eyes in the mirror is a little unnerving. Concentrating on your eyes while you recall the information helps solidify the memory.

2. Teach the concept to someone else. Ask students to teach classmates, students in other grade levels, or adults in their lives. Ask them to create a lesson plan and execute it, complete with

the objectives, methods of instruction, practice activities, and a final quiz on the topic. By designing all this and interacting with their "students," they actually memorize the information themselves. Teaching a topic is one of the best ways to learn that topic.

3. Practice reciting lines or information while standing in front of your family or friends. This simulates the pressure we'll feel when reciting the lines for performance or test, and we need to condition our minds to be able to do this prior to the actual assessment.

4. Start from the end and move backward to the beginning. Begin by memorizing the last few words of the last line. Then add the word or few words in front of that and continue all the way to the end of the phrase you already memorized. Then memorize the word or few words in front of that and go all the way to the end, and so on. Starting from the end and working backward to the beginning eases the mind, almost like breaking off chunks of a task to make it doable. By the time we work our way back to memorizing the text's very first words, the rest of the passage has been repeated many, many times, and we know it well.

5. After memorizing for a while, go do something else. Let some time pass. Then, recite your lines/concepts again. In her book *How to Teach So Students Remember* (2005), Marilee Sprenger reminds us that when first memorizing, the reciting/practice sessions should be frequent and with short time periods between each one. As we move further from the original learning, however, we need to space out the sessions.

6. At every waiting time in your life, practice the lines or information. This keeps the information on our mental radar scope and memorized under a wide variety of conditions, which creates a memorization dexterity that's important to recalling the lines when we most need them—for a performance or test.

The more contexts in which we recite the information, the more versatile we are with that information.

7. Use different voices to recite the lines. I know this is weird, but try saying the lines with different accents or impersonated voices. Again, we're creating some additional variables, but each one provides more access points and makes the lines more vivid in our minds.

8. Practice reciting the lines or concepts in the same place you'll be asked to remember them. The familiarity will make it easier to recall the lines. Students who learn math formulas while staring at your Calvin and Hobbes cartoon collection on the wall will remember the formulas when they see those cartoons. Many colleges and university classrooms are open at night for students to study in the same place in which they will take their exams. Context has great impact on memorization.

9. Express the information to be memorized through a different medium. Draw a picture, do a dance, or play music on an instrument that represents the information. Reexpressing the information in another domain, such as art, dance, or music, helps our minds recall the information later. Once again, we like multiple access points!

10. Use memory devices (mnemonics). Many of us know the popular mnemonic for the order of operations in math: "Please Excuse My Dear Aunt Sally," in which each word begins with same letter as each math operation in the proper sequence of their executions in a math problem: parentheses, exponents, multiply, divide, add, subtract.

Another example of a mnemonic is to use a familiar structure in our lives such as a bedroom, apartment, or house, and imagining different elements in that structure representing different items we need to memorize. When recalling the items later for a test or application, we imagine walking through the structure and looking at each element in the room. My students became quite good at this, often setting up large, colorful signs with vivid wording they actually displayed in different parts of the room, so all they had to do was walk a path in their minds to remember the items in their proper order. Students would imagine arriving home from school and immediately seeing a sign on the floor declaring, "kingdom." From here, they know they would throw their book bag on the kitchen table, so on the table was the sign, "phylum." Moving to the refrigerator, they'd see, "class." As they moved around the kitchen, then on to their bedrooms, they'd see the signs for the remaining taxonomic references, "order," "family," "genus," and, "species." During the test, they just remembered coming home at the end of the school day, and each of the items came to mind in their correct order.

11. Make an outline of the lines or concepts, and memorize just that. This is kind of a mnemonic, of course, but it's more a virtual metaphor for packaging the information. Students tend to be able to remember five or fewer unrelated items at a time. This means we should do lectures in terms of five or fewer major points, speak in terms of five or fewer steps in the math algorithm, and ask them to memorize five or fewer aspects of a particular historical era. The great thing, however, is that they can actually memorize more, if it's compartmentalized.

12. Use props. The mind likes prompting. If we memorize a section of text about the way Eratosthenes discovered the circumference of the earth, while placing a cloth tape measure used for measuring waistlines around the classroom globe, we remember the material better. If we can use the props in our performance or test, they will trigger our memories of the information. If we can't use the props at our desk or on stage, we can still line them up in the back of the room where we can see them and get the trigger that way, too. As we recall each prop, we recall the information associated with each one.

13. Make a chain. This is good for lists or groups of unrelated items that have to be remembered. In a chain, we create a story or picture that incorporates every item in the list or group. For example, if we had to memorize horse, candle, dictionary, cryptology, violin, and thunderstorm, we'd imagine riding a horse through a midnight thunderstorm that threatened to extinguish the candle flickering in the lantern we carried in one hand above the horse's head. If it goes out, we won't be able to find our way to the cryptologist's home to give him the secret code dictionary carried in our other hand that he needs to save the country. If the sequence of the items to be memorized is important, then each item should occur in the story or picture in the order that reflects that sequence.

To really hit a home run with your students, use these strategies yourself and walk into class on the first day of teaching the techniques with a famous poem, intricate scientific process, or a section of the textbook fully memorized. Dazzle your class with your recall. Seriously, show off; this is a time to "wow" the students. Students are often astounded by what their minds can accomplish if they only put some effort into the task.

Plan Now for Those Last Few Weeks

The post-standardized-test last few weeks of school every year can be among the most difficult. Many of us wonder if it might be better to end school early; everyone's tired and what's done is done. During these weeks we show up to fill out the required number of days, biding our time until we can all yield to summer's call. Some teachers rationalize that these days are inert because no one's paying attention. These teachers are wrong.

Effective teachers realize that the last weeks of school have great impact. Most of my students actually become more engaged in learning during the last few weeks of the year, not less. They realize the cocoon in which they've been nurtured is about to unravel, and they're wistful, almost nostalgic about their year. Sure, they can finish my sentences, they know all my jokes, and they're eager to unshackle the chains of homework, but they sense the bittersweet separation about to happen.

If we want the last few weeks of school to be interesting and result in real learning, we have to start planning now. These days will bring some of the most vivid and lasting memories of the year; let's make them worth remembering. We should be doing things in our classrooms that we can only do when we are gathered together with the support of the school's resources. Yes, some popular DVDs have great stories, but students can watch them at home. Shoot for something more interactive in those last weeks of the year.

Use the following ideas as starting points for your own activities. Some of them are my own and some are taken with permission from contributors to AMLE's Listserve, MiddleTalk.

From my classroom

Here are some suggestions from my classroom:

- Ask students to write and shoot a short video about a topic from the year.
- Ask students to dress as historical figures and debate modern world issues.
- Ask students to paint a wall inside or outside the school that expresses the curriculum or students' unique nature.
- Connect with a local or national museum and conduct an electronic fieldtrip via videophone with scientists and researchers in the field. At my school, we once had a sleepover in which we

held a 1:30 a.m. video conference with Dr. Clyde Roper who was searching for giant squid off the coast of New Zealand.

- Ask students to give speeches on an important topic and invite the local press.

- Ask students to record books, newspapers, and magazines on tape for younger students, homeless shelter residents, or nursing home residents.

- Ask students to participate in a large service-learning project.

- Ask students to build benches for the school's courtyard or grounds.

- Ask students to write letters to be placed on hospital patients' food trays.

- Ask students to write letters to themselves that you will send them one year from now.

- Ask students to write letters of advice to next year's students who take your course.

- Ask students to create string art designs, computer-aided designs, or any other projects with a partner.

- Ask students to evaluate your class and their learning with you.

- Conduct a fun contest in which students problem solve or work in teams. Odyssey of the Mind and Math Olympiad programs have great suggestions.

- Take students on a ropes initiatives or Project Adventure Course.

- Conduct board game tournaments with interactive, subject-based board games created by students.

- Play word games based on this year's curriculum (Taboo, Pictionary, $25,000 Pyramid, Password).

- Teach students to play bridge. The American Contract Bridge League (www.acbl.org) provides instructors free of charge.

- Ask students to do body statues of topics: Small groups of students use every person's body to sculpt a frozen tableau that symbolically portrays a concept or topic of study. The rest of the class identifies what's being portrayed and critiques the group's portrayal.
- Conduct a paper airplane construction and flying contest.
- Conduct a poetry festival or poetry slam. Check out Taylor Mali's website (www.Taylormali.com) for more details.

From your classrooms

Here are some great ideas from AMLE's MiddleTalk participants:

Tena Linsbeck-Perron of Maine's Scarborough Middle School conducts a coffee-shop-style poetry and readers' theater program, including her students' own version of the Broadway hit, "Stomp." She also asked her daughter, a recent theater program graduate, to teach students theater games.

A favorite activity of hers, however, is to share the poem by Maria Mazziotti Gillan, "After School on Ordinary Days" (www. poetrymagazine.com/archives/2003/Summer2003/gillan.htm). After students interact with the poem in multiple discussions, she asks them to create their own version of "After School on Ordinary Days." Samples can be found on their poetry slam pages: http://www.literacyworkshop. org/plslam07-1/perron/after_school_on_ordinary_days).

Alternative history author Harry Turtledove would be thrilled with this idea from Anne Van Meter at Jenkintown Middle/High School in Pennsylvania. Working with her language arts partner, Anne asks students to do a Turning Point in History fantasy/science fiction writing project in which students explore how our lives would be different if certain historical events had not occurred.

Kim, in North Carolina asks her students to weave technology into their final project of the year:

> As part of our year-end reflection, each student takes a digital camera, walks around the school, and takes one picture that sums up their year in eighth grade. They then write a one-page explanation on why they chose that particular scene/item/person/room etc. to capture. One student took a picture of a beautiful old oak tree because it was where he asked a girl out for the first time in his life. Another took a picture of the section in the cafeteria where she sat with all her friends. Another student took a picture of a book in the library because it was the book that turned him on to reading. The students really loved this assignment—even my reluctant writers were excited to write about their picture. Their reflections end up being about so much more than the pictures.

Pam Tempest at Hudson Middle School in Florida asks her students to write a script and create an iMovie/music video that gives next year's incoming sixth graders tips on how to succeed in middle school. Pam was ready for the kids who chose not to do the project, however: "The six or seven kids who didn't participate in that project created a welcoming bulletin board complete with personal letters full of tips on how to succeed in middle school. I think that was my favorite as it also helped me with the first hallway bulletin board of the year."

Lisa Drew at California's St. Mark's Episcopal School has students design their own math game, including all rules. "Rumor has it," she says, "that the designer of the excellent factoring game 24 was a sixth grader completing just such an activity." She also asks students to design, draw to scale, and build models of parks, zoos, malls, houses, and other structures that incorporate geometry skills. "When I did this activity, I took digital camera pictures of the results and then switched the pictures in and out of my math class website the following year, so there was a bit of fame associated with the activity."

New Jersey science teacher Eileen Bendixsen ends her year in CSI mode: "In science our part of the unit is a crime scene. We set up a crime scene on the stage in the cafeteria and the kids spend the next couple of weeks looking at the evidence. In the end they each come up with what they think happened based on the scientific evidence."

Wendy Goldfein in Fairfax County, Virginia, has her students produce, design, and star in a Shakespeare play. She personalizes the experience for students each year: "Everyone has a part (we add parts so there is enough for everyone). The students pick the setting so we have done A Midsummer Night's Dream as a tropical beach excursion, a 50s rock and roll romp, a western along with traditional Ancient Greece and medieval settings."

Karen Onyx at Carusi Middle School asks her students to create a brochure to "sell" their week-long visit to Mt. Misery, their environmental camp. She explains the substantive nature of the task: "The piece pulled together their research, presentation skills, persuasive writing, and descriptive writing, and it gave them a professional-looking product for which they were responsible."

Kansas middle level teacher and technology leader Marsha Ratzel is a goldmine of end-of-the-year substance and engagement. "In science, I try to save force and motion (F&M) for the end of the year. I bought skateboards for them to use with brick riders and they are allowed to bring in their scooters, bikes, or rollerblades for some experiments …. I end the F&M unit with simple machines—and who wouldn't want to use Legos? To do this, I've combed garage sales and now have a pretty big collection. We build robots (non-moving) to lift loads via levels, pulleys, wheels, inclined planes, et al. All of these are loud and feel chaotic … but if I recruit enough parent helpers, it works out pretty well: I know they're still engaged and they fall in love with science again."

Every day counts

Reread Marsha's last seven words. Does it get any better than that? Don't waste the last few weeks of school on fluff and babysitting experiences. It's not only boring to students, it's unethical. Choose a day very soon to begin planning for one of the highlights of the year: the experiences of those last few weeks.

Assessment

Curriculum Clarity: Teaching What We Think We're Teaching

Four teachers in the same building teach 9th grade English, but that doesn't mean their students learn the same curriculum. As teachers, we elevate and prune content every week depending on our strengths, interests, and personal investment in the cause.

Some of us display a moderate bravado in our curriculum claims because we want everyone to think we know what we are doing, even when we don't. We can become so territorial and myopic that we march through our lesson plans for years without updating their content. We've already invested so much time and energy into what we currently deliver, it's become our identity, and it hurts to find out our identity needs retooling.

Curriculum inconsistency runs through every subject. A science teacher states, "My students must understand entropy," and describes each element of thermodynamics that she requires students to know. Her colleague teaches entropy as well, but her requirements are dramatically different. Content demonstration that in one class receives an A may generate only a C in the other class.

These teachers declare their grades are accurate reports of student learning and their lesson objectives match district curriculum mandates, but how can wildly varying teachers' criteria live up to claims of integrity and consistency? And what if the new Common Core Standards mandated by my district differ in expectations from my own professional expertise in the subject? How will I reconcile these two perspectives? Which ones better prepare students for the world? Alternatively, who am I to question the larger education circles of my discipline?

In our rush to put quantifiable data on a pedestal just because it's measurable and measurability makes us feel secure in an insecure world, we can lose sight of what truly matters in our content and daily teaching. Effective teachers reexamine their curriculum through the lens of subject expertise at least yearly and adjust lesson content as needed. Knowing what we're supposed to teach plays a huge role in three of the biggest elements of teaching: lesson design and implementation, assessment, and grading. Clearly identifying that content is key to monitoring whether we are making progress with students.

Great practices in clarity

Fortunately, there are specific practices that clarify what we're supposed to teach in each standard or outcome. They not only increase the accuracy of student grades, they keep our lessons effective and up-to-date. Great practices for clarifying curriculum include the following:

Identify the verbs.

Your standard states, "Students will understand the difference between fact and opinion." What does "understand" mean? Let's break it down. Students need to identify fact and identify opinion. Should they also be able to create fact and create opinion? How about revising a piece of writing to make it more factual and less opinionated? Already, we've identified identify, create, and revise as subsets of "understand." Capturing the inherent verbs of a standard goes a long way toward figuring out what we're supposed to teach.

For each standard or outcome, identify the specific knowledge students should know and understand, have at their mental fingertips and what they should be able to do with it. For example, we may teach students about humans developing from hunters and gatherers to farmers, but we also want them to use this knowledge to note similarities in the development of other cultures and to see how this change was a catalyst for the development of record-keeping, writing, and new societal roles.

Practice making the invisible, visible.

Don't assume everyone understands what you mean, particularly young adolescents. Spell it out. If you ask students to put some of their personality into a task, demonstrate vividly and repeatedly what you mean. If we assign students a project, we give them the evaluative criteria and present multiple think-alouds (self-talks) as we work on a mock version for the class. We display examples from last year's students, if we have them, or we make some ourselves. We ask students to evaluate these samples and their own efforts against the standards of excellence presented. We tell students what they're going to learn, we help them learn it, then we remind them what they learned.

Divide and conquer.

Ask some teachers in the department to unpack the standards/outcomes for some units, while other teachers do the same with other units. We distribute these parsings to the entire department for professional response. An hour or two spent online looking at others' unpacking saves us a lot of time and gives us language and hierarchy we may not have considered. Do it right: Let the initial attempts at unpacking standards/outcomes take a whole school year or two. When you take your time, you allow for serious reflection.

Identify the standards that provide leverage.

Larry Ainsworth, Doug Reeves, and others recommend teachers consider whether proficiency in one standard leads to proficiency in a subsequent standard. Is the standard we're currently teaching so foundational that not learning it will dramatically limit students' future learning? If there is a direct impact on future learning, we need to elevate this standard and its careful unpacking.

Elevated standards such as these are often referred to as power standards. They are salient and nonnegotiable concepts and skills in our curriculum that provide the most utility to students' learning. They loom large on the curriculum radar, and students' marks and scores rally around them.

Power standards are present in all areas of the curriculum. Students learn about elements, atoms, molecules, and electromagnetic forces before learning how to balance chemical equations. They learn about cells in general before studying their specific parts. We teach the Middle Ages prior to the European Renaissance, so students can appreciate the phenomenal changes in thinking that occurred between the 14th and 17th centuries.

Be careful with pure sequential thinking, however. Some teachers disparage students' poor math skills, for example, using that lack of proficiency in earlier skills as justification to give up on teaching students advanced ideas in pre-algebra or algebra. Lack of proficiency is not always an impediment, however. Students may not know their multiplication facts as well as they should, but with varied levels of support, they can still isolate a variable to one side of the equation, identify the cubed root of 125, and determine rate of speed when given distance and time.

It's not always the case, of course, but we can teach many advanced concepts to secondary students even when they don't fully grasp some of the basics from earlier units. Larger units of study provide meaningful context for learning smaller, discrete skills that would be lost if taught earlier in isolation. Often, large context instruction helps students see the value of learning those earlier foundational skills and knowledge, and they invest in them.

Share your thinking.

None of us holds a sufficiently broad perspective to unpack any one standard in its entirety in a meaningful way for students. We need interaction. I declare aspects of the curriculum nonnegotiable, but you point out how students can learn beautifully without those esoterica, and that there is no mention of those aspects in the state or provincial curriculum. You tell me that the author of a commonly taught novel symbolized the fragile nature of man's ego, but I cite several literary critics who provide ample evidence otherwise. Wow, do we need each other! These conversations are not a luxury if time allows; they're important enough to change schedules in order to conduct them.

You can begin and maintain these professional discussions in many ways. In the year ahead, participate in professional Listservs within your own subject associations. Teacher unions and other associations often have multiple Listservs as well.

Move from standards to evidence or outcome.

Instead of confirming with colleagues that we have the same interpretation of the standard, we should ask each other, "What evidence of the standard will we tolerate?" The standard might state, "The student will read and write in a variety of formats," and it might list suggested formats, but as a grade level or department representative, we have to decide what formats students will read and write, and what level of proficiency for each one constitutes meeting the standard.

Consistency weakens if we don't have these conversations with each other, although in an innovative society, inconsistency is not always a bad thing. We want students to color outside the lines. Most innovations in the world today came from individuals who didn't follow the rules, who questioned the status quo, and who didn't succumb to the lockstep march through the mandated pacing guide. Thankfully, we have educators who look for opportunities for students to transcend conventional thinking.

I'm not advocating that we dismantle standards, only that we guard against blind adherence to them. We use standards to reflect on what students are learning and to create the road map for their future learning. Candid discussions of standards provide the compass rose for knowing which way is up and how to hold the map. Without clarifying those standards with each other, we all touch the elephant at different points of its body and claim we know the whole from perceiving just one part.

Our students succeed best with fully explored and well-communicated content. We have to know it ourselves before we can teach it to others. It takes practice and specific skills to forge these clarifications, but let's start doing it now, in the middle of the school year. If we wait until we think we have time to do it, we'll never learn what the Age of Enlightenment really was.

"Evidence-Based" vs. "Research-Based" and RTI

MiddleTalk posting January 2009

Research-based" myopia is part of our downfall as a profession. So is everything being "data-driven." Not that I want to perpetuate another buzzword, but at least a little bit more appropriate is the term "evidence-based." Subtle difference, I know, but "evidence" opens the door to other indicators than just test scores, percentages, and tallies. As others have stated, there are multitudes of outstanding instructional practices without official research bases, yet they are wonderfully effective.

When they use the term "research-based," most government bodies are referring to scientific studies using professionally accepted research protocols that found empirical evidence for or against a hypothesis and were published in esteemed juried magazines or journals. In my work with teachers across the nation, I find good teachers' anecdotal records; student products born of spur-of-the-moment inspirations; PLCs; and common sense, practical methodologies just as valuable to our collective wisdom and research base; they should be honored as such.

Because they are not easily quantifiable and repeatable, these types of classroom research seem "softer" than those fitting the hard-core research definitions. But, as we know, they are just as empirical as the material in our education and psychology journals and often more applicable. I don't want to downgrade those official studies—they are tremendously helpful—but they must always be reinterpreted in terms of our own individual schools and classrooms: "What aspects can I take and apply here, given the parameters and findings of the study?"

In the fine print of NCLB are paragraphs declaring that everything funded by government monies must have a solid research base behind it, yet in the very next paragraphs are statements indicating the government recognizes not all that is good in teaching has a research base. This is rather contradictory and very frustrating.

A lot of that conversation was born from the past President's Reading Panel's discussions about early reading development. I gleaned from my graduate program and a series of literacy conferences, readings, and further conversations with those in play at that level that the Reading Panel was comprised primarily of representatives from published phonics-based reading programs, all with the same ideology—political and pedagogical—and they had vested interests in wording the law in such a way. Rather than "Let's get the best minds in the country together around the table and figure out how to solve our education problems," it was "Let's get the people who share our same political ideology around the table and make a law." This is not the wisest course for making long-term effective decisions.

The public wants results, and in particular, something well-defined, something upon which they can place their fingers. That's hard in a messy enterprise like teaching humans how to read, do math, understand abstract concepts, reason, and show compassion for one another. Society is an ever-changing foundation on which we base what is important and what is not. In an insecure world, we cry for clear vision and proof that we are on the right track. Sometimes it gets so bad that we find fault with anything that didn't work one time or with one student, when, under different circumstances, we would have said, "Well, it didn't work this time, but it might work within a couple of weeks or with those other students." To appease everyone's general sense of needing to know and to ease our worries, politicians cry for research-based practices in everything we do. Sadly, some educators who were never in the classroom (are they really educators?) make the same declarations. Those in the classroom would never declare such limitations. Many of the best things ever to occur in education came at the play of a hunch.

Yes, there are teachers who coast. They do things with students without consideration about whether or not they are effective strategies, and even worse, they blame the student when their ill-considered strategies don't work. These teachers should be given intense intervention and remediation, of course, and if these don't work, they should be removed from their influence over the next generation. Most teachers, however, try to do right by their students, and they are very conscientious individuals who are more than willing to use effective practices, if they only knew what they were. This is a clear bell ringing for increased professional development and professional interaction opportunities. Heck, those two developments alone would cut in half the number of students who drop out every year.

We don't want teachers or principals not to use something a teacher or group of teachers has found useful, however, because there is no official research base behind it. RTI's bottom-line goal is that students move through the tiers and no longer need the interventions. If something works to create that movement and overall growth, then, "damn the torpedoes, full speed ahead" without apologies to anyone. I submit that you CAN use those alternative, outside resources as legitimate practices in an RTI intervention program as long as you get the results you are seeking. The results can be shown using whatever instrument we have agreed would provide valid evidence of growth by the student.

One of the numerous RTI websites defines "data-based/data-driven decision making" as: "A process of collecting, analyzing, and summarizing information to answer a question and to guide development, implementation, and evaluation of an action. Data-based decision making is continuous and regular, and most importantly linked to educational/socially important questions." This is very appropriate for our classrooms and it is consistent with the intended spirit of RTI legislation.

Teachers can definitely do this without constantly referring to published studies. They can this process themselves, in fact. We need to be very focused on the decisions we make and the impact on students, and if something isn't working, we have to find quick ways to perceive that lack of effectiveness. Then we change what we are doing so we are effective instead of thinking, "Oh well, maybe she'll learn it next year." Another RTI website states the evidence-based classroom has the "...practice of providing high-quality instruction and interventions matched to student need, monitoring progress frequently to make changes in instruction or goals, and applying child response data to important educational decisions." Again, this very important and exactly what great teachers already do as they differentiate instruction and assessment.

If those who mandate policy upon us say that without the scientific research-base, "...our attempts may be considered futile, and there is no way to monitor progress to determine whether or not this intervention was helpful." By whose opinion are our attempts futile? We do not have to succumb to policymakers' lack of experience and knowledge. What is policy is infinitely changeable, for it is arbitrary at best. We can teach and monitor in a scientific manner, even with newspapers, comic books, text messaging, and video games. Our progress monitor would identify the acceptable evidence; once the student produces it, our intervention is proven effective, and we have met the RTI goals.

Although we are being held accountable for the choices we make, what everyone is really seeking is that we do whatever it takes to be effective. While there is a lot of RTI literature mentioning scientifically-based research curriculum to use as the intervention strategy, there is more literature sharing wonderfully effective ideas with clear proof of their positive impact that should not be discarded.

Most education and psychology researchers indicate there has not been enough time and human power to design and test scientific, official research studies in all that we do in education. Our education knowledge base is expanding geometrically. Our current students need effective interventions now, not after research has been done. Why would any dedicated, professional educator sacrifice sound interventions because they weren't on someone's official list of what's acceptable or not? Sure, we should spend time weeding out those practices that don't show positive effect, and we should make teachers explain/justify their decisions as they work with struggling students. If they are unprepared to meet those struggling needs, let's prepare them, but let's not hide behind the altar of an almighty research-based idol.

Building our Data Analysis Skills

Half of all Pacific Islanders fail at my school. That was a startling claim. The parent making it said that she found the fact on the district website where they had just posted new test data. She asked us what we were going to do about it.

My team went to the website. It said 50% of Pacific Islanders passed the exam, which means half of them didn't pass. We turned to each other for professional soul-searching: *What is it about Pacific Islanders that we don't understand? Are we lumping all Pacific Islanders together? Aren't students from Samoa different than those from Fiji or Tahiti? How could we be so oblivious to their academic problems?*

Then a colleague interjected, "Before we get too upset about this, we should look at the demographics of our school." He tapped the data printout and we leaned forward to read it. There were only two Pacific Islanders in the school. One passed, the other did not. 50%. We needed to respond to one student's unique needs, not the entire spectrum of Pacific Islander cultures.

In addition to missing the larger picture from time to time, many schools use supposedly "catalyst" data measures that require schools to improve test scores by 2.5% every year or face sanctions and labels of failure. Some of these schools perform consistently at the 95% or higher level, however, so there is little opportunity to show growth every year. As a result, these schools are labeled as failures with close to 100% achievement in the student body.

Because of the Race-to-the-Top programs and rising accountability rhetoric among politicians, value-added measures have been added to teacher accountability programs in many states. There are significant limitations and issues with their use, of course, but the general public feels safer with such measures in place because it makes the messy, complex job of teaching quantifiable. They reason that if it has a metric and is mathematically calculable, it must be legitimate.

The problem, however, is that not all that is good in teaching has a research base or is measurable, and just because we have data doesn't mean we have causation or correlation. Most of us in education can cite reckless data interpretations made by policy makers to justify millions of dollars spent on programs and tactics that resulted in little to no change in student learning, or worse, decreases in their learning.

And many of us are put off by data analysis. We took statistics and education measurement courses in college, but now that we're employed and working until all hours of the night on papers, committees, and professional development, we're happy to let someone else do the heavy lifting when it comes to extrapolation and standard deviations.

Educators, writers, and professional developers use data to convince others of our point of view and credibility. We're in the art of persuasion. We must be careful, though, not to misrepresent the data or overstep what we can claim based on the data. We need a workable relationship with data interpretation and application. These skills are not the exclusive domain of the district, state, or provincial data specialist. They are helpful tools for each of us as we conduct our classrooms or schools and participate in the education world on a daily basis.

Let's take a look at some of the cautions and tenets of data analysis as we use data to make instructional decisions:

New homework studies come out every other year, some claiming that homework has great impact on student achievement and others saying it has no impact. When we read the actual studies, we find that most of them don't control for influencing factors such as access to resources, parent support, students' other responsibilities at home and work, sleep deprivation, the engaging nature of the assignment or lack thereof, the time of year, positive/negative student-to-teacher relations that affect homework motivation, level of English proficiency, and students' readiness for the assignment.

Read every line of studies on topics important to you, including the study design, participants, mitigating factors, researchers' declaration of study limitations, and specific conclusions. By the time we get the information, it can be encapsulated and massaged so much that it barely resembles the original report.

Be careful of the rearview mirror effect. It's June, and according to the results of February's state exam just delivered to our computer screens, eighth grader Carrie and 81 of her classmates struggle to find main ideas and their supporting details in grade-level expository text. We look back at the months since February and wonder what we were doing about this problem.

Now that we have these results, do we know whether she and her classmates still have this problem? And if they do, what can we do about it over the summer or as they start their next year? Or, did someone pick up on this problem using another assessment measure and do something about it? Did Carrie and her classmates mature in their reading since February and might some of them be at a higher proficiency now? We don't know which way to steer.

Former principal turned author and consultant Stephen H. White, author of *Show Me the Proof! Tools and Strategies to Make Data Work for the Common Core State Standards* (2011) and *Beyond the Numbers: Making Data Work for Teachers & School Leaders* (2011), points out that we don't drive very well by looking only into the rearview mirror. Imagine navigating a crowded highway at high speed using only the small, reverse image of the road we've already passed. How would we respond to the current and future bumps and turns in the road? We couldn't, of course, because we wouldn't be looking.

Many schools get test results months after students finish those tests. After the results are in, everyone gathers to look through the data and plan how to respond to low-scoring students. Their move forward is not based on what's currently happening or what's needed in the future, only on a single snapshot from months ago.

Instead of relying on that rearview mirror for making decisions, we should assume that standardized test results that arrive months after administration are closer to being politically motivated than pedagogically helpful. It's up to us as individual teachers and schools to design and implement our own useful assessments.

Designing common formative assessments and conducting professional learning communities are effective strategies for generating these tools, as are teacher action research teams, lab schools connected with local research universities, and schools that dedicate considerable professional development to standards-based assessment training.

Look to data to reveal the student's story.

The unit test assesses seven different standards or outcomes, yet the student gets a single "86%" written at the top of the first page and a bunch of "-1/2" and "+3" indicators in the margins of each response. The composite 86 doesn't tell us or the student how she did on any one of the seven standards. We can't make instructional decisions, document proficiencies, or provide descriptive feedback with such a general score.

We should break down composite scores into specific domains and standards as much as we can. One student does well on the first standard but poorly on the second, and another student does the reverse: poorly on the first and well on the second. A third student performs poorly on both. All three students tell a different story, and all three should receive a different instructional response from their teacher. If the teacher never disaggregated the data, however, she wouldn't know different responses were needed.

We can help identify areas of challenge and success by using assessment prompts that require complex applications of content and skills as well as prompts that assess individual content and skills within those larger applications. For example, if we're assessing where Javier struggles with determining the total area of irregular shapes made of attached regular shapes, it would be helpful if (1)we included other problems on the test asking him to find areas of individual regular shapes, (2) we gave him written steps for finding the total area of two attached shapes and determining the length of one side based on the length of the corresponding side, and (3) we provided prompts that ask him to demonstrate his capacity to think spatially and see the regular shapes within the larger, irregular shape.

Students can be taught to reveal their story as well. In his May 2007 *Education Leadership* article "Assessment Through the Student's Eyes," Rick Stiggins shares a wonderful idea for teachers: ask students to do item analyses of their own tests. When I've done this with students, it's given them renewed investment in their learning, and in my experience, increased their achievement. As often as possible, distribute an item analysis chart when returning papers and tasks that you have marked. Ask students to record how they performed on each standard and then write a letter to you summarizing the results. Figure 1 illustrates the item analysis chart. In the student's letter, he describes how he did well with reciprocals and admits he was careless in checking his work when doing fraction/decimal equivalents. He's done self-assessment, graphically portrayed his performance against standards, and is creating a plan for moving forward, asking for assistance—all important components of learning. Data and their analyses that do not provide information leading to improved learning aren't worth discussing or imposing on others. The most helpful data are disaggregated for more focused use.

Contradictions are okay.

A study says teachers should teach one way, but another says they should not use that method. This happens a lot, and we can't get too upset about the apparent contradiction. It's the nature of the scientific process. When we look further into studies that appear contrarian, we often find significant differences in hypotheses, methodology, sample groups, and other factors that were not related in the summation of the studies' conclusions. Only by exploring two studies beyond their initial reports do we see that both of their conclusions are accurate. We use the insights from both studies and see how they might play out in our own classrooms and schools.

From politics and the economy to blowing up things on the Discovery Channel, it's popular these days to be a myth buster. We can't overly generalize, however. In a bid to bust a supposed education myth, Daniel Willingham of the University of Virginia declared differentiated instruction as highly overrated and ineffective in his book *Why Don't Students Like School? A Cognitive Scientist Answers Questions About How the Mind Works and What It Means for the Classroom* (2009). He based his conclusion on a misinterpretation of differentiation as the exclusive use of learning styles as the sole differentiation delivery vehicle. Upon further reflection and some education by differentiation experts, he posted a video and writings in which he stepped back from those generalizations, and instead limited his declarations to learning styles alone.

Leading with data

In a world drowning in sound bites and accountability measures, it's hard to discern facts amidst the cacophony, effectiveness among the politics. Reflective practitioners build their professional critical thinking capacity as often as they can. Accurate data analysis and vigilant questioning of their interpretations are skills worth pursuing. The insights gained affect more than just our anxieties about wandering Pacific Islanders or whether we can meet our goal of a 2.5% improvement in school-wide test scores. Real individuals with real, yet unwritten, futures hang in the balance. They deserve wonderful journeys with skilled guides.

Figure 1

Item	Standard/ Outcome	Correct	Incorrect	Careless Error	I really don't understand this
1	Dividing fractions		√		√
2	Dividing fractions		√		√
3	Reciprocals				
4	Reciprocals	√			
5	Fraction/ decimal equivalents		√	√	
6	Fraction/ decimal equivalents		√	√	

Staying Focused on Formative Assessment

I have two fears about formative assessment: First, unless we're careful, it will become a buzz phrase lost to the cacophony of jargon that surrounds every teacher, thus generating indifference. Second, many educators, including whole school districts, think they are incorporating formative assessment when they are not. This spreads cynicism regarding what should be a very healthy and nonnegotiable tool of learning. Let's do what we can to make sure these fears don't see the light of day.

True formative assessment is neither safe nor passive; it provokes. It compels a response in the teacher and student. "You earned a 92%, Joel," says the teacher as she passes back test papers, "better than most of the class." There's no spark that ignites further contemplation. There's no specific feedback, no invitation to engage with the results or the material any further. The assessment was instructionally inert.

"Let's explore this section here," says the teacher, pointing to the middle of the student's lab write-up. "You claim that you identified all dependent and independent variables, but I couldn't find any mention of the water's salinity. Can you help me find it? If we look at this and find you forgot about salinity, what will you have to adjust in the lab to prove you understand the roles of independent and dependent variables?"

Here, the feedback is contextualized and the student is given the opportunity to revise his thinking and subsequent performance in light of that feedback. There's no comparing students to other students, and there's no giving tests just to have enough grades in the grade book. This assessment is an opportunity for progress, not a declaration of deficiency.

Notice the focus on the standards or learner outcomes in the second example. This is key. Over the years, I noticed that students who repeatedly struggled were the least likely to know where they stood against the lesson's goals. Students who did well were more likely to know the lesson's goals and where they stood against them. Frequent formative assessment provides this awareness. When I give struggling students information about the lesson's goals and their personal progress toward them each week, their learning improves.

Beyond the format

When colleagues ask me to show them an example of both a formative and a summative assessment so they know how to design each kind, I show them the same assessment task. It's not the format that makes an assessment formative or summative; it's when we give the assessment and how we use the data from it that makes it formative or summative.

Formative assessments happen during the course of learning and summative assessments happen after the learning is done. Teachers could use an official final exam as a formative assessment during the unit of study if they used the scores on the exam to adjust later instruction, and, after taking it, the students could go back, learn from their mistakes, and take a new exam to better demonstrate their updated competencies.

Formative assessments are purposeful and ongoing checks for understanding that cause teachers to revise instruction based on assessment data and cause students to learn more ways to learn. Just as importantly, teachers give students opportunities to pursue those new strategies. Because of their immediate applications to the current learning sequence, most formative assessments tend to be shorter than summative versions, but not always. They assess focused areas of the curriculum. This way, teachers can consider their results quickly as they make weekly and sometimes daily instructional decisions.

Half- to one-page quick writes, exit cards, oral responses to clarifying questions, thumbs-up/down, buttons pressed on audience response system "clickers," metaphor/analogy generation, completing graphic organizers, observing body language and facial expressions, practice problems/sentences, skill demonstrations, and think-alouds are all examples of useful formative assessments.

Summative assessments can use these same tools, of course, but they tend to encompass more curriculum and take longer to consider—but not always. Summative assessments can be just as cut-to-the-chase short as formative assessments, and formative assessments can require students to weave together complex understanding and applications, just like summative ones. The difference is to what degree the assessment shapes subsequent instruction and student growth.

Formative assessment almost rivals the quality of the teacher when it comes to its positive impact on students' learning. For many of my own students, it is formative assessment that creates the most transformation, particularly with diverse populations. It's the en route assessments that change everything, so much so, that we should be able to see formal formative assessments listed in our daily lesson plans. If we don't see them there, the lessons aren't as powerful as we think they are.

Transforming assessment

Ideas for formative assessments usually come from teachers breaking down the standards or outcomes required in the summative assessments. This means we should design the summative assessments first, basing them on the standards or outcomes. Then, we break off smaller pieces of those summative tasks/prompts to use for our formative assessments during instruction. For example:

> Summative Assessment: The student will translate a paragraph written in English into Spanish, accounting for correct vocabulary, verb conjugation, sentence structure, and other nuances of the Spanish language.

> Formative Assessment: The student conjugates regular and irregular verbs, translates single sentences, defines vocabulary terms, identifies errors in others' translations and corrects them, justifies pronoun/verb/noun/adjective sequences, and receives descriptive feedback about his performance with each element.

Anything can be broken down into focus areas for formative assessments, and by tying them closely to summative assessments, we create a clear picture of students' readiness and what we need to provide next in their development. Will students have to think of novel applications of a concept on the final exam? During instruction, we provide frequent formative assessments dealing with "curve balls" in applying the concepts. Will students have to write a compare-and-contrast essay? We give them ample formative assessments on each portion of essay writing: drafting introductions, body paragraphs, conclusions, transitions, revisions, as well as assessing their capacity to identify substantive similarities and differences.

About the grades

Formative assessment isn't graded. It can be marked, but not with letter grades or percentages. If we have to grade it for some reason, we make sure it isn't included in the final summative report of students' performance against standards, i.e., academic achievement grades on report cards. For formative assessment to be effective, students must feel free to explore content without fear that their first and continued wrestlings with new ideas are the final declarations of their proficiencies with those ideas. This not only diminishes learning, it's unethical because the grade is inaccurate. Letter grades and percentage are associated with final declarations of mastery, not the early and ongoing explorations of students moving toward that mastery.

Some teachers claim that students won't do assignments if they aren't graded. My response to this issue is fourfold:

1. We can comment on these assessments, just not letter grade them. We give students very clear feedback that will serve them better than an abstract symbol ever will. We record these comments somewhere for documentation purposes.

2. We can change our assignments. We can make them compelling enough to warrant students' investment of time and energy.

3. Students want to be productive; they're wired that way. When they are not productive, there's something going on we need to investigate and help resolve: Time management issues? Auditory processing issue? Learned helplessness? Intimidation? Test anxiety? Trouble at home? When students struggle to complete work, it's usually not for unimportant reasons.

4. Grades are poor motivators. It's a mistake to think that students do tasks simply because of a lure or threat of grades. The instructional power of formative assessments is too important to diminish because we felt compelled to put a grade or percentage on a formative experience. We should be strong enough to keep formative assessment instructional.

An emphasis on formative assessment also translates into a focus on student self-assessment. To provide the timely and helpful feedback associated with formative assessment, the assessment can't be limited to the teacher's one perspective. The students will need to do a lot more assessing.

Making the right noise

Just like most important elements in sound instruction, formative assessment is a mindset. A basic tenet of this mindset is that teaching and learning are interactive, not one-way streets. Students learn how to learn for themselves using teacher and classmate connections, and teachers adjust instruction in light of evidence gathered in assessments.

Now we have to make a decision: Do we do whatever it takes to keep formative assessment on our radar scope this school year, or do we let it slip into the land of wishful thinking, only to be brought to life during teacher evaluation cycles? There's enough going for it, including its real impact on students' personal lives, to keep our scope sharply focused on formative assessment.

Let's do it correctly, and let's still the education-speak cacophony with formative assessment's clear high notes—critical elements of successful instruction.

Aim for More Authentic Assessment

"Explain it to me," I said to Kalyani in my fifth period class. "Well," she responded, "a hybrid is like when you combine the genetic codes between two types of tomatoes, one that's bright red but doesn't last a long time, and one that's mostly green but lasts a long time. The hybrid uses the genes that make the tomato red and the ones that make it last a long time."

"Excellent," I said and then asked her, "Can you find examples of hybrids in math? In English? In history? What would it take to build a model to demonstrate the nature of a hybrid?"

Education researcher and author Jay McTigue is fond of saying that assessment should promote learning, not just measure it. He's right. Assessment is a coaching tool. It doesn't only document the quality of a performance; it demonstrates the depth of understanding, which shows both the teacher and the student what they need to do next.

Whether formal or informal, good assessment is connected to the learning, giving students regular feedback. Track coaches don't wait until the meet is over to tell their promising young athletes what they did right and wrong. They assess performance weekly (if not daily) and offer tips for improvement, so the athletes can practice before the big event. Based on the athletes' performance during practice, the coach might adjust the training; just as a classroom teacher might change the lesson based on indicators of student comprehension.

I try to coach my students while they're learning new concepts and skills. When we use peer critiques, for example, students comment on their classmates' work using the same rubric that I refer to when grading the final product. When I post samples of successful products on an overhead projector, we discuss what made them strong. Periodically, we film students as they're reporting on their research, and we provide helpful advice by analyzing the video.

As I work with students, I jot notes on yellow sticky pads (PDA or iPad), indicating what I need to teach or reteach. I know some teachers who carry clipboards containing charts of students' progress. Either way, the goal is finding out what skills and information we still need to convey. In the past, I've thrown out the rest of the week's lessons because the feedback I received on Tuesday indicated that students didn't understand the basic steps well enough to move on to more complex applications.

Good assessment defines the goal at the beginning, not the end. In the real world, we usually know what success looks like. A television repairer knows that his goal is a functioning television set. A webmaster knows that her job is to produce an attractive Internet site that encourages visitors and provides useful and timely information. If most adults know the expected outcome of their efforts, shouldn't students know, too? Why should a student ever have to ask, "What's going to be on the test?"

I know it's a bit radical, but I advocate giving students a copy of the test or expected performance when starting a new unit. Make the questions or standard rigorous so students can't easily memorize the answers as in a list. But the goal of learning should never be a mystery. I've seen a significant increase in subject mastery among students who received the assessments in advance of the evaluation compared to those I taught years ago when I still kept my test formats secret. In years past, my students used to say, "I didn't know you wanted that," or "You never told us it had to be in cursive," or "I thought one supporting detail was enough." Students with learning disabilities were overwhelmed by the need to study everything, so they studied nothing or the wrong things. Ambiguity bred stress. It also made the learning a teacher-driven process. I was the big answer man, and I would bestow the mark of acceptance on selected individuals who were able to guess what I had in mind.

Today, my students focus on key concepts and how to learn them, instead of playing guessing games with me. The content and skills are the hub around which we revolve. I am the liberator, not the gatekeeper, and my students are achieving more as a result. One important note: I didn't say my students' grades have improved as a result of this change in my assessment process. My grade book includes roughly the same distribution of As, Bs, Cs, Ds and Fs as before. I said that their subject mastery had improved. In good assessment practices, grades aren't the goal; learning is.

Pursue the essential and enduring knowledge.

The first thing we should think about before teaching any unit is what we want our students to know at the end. For me, such reflection creates objectives that demand more from my students and gives me the courage to eliminate activities that serve no real purpose. Students need to do important work, not busy work. Hard work can be inspiring when it seems to matter, which means it either must target a specific audience that will respond to it, be useful to someone else, or be relevant to the student. When I teach students how to write editorials, draw political cartoons, or report events, I let them create a real newspaper and put it in local businesses or doctors' waiting rooms. Students' efforts and skills increase dramatically because they know someone besides the teacher will read their work.

Good assessment also must have depth. For example, when I use the computer software program, SimCity™, I don't ask students to play the game for the fun of it, but to further their understanding of a topic. SimCity™ lets players build a city, using finite resources, a growing population, and variables such as traffic congestion, fires, and underfunded government departments. With a unit on communities or habitats, I would use the software program to teach the basic elements of city planning, then ask groups of students to plan an underwater city based on the principles they learned from the SimCity™ game. Specifically, students would have to investigate oxygen supply, salinity, sea life, corrosion, diminished sunlight, underwater topography, the three-dimensional nature of underwater transportation, and other factors. Multiple-choice tests might be administratively easier to produce and to score than such assessments, but they won't give you as much information about what your students can do with what they've learned.

For many years, I've asked students to research and portray ancient cultures such as the Babylonians, the Assyrians, the Anasazi, the Mayans, and the Phoenicians, in a United Nations-style debate on modern world issues. Students set up booths of cultural artifacts; other classes visit the exhibits, ask questions, sample items, and listen to the debates. Using their knowledge of ancient cultures, my students tackle compelling questions, such as "Should rap music lyrics be censored?" "Should our planet have one language instead of many?" "Is formal schooling useful?" and "What are the qualities of an effective leader?"

Another teacher I know put a different spin on this by asking students to portray endangered animals in a debate about environmental issues. I also like to use the format from Steve Allen's Meeting of the Minds television series, asking students to portray historical figures and debate modern world issues. In the assessment stage, I look for the accuracy of the dramatic portrayal, including whether students have woven facts into their conversations and have made reasonable predictions about how a person (or animal) would respond to the given issue. They write reports of what they've found out about the culture or person and present these to the class. To defend a belief intelligently and accurately, students must understand the people, their history, and the issue itself. The assessment guides the learning.

On other occasions, I have asked students to write sonnets (using as a model Shakespeare's 18th Sonnet, which begins, "Shall I compare thee to a summer's day?") to demonstrate their understanding of blood from a unit on human health. Modeling Shakespeare's comparison of his love to a summer day, I asked my students to compare the different parts of blood—red cells, white cells, plasma, and platelets—using the sonnet structure. For example, red cells are small, round donut shapes that are indented in the middle and have no nucleus in the mature state. White cells, by contrast, are large blobs with mature nuclei. I still remember the first two lines of one student's sonnet: "Shall I compare thee to a white corpuscle? Thou art more pinched and have no brains!" Through this process, students learned how to synthesize information—a higher-order thinking skill and a habit of mind applicable to other disciplines.

Ask students to design the assessment.

Effective assessment should involve the people we're evaluating. If we do this in our classrooms, we help students understand the characteristics of excellent work. To encourage students to use different assessment formats, we can provide three or four samples and ask them to brainstorm at least 10 others. So, for a demonstration of the differences between plant and animal cells, I might show the class a comic strip that includes superhero plant and animal cells, a clay sculpture, a poem, and a video of a mime act. Then I would ask the class to list the common characteristics of the various products and the qualities that made them good. After some probing questions and a discussion, we would revise the list and pare it down to a few important attributes that comprise our standard of excellence.

At this point, I would bring out another product that I consider excellent and apply the new rubric to it. If it matches our criteria for success, then we move on. If it doesn't, we rewrite the rubric. As often as I think of it, I throw out a few questions that I can expect students to ask later in the process: "What if the product gets high scores in organization and mechanics but really doesn't say much?" or "What if it demonstrates full knowledge of the concept but is sloppily done?" or "What if they do more than what is required and some of the required items aren't as good as others?" By learning how to evaluate the sample products, how to construct the standard for assessing future products, and how to evaluate the rubric itself, the students know what I expect them to learn and how I will grade their performance.

Good assessment ensures validity. If we want to know whether students "Can conduct research using primary and secondary sources," a paper and pencil test asking them to list library sources won't prove whether or not they can use those sources for actual research. Instead, expect students to demonstrate that they have obtained information from observations or interviews with people directly connected to the topic. Summaries of what others have reported will do for secondary sources.

Researching alternative assessments has opened my eyes to the many ways students can express their knowledge. Some popular alternatives to traditional tests or writing assignments include:

- Pop-up or alphabet books
- Restaurant menus
- Journal or diary entries
- Annotated catalogues of artifacts
- Correspondence (letters) between two people
- Radio plays
- Videos
- Drawings/illustrations
- Games/puzzles
- Debates
- Puppet shows
- Interviews with an expert
- How-to books
- Field guides/museum guides
- News or feature articles
- Murals or timelines
- Spreadsheets/graphs
- Advertisements
- Speeches/oral presentations
- Owner's manuals
- Almanacs
- Musical compositions

Before anyone judges these as too soft or simplistic, consider what students have to do to create them. They must have accurate and complete information presented with style and an awareness of the audience. To manipulate information in this manner requires mastery of the material.

Instead of taking a test on Latin word roots a few years ago, two of my students created a huge board game. They included game cards, spinners, markers, a colorful and organized game board, elaborate rules, and compelling twists in the progression of the game. Players encountered every Latin root in the course of playing the game. I read the cards, board, and directions for accuracy, then verbally spot-checked the girls. They knew everything.

Some educators treat assessment as an affliction, rather than as a tool. Like most things in middle schools, assessment will be successful if it's proactive and interactive. Include small, specific skill assessments during a unit, if you want, but push students toward complexity. The best assessments integrate more than one subject, include real-world applications, and test mastery in the same format in which students learned the concepts and skills.

Assessment shows students and the community how we use instruction and evaluation to promote learning. If the tools we use are significant, then they deserve reflection and renewal. We don't want people to think we only document deficiencies. We want to be known as educators who teach students well. Good assessment practices let us do that.

Creating Good
Test Questions

Question #13: What is the best way to describe the Renaissance Age?

a   All of the below accept "d"

b.   A period in which all the great artists lived

c.   An age of widespread feudalism and rampant religious "correctness"

d.   An age that turned scientific and artistic pursuits toward humankind instead of the church

e.   An age of rebirth

f.   None of the above

'It could be "d" and "e," but also "b,"' Raul thinks. 'Am I supposed to circle the one with the most correct information? Maybe there's one word that's incorrect, and my teacher wants to see if we're smart enough to catch it. Wait, it can't be "b" because other great artists lived in other time periods. Now we're getting somewhere…uh oh, wasn't there worry over "correctness" in the Renaissance as well as the Middle Ages? Okay. Skip this one for now, and see if answering some other question might give me a clue.'

Questions like the one above have no business in a middle school classroom. They do not assess a student's knowledge and skill, only the extent to which he or she can guess what's on the teacher's mind. Nor do they instruct as all good assessments should. In short, this question and others like it are a waste of time that we don't have to waste. Every test question should be important enough to ask and clear enough to answer.

Designing smart tests

Designing smart test questions gets easier with practice. In the back of our minds, of course, we're also thinking about how we're going to grade students' responses efficiently. Here are some effective strategies that successful middle school teachers use to design and grade tests:

- Use a variety of questions/prompts, such as matching, true/false, fill in the missing word, multiple choice, definition, and essay or short answer.

- Use innovative questions/prompts such as analogies, drawings, diagrams, analyzing real-life applications, critiquing others' performance or responses, demonstration/performance, integrating more than one topic, and exclusion brainstorming ("Circle the item that does not belong in the five words listed and explain why it doesn't belong.")

- Consider using non-traditional formats such as asking students to design a new country to demonstrate geography proficiency, creating an accurate coloring book on the topic for younger students, or deciphering content clues that, when put together, reveal a secret message or conclusion.

A traditional test question would be, "Define the Latin word root terra." A test question that pushes students a bit farther is, "In the spaces below, write what you think each real or nonsense word means or could mean. As long as you capture the essence of the root words, the answer will be correct."

Terratempo:	Thermairnaria:
Zotox:	Photophobia:
Noveloc:	Protophytop:
Lithjector:	Patripathy:
Sophipsychia:	Magnijuris:

Efficient and effective

Make tests efficient for students and for you. Don't ask students to write a "T" or "F" for "true" and "false." Sometimes we can't tell the difference when we're grading the test. Instead, provide a "T" or an "F" for students to circle, or require students to write out the full words.

When asking students to do a matching activity, write the definitions on the left or at the top and list the words from which they are to match their answers on the right or the bottom. This way, students are scanning word lists to find the correct response, not reading through every single definition. It's faster and less tiring for them, but serves the same purpose.

Format tests efficiently for grading. If possible, ask students to record their answers on an answer sheet. This has several advantages. First, if you teach more than one period of a subject, you only need to make one class set of tests. Second, when you grade the tests, you have fewer papers to carry home to grade. As you grade, you don't have to scan through the pages of the test looking for the answers—you just run your eyes down the answer sheet. Efficient teachers arrange the answers to their multiple choice, matching, or true/false questions to create a pattern when recorded. This makes for easy grading. For example, an answer pattern might be "dabadacadaba." Scanning can quickly target a letter that's out of the sequence. Of course, the moment our test answers reveal a pattern, we have to throw a curve ball into the pattern so students don't just record answers according to the pattern.

To accurately diagnose students' proficiencies, put in common errors as candidates for multiple-choice responses. In math, for example, the answer could be the same sequence of digits, but the decimal is placed in different positions among them. Commonly confused words can share definition possibilities, and graphs can have multiple misinterpretations in the mix of possible responses.

But, please do not insert choices that make students stumble over wording or logic: "All of the above except C and E," "Which of these is NOT associated with...," and "All of these." Such statements don't really assess student's knowledge and skill with the topic. Any error on these items is related more to reading and logical thinking ability than students' understanding of content.

Put some fun into your test questions as well. Incorporate students' names and aspects of their culture into the test items. Students will actually look forward to reading the test items, and a little smile here and there on a test is a good thing. Instead of, "A community playground needs enough small gravel to fill the swing set area with dimensions, 40' x 65' x 1', how many cubic feet of gravel will they need to purchase?" how about, "Abdul is building a rectangular practice hockey rink for his championship-winning Mighty Anoles hockey team. How much water must he pour into the containing walls and then freeze, if the frozen ice is twice the volume of the liquid water, and the dimensions are 100' x 50' x 2'?" Or instead of, "Describe the main character," how about, "Create the lyrics to two verses of an Avril Lavigne tune that accurately portrays the main character's feelings."

Be sure that the questions you're asking students will enable them to express the information you want to assess. Go back to the essential understandings you've established for the unit of study and design questions that elicit that information. If one of your objectives is for students to identify a country based on latitude/longitude coordinates, then provide two different pairs of coordinates and ask students to identify those two different countries. If you want to raise the complexity a bit, provide those same coordinates, but ask "Before traveling to which location would it first be wise to learn to speak French?

Keep it efficient, too. We don't need 10 similar questions when we can determine in two questions whether or not a student understands the concept. Let's make our questions match our lessons. For example, if you taught a procedure one way, don't call for students to use another approach on a test question. That's unfair and unprofessional. Test questions should be reliable and valid indicators of what was taught.

Include items that challenge students to generate information or manipulate information. Simply reporting what they have memorized isn't always a sign of understanding and longterm retention, which are our goals. It's easy to parrot information; it's masterful to apply it.

Testing with a twist

Rigor in testing does not mean more tests, more test items, or more difficult test items. It means increasing the complexity of the required responses—enhancing the required reasoning and thoughtfulness. We can do that through traditional and non-traditional test questions.

Let's make tests that can be completed during one period or let's make take-home tests. Let's share our tests with one another and get advice on how to improve the questions and their grading. With so much riding on tests, every item deserves careful consideration.

Grading

Standards-Based Grading: Taking the Leap

A member of MiddleTalk asked Listserv members for advice on implementing standards-based grading in his classroom. My response follows.

I used standards-based grading (SBG) in my classroom for years, but now I'm out working with teachers and principals on SBG, among other topics. I'd be glad to join the conversation with others as you post concerns and insights.

Criteria for grades

You wrote that you use the following ratios to establish a grade:

80%: Assessments on mastery of learning targets. Quizzes, tests, etc.

10%: Homework completion.

10%: Class participation.

My first thought is that something over 20% of your grade has nothing to do with mastery, which means you grades are probably not as accurate as you'd like them to be. Homework and classwork aren't considered final declarations of mastery, nor are quizzes, if the material on the quiz occurs on the final test as well. Weaving quizzes into a summative test grade distorts the accuracy of the grade. You said that you also added compliance, work habits, and behavior, too, so gosh, I'm thinking the grades are really far from their intended goal: an accurate accounting. I can tell that you probably already know this, but I just wanted to give an outside view.

Scale for tracking learning objectives

You asked about what scale to use for tracking each learning standard—not rubrics for specific assignments (such as a lab report or a project), but rather, a learning target such as "I can create a well-designed experiment." You proposed two options:

Choice A:

2 — Mastered

1 — On my way

0 — No evidence available

Choice B:

4 — Advanced; Extended and Connected with Other Skills

3 — Proficient

2 — Needs Improvement

1 — No evidence of mastery

As far as scales go, I like the first one best, though I would change it to, "Not enough evidence presented," not, "No evidence available." You can use the upper symbol as, "mastered," if standard is a standard of excellence. If the standard is just a promotional benchmark minimum, however, Scale B may be the better one to use. A regular report can only report against regular, publicly determined and posted objectives, not something above and beyond, something not listed in the course curriculum. Robert Marzano and I differ on this, just so you know.

How many learning objectives to track

You describe your curriculum as divided into roughly 12 "units," with each unit currently having 10 to 12 learning objectives including science inquiry and literacy skills that apply to all the units. No wonder you are overwhelmed by the number of objectives to track! You give your options as

A. Track 'em all! They are all important!

B. Create a handful of meatier objectives per unit, and make the smaller objectives part of the larger ones.

And you go on to say that you are leaning towards B for sanity's sake. You're right, Choice B is better. It's prohibitively cumbersome and reductive to track every single thing, though you can have a very clear posting—hardcopy, online, and in students' hands—of each large umbrella and medium umbrella topic and the subtopics underneath each. You will still need to confirm what you and your subject-like colleagues will tolerate as evidence of each standard, however, even those smaller ones.

How to track habits of mind/work habits?

You wrote:

> How should I track habits of mind/work habits? I teach middle school, and I don't just teach "science". I teach the whole kid, and a big part of that includes trying to help them develop good work habits and use effective effort. For example, one of my objectives for effective effort relates to persistence: "I demonstrate persistence by trying different learning strategies until I find one that works."
>
> I am struggling between two perspectives:

A. Teach the work and effort skills, but only assess the learning that results from them. In other words, if kids apply the effective effort principles, they will be more successful in mastering the learning targets and the fruits of their labor will be assessed there.

B. You get what you measure (especially with middle school students who are not used to SBG!). If students are assessed explicitly on effort objectives, they will be more conscious about them.

> My heart is with A, but my gut is telling me B!

I suggest you teach and assess them quite intensely—they are super-important! Just be very transparent, criterion-referenced, vet the criteria with colleagues, and report them in a separate column in your grade book and on the report card. If your system doesn't allow you to do that, there's nothing stopping you from designing your own report card on these very important characteristics and sending it home as an addendum. Be aware, however, that just because there's no place to record them on a current report card (if that's your situation) doesn't mean a teacher has a right to aggregate them into the academic report and knowingly falsify the academic report (grade).

Differentiated Grading: Treating Students Fairly

Differentiating instruction means doing what's fair for students. It's a collection of best practices used to maximize students' learning at every turn—including giving them the tools to handle anything that is undifferentiated. In short, it's highly effective teaching.

Most of us try to live up to the promise of differentiated instruction, but when it comes to grading and report cards, our resolve weakens. We question the legitimacy of giving equally weighted grades to students who demonstrate mastery in alternative formats or through alternative means: Was it fair that one student did an essay while another did artwork? Are both assessments challenging? Was it fair for some students to receive additional support (scaffolding) to accomplish the task while others did not? What about redos? Do all students get full credit if they redo assessments?

Why give grades?

For many teachers, a grade represents a valid and undiluted indicator of mastery—what a student knows and is able to do. Anything that dilutes that grade—penalizing students' multiple attempts at mastery, incorporating non-academic factors (behavior, attendance, and effort), and assessing students in ways that do not accurately indicate students' mastery, for example—is suspect. To dilute a final grade because of such factors demonstrates a teacher's interest in holding students accountable, not teaching. It promotes a "learn-or-we-will-hurt-you" mentality, a red flag, as pointed out by middle level educator Nancy Doda.

Class after class, week after week, grading period after grading period, year after year, we scramble to boil a student's learning journey down to a single symbol in a tiny box on a thin piece of paper that may or may not make it out from the crumpled darkness of a book bag. That one little mark has the power to transform not just that evening, but a whole month and beyond into a morass of angst, guilt, self-doubt, dysfunction, and fear in both students and their parents. We tell students that grades let them know how they're doing. But we know it's not possible for one symbol to provide clear feedback of all the information and skills assessed for a grading period. Given this perspective and the need to be fair with students, maybe we can make the best of such inaccurate yet popular conventions and focus on the instructional uses of grades.

Grades and instruction

We must make a decision: Do we grade students against the standards, against their own progress, or both? Most of us use the standards, but there are times when this isn't appropriate, such as when the student is new to the country, doesn't speak our language, or is working with an advanced curriculum. With these students, conventional grading doesn't work. Rather than using a contrivance like equal grading for all, we can alter the report card format to promote a more accurate reflection of a student's achievement. For example:

- Grading the student against his own progress, but indicating that the grade reflects an adjusted curriculum. An asterisk is placed next to the grade or a box is checked on the report card indicating such, and a narrative comment is included in the cumulative folder to explain the adjustment.

- Giving the student two grades: one indicating her performance relative to the standards and another indicating her own progression. A, B, C, D, or F might indicate a student's progress against state standards, while 3, 2, or 1 might indicate her personal progress. A student with an average performance but exceptional growth during the year, for example, would earn a C3.

- Dividing the grade into its component pieces. For example, a B in science can be subdivided into specific standards or benchmarks such as, "Demonstrates proper lab procedure" or "Successfully employs the scientific method." In *Transforming Grading Practice* (2001), Robert Marzano reminds us that multiple subcategory evaluations within subjects are more accurate indicators of mastery than a single symbol.

For a grade to be a valid mechanism for feedback and instructional planning, we cannot grade the practice or effort that went into the pursuit of mastery. No adult would tolerate being graded on his or her practice while mastering something. We accept graded critique only when we're ready to be licensed or certified. We need to extend this same consideration to our students. For example, if a student does none of the homework assignments, yet aces every formal assessment, does he earn anything less than an A on his report card? No, he deserves the A. The homework would have served no purpose for that student.

Of course, completing homework usually leads to academic success and higher grades. However, if we lower his grade because of an issue like immaturity for not doing his assignments, the grade no longer reflects the student's mastery of standards, nor can it be used to guide future instructional decisions.

The subjectivity of grades

Grades are subjective. As Marzano points out, pure mathematical averages of grades for a grading period are inaccurate indicators of students' true mastery. He contends that a teacher's professional judgment via clear descriptors on a rubric actually increases the accuracy of students' final grades as an indicator of what they learned.

Marzano also presents research demonstrating how a teacher's judgment via rubrics has a stronger correlation with performance on standardized tests than do point or average calculations. Whoops. We think that using points and averaging mitigate our subjective opinion of students' achievement and are supposedly unbiased, when really, the reverse is true. Use of pure mathematical averages of grades often exacerbates grade distortions that stem from a teacher's frame of mind while grading, but use of rubrics with standards is better suited for evening out such distortions over time.

This subjectivity and students' varied states of readiness and learning styles make strict adherence to equal grading for all disquieting. Regardless of how "teacher-proof" a curriculum becomes, we all emphasize some aspects over others. The curriculum is too huge for student mastery, so we're always deciding what to prune and what to keep and when to push for mastery—and what constitutes mastery varies from teacher to teacher, no matter how scripted the lessons.

The only ethical thing to do, then, is to abandon one-size-fits-all grading practices in favor of grading students in whatever manner will maximize their learning at every turn. Such a policy may be uncomfortable at first. For example, this means we allow assignments and tests to be redone for full credit as long as students are truly trying to learn, and it's within reason. We require students to submit a plan of study that will enable them to improve their performance the second time around. We identify a deadline by which this will be accomplished or the grade is permanent. Then we help students create a calendar of completion that will help them succeed.

If we want grades to inform and help students achieve, they must come regularly. Successful differentiated grading emphasizes formative assessment over summative. This means we shorten assignments (example: change multi-page writings to a series of one-page writings), find ways to provide feedback other than from the teacher, and make sure students get feedback within three days of submitting assignments, if possible. Students will hear and use a continuous cycle of quick feedback in smaller doses. It's more powerful than extended feedback weeks after the assignment's due. We must also plan how students will receive timely feedback on every assignment.

Differentiating assessment

When we differentiate teaching strategies, we sometimes have to differentiate the assessment. This may require "tiering" our tests: providing a level 1and a level 2 test. The level 1 test assesses three of five standards, while level 2 assesses all five standards. Most of the students are assigned to one or the other—it's non-negotiable unless a student really wants to try the more-encompassing test to see what it's like. We keep track of which objectives/standards have been mastered and work with students in tiered lessons on the objectives they have not yet mastered.

What happens if a student gets a high grade on a lower tiered test? What grade does he get on the report card? Remember, it doesn't matter where in the grading period a student demonstrates mastery. To require all students to demonstrate mastery on Tuesday of this particular week at 10:00 a.m. in this particular format is absurd. Within reason, give students the whole grading period to receive what you have to offer. If you need to limit the window of opportunity to learn and demonstrate mastery to protect your sanity, that's fine, but don't hold everyone to demonstrating mastery with no chance to improve. If students are working diligently, yet demonstrate mastery of all objectives three weeks after everyone else, they get the same high grade as their classmates.

If they don't yet demonstrate full mastery by the end of the grading period, we're back to the central question: Do we grade students against their own progression, against standards, or both? It does students no service to record a D on the report card when they have grown tremendously throughout the quarter. I'd rather give them the B or A and indicate somewhere on the card that it was with an adjusted curriculum.

The issue is not, "How do I equitably assign grades? Instead, it's, "What is fair for each child?" and "What report card feedback best represents what a child truly learns and promotes the most learning?" If living up to the promise of differentiated practice means redesigning report cards and grade books, let's do it. Let's be consistent in our pedagogy: Differentiated instruction means we differentiate grading from time to time, and this does not mean we are weakening our curriculum or lessons. On the contrary, it's making learning more demanding. Students have little opportunity to escape the challenges; accountability and feedback are specific, vigorous, and frequent. It's what's fair.

It's Time to Stop Averaging Grades

Then there is the man who drowned crossing a stream with an average depth of six inches. —W.I.E. Gates

I abhor averages. I like the individual case. A man may have six meals one day and none the next, making an average of three meals per day, but that is not a good way to live. —Supreme Court Justice, Louis D. Brandeis

While the individual man is an insoluble puzzle, in the aggregate he becomes a mathematical certainty. You can, for example, never foretell what any one man will be up to, but you can say with precision what an average number will be up to. Individuals vary, but percentages remain constant. So says the statistician. —Arthur Conan Doyle

The average human has one breast and one testicle. —Des McHale

For too long and from too many teachers, students have received false reports of their performance against standards. The practice that creates these false reports is so entrenched in our profession, it has won general fiat and seems irreproachable. Its continued use, however, thwarts students' learning and casts doubt on our instructional decisions.

Let's right the wrong: It's time to stop averaging students' grades. All of our assessment and grading leaders: Guskey, Reeves, O'Connor, Popham, Wiggins, Brookhart, McTighe, Marzano, Yolen, Davies, Stiggins, and Cooper, among others, agree that averaging marks/grades creates inaccurate reports and leads to poor decisions and feedback. Let's find the political and professional will to join them and start dismantling this practice this year.

"But I've always averaged grades," some teachers say, "and my teachers averaged my grades when I was in school, too. It works fine."

Does it? Just as we teach our students, we don't want to fall for argumentum ad populum: something is true or good just because a lot of people think it's true or good. Let's take a look at the case against averaging grades.

Hiding behind the math

Just because something is mathematically easy to calculate doesn't mean it's pedagogically sound. The 100-point scale makes averaging very attractive to teachers, and averaging implies credible, mathematical objectivity. Statistics can be manipulated and manipulative in many ways, however. One percentage point is the arbitrary cut-off between getting into, or being denied, graduate school. One student gets a 90% and another gets an 89%, but the first is an A and the second is a B, yet we can't discern mastery of content to this level of specificity. These students are effectively even in mastery of content, but we declare a difference based only on the single percentage point nonetheless. The student with 90% gets scholarships and advanced class placements while the student with 89% is left to a lesser path. Something's wrong with this picture.

Early in my career, one of my students had a 93.4% in my class. Ninety-four to 100 was the A range set for that school, so he was 0.6% from achieving an A. The student asked if I would be willing to round up the score up to the 94%, so he could have straight As in all his classes. I reminded him that it was 93.4, not 93.5, so if I rounded anything, I would round down, not up. I told him that if it was 93.5, I could justify rounding up, but not with a 93.4.

I was hiding behind one-tenth of a percentage point. I should have interviewed the student intensely about what he had learned that grading period and made an executive decision about his grade based on the evidence of learning he presented in that moment. The math felt so safe, however, and I was weak. It wasn't one of my prouder moments. We can't resort to averaging just because it feels credible by virtue of its mathematics. There's too much at stake.

Simple averaging falsifies grade reports

For a quick proof of averaging's fallacy, consider the teacher who gives Martin two chances to do well on the final exam and then averages the two grades. The first attempt resulted in an F grade, but after re-learning and a lot of hard work, the second attempt resulted in an A. We trust the exam to be a highly valid indicator of student proficiency in the subject, and Martin has clearly demonstrated excellent mastery in the subject. When the two grades are averaged, however, the teacher records a C in the gradebook for Martin—falsely reporting his performance against the standards.

While this is strikingly inaccurate when using grading scale endpoints such as A and F, it creates just as inaccurate, "blow to grade integrity" reporting as when we average grades closer to one another on the scale: B with D, B with F, A with C, A with D, C with F, and C with A.

Consider a sample with more data: Cheryl gets a 97, 94, 26, 35, and 83 on her tests which correspond to an A, A, F, F, and a B on the school grading scale. When the numbers are averaged, however, everything is given equal weight, and the score is 67, which is a D. This is an incorrect report of her performance against individual standards. This happens in a 4.0 scale as well: Cheryl gets a 4.0, 4.0, 0.0, 0.0, and 3.0, which is also an A, A, F, F, and a B. Numerically, however, this averages to a 2.2, which is a C. Again, it doesn't adequately report how Cheryl is doing against specific standards.

Thankfully, many schools are moving toward disaggregation in which students receive separate scores/marks/grades for individual standards. This will cut down dramatically on the distortions caused by aggregate grades that combine everything into one small symbol. Disaggregation, stopping averaging, and focusing on patterns of performance over time eliminate teacher concerns about students who "game" the system when their teachers re-declare zeroes as 50s on the 100-point scale. These students try to do just enough—skipping some assessments, scoring well on others—to pass mathematically. In classrooms where teachers do not average grades, students can't do this. No more mind games; students have to learn the material.

Averaging grades counters the charge to be criterion-referenced.

"Average," "above average," and "below average" are norm references, but in today's successful classrooms, we claim to be standards(outcomes)-based. This means that assessments and grading are evidentiary, criterion-referenced. A teacher declares Toby is above average, but we're not interested in that because it provides testimony of Toby's proficiencies only in relation to others' performance, which may be high or low, depending on the group. Instead, we want to know if Toby can write an expository essay, stretch correctly before running a long distance, classify cephalopods, and interpret graphs accurately. We don't need to know how well he's doing in relation to classmates nearly so much as how he's doing in relation to his own progress and to societal standards declared for this grade level and subject.

We can't make specific instructional decisions, provide descriptive feedback, or document progress without being criterion-referenced. Declarations of average-ness muddle our thinking and create a false sense of reporting against standards. We need grade reports to be accurate.

We've distorted averaging's intended use.

One of the reasons we developed averaging in statistics was to limit the influence of any one sample error on experimental design. We don't want any one sample error to have undue influence in an experiment or test. For example, in the Cub Scouts' Pinewood Derby, small wooden cars carved and decorated by individual Cub Scouts are raced down a track. The track begins at 4 feet off the floor and curves into a flat section, covering about 40 feet in total length. Gravity pulls the car down the track with the release of a starting lever at the top. We want to know how long it takes a car to travel the length of the track.

If we ran just one trial run of a car down the track, any number of sample errors could creep into the equation and distort the results dramatically: Cub Scouts spilled soda pop at the bottom of the track and tried to wipe it clean but they were not thorough; sticky residue remains in that spot and it affects car speed through that spot. After 20 races, however, a solid wheel groove is molded through the sticky spot and the cars roll through it freely. In another sample error, a car is placed at a slight angle at the starting gate so when it starts rolling, it shimmies against the raised edge of the track, causing friction and thereby slowing down the car. In yet another sample error, some of the races were very exciting, and Cub Scouts jumped in the air and landed on the flimsy school cafeteria floor repeatedly, which jarred the cars as they bounced down the track.

As we run 100 time trials in order to increase our sample size, we never change the experimental design: we don't raise or lower the slope or length of the track, we don't spray powdered graphic into the axles or glue-gun pennies to one side of the car to redistribute its weight. The design remains consistent. After 100 races, we average the times and this gets us a nearly accurate report of how long it takes a car to travel the length of the track. We can average all these times because the design remained the same.

Consider, though, a student taking a test in our classroom. The test is on a particular topic and in a particular format. The student ate a breakfast, or he did not. He slept well, or he did not. His parents are divorcing, or they are not. He has a girlfriend, or he does not. He studied for this test, or he did not. A high-stakes drama/music/sports competition is later this afternoon, or it is not. Whatever the combination, all these factors conspire to create this student's specific performance on this test, on this day, at this time of day.

Three weeks later, we give students another test about the next material in our unit of study. Have students changed over three weeks? Yes, hormonally, if nothing else. Add to those changes that the second test is on a different topic and perhaps in a different format. On the first test, the student ate well, but didn't study. He slept well, but his parents are arguing each night. The drama/music/sports performance came and went and he did well in it. He didn't have a girlfriend. In the second test, however, he now has a girlfriend, and he studies well. He didn't sleep well, however, nor did he eat breakfast, and his parents have stopped arguing, which has calmed things down at home.

The second test situation is dramatically altered. The integrity of maintaining consistent experimental design is violated. We can no longer justify averaging the score of the first test with the score of the second test just to limit the influence of any one sample error. The only way we could justify averaging two test scores would be if we erased students' minds and re-created the exact same test—same questions, same format—as well as the exact same testing conditions (blood sugar levels, extent of preparation, emotional atmosphere, everything). Only with such design consistency could we justify averaging scores to minimize the influences of sample error.

Mode has higher correlation with testing done outside the classroom.

According to the assessment researchers listed above, if we look at the pattern of performance over time, the greatest preponderance of evidence, it correlates with outside the classroom testing better than averaging (mean) does. This observation is furthered by one of effective assessment's central tenets: Accurate assessments are based on clear and consistent evidence over time. It would be very uncomfortable for a teacher to be confronted with the question: "Your student received an A grade in your class, but failed the state (provincial) exam. How do you explain this?" or the reverse: the student fails the class, but excels on the standardized test in your subject area. We want our grades to have integrity, which means we need curriculum to align with assessments, and we need to use mode (and in some situations, median) instead of mean.

For high school teacher testimony on this, visit www.stenhouse.com/fiae (free registration), a website related to a book I wrote on assessment and grading. Baker High School biology teacher Eric Ziegler considered these ideas about mode, mean, and correlations while getting his students ready for the New York state Regents Exams. His experimentation and insights are compelling.

The electronic gradebook we use only averages grades—what do I do about that?

The only reason our electronic gradebooks average grades is because someone in a policymaking decision capacity declared it so, not because it was the educationally wise thing to do. Almost all gradebook software available today allows schools to choose its own procedures for grade calculation—mode, mean, median, not using central tendency, narrative commentary, weighting or not weighting, formative separated from summative. Let's choose our grading philosophy first, then find the technology to support it rather than sacrificing good grading practices because we can't figure out a way to make the technology work. The cool thing is that current technology can really do these wonderful things pretty well.

What we are really asking with the question above is: What do we do when we are asked by administrators or a school board to do something that we know is educationally wrong? This is a tough situation. I suggest we do the ethical thing in the microcosm of our own classrooms, but then translate that into the language of the school or district so that we can keep our jobs.

In addition, when bringing a problem to a busy administrator or policymaker, it's always better if we bring a solution or three for that problem at the same time. Our concerns are more likely to be given serious attention when we do this. We can also volunteer to be on the committee to revise the gradebook format to more thoughtfully reflect modern pedagogy. We can inform parents and business leaders so constituencies ask policymakers for the positive changes.

We can experiment in our own classes by reporting a subset of students' grades with and without averaging them just to see how they align with standardized testing. Sometimes running the numbers/grades ourselves helps us see with greater clarity than just hearing about ideas secondhand. We can read articles on grading and averaging and participate in online and faculty conversations on the topic.

We're working with real individuals, not statistics. Our students have deeply felt hopes and worries and wonderfully bright futures. They deserve thoughtful teachers who transcend conventional practices and recognize the ethical breach in knowingly falsifying grades. Let's live up to that charge and liberate the next generation from the oppression of averaging.

The Test of Accountability in School

Jared was presenting an oral report on Aristotle's Rhetorical Triangle (ethos, pathos, logos), and he was floundering. Embarrassed because he kept forgetting his memorized speech, he begged me to let him take an "F" and let him sit down. Instead, I asked Jared to take a few deep breaths and try again.

He did, but again, he bombed. I explained that an oral report is not just about delivering information; it's also about taking risks and developing confidence. After his classmates offered encouraging comments, Jared tried a third time and got a little farther before stopping his speech. I suggested that he repeat the presentation in short segments, resting between each one. This approach proved successful. After Jared finished, he moved to take his seat, but again I stopped him and asked him to repeat the entire presentation from the top without rests.

As his classmates grinned and nodded, Jared returned to the front of the room. This time he made it through his presentation without a mistake. His classmates cheered. Jared bowed, smiled, and took his seat. It was a wonderful exercise in perseverance, risk-taking, and accountability. Many educators dismiss accountability as a futile paper chase or an undeserved burden, yet it is actually an essential and desirable part of education. Accountability shouldn't just be about documenting academic deficiencies or pushing adolescents to pass politically motivated standardized tests. The real purpose of accountability is helping students achieve authentic accomplishments and giving teachers a valid measure of their professional success.

To hold students accountable for excellence, we need to provide models of success. We can't expect them to demonstrate excellence when they have no idea what it looks like. In the classroom, we can post examples of outstanding projects and papers, discuss the characteristics of excellent work, and encourage students to think about how they can reach the same levels. We can teach them how to break large assignments into smaller tasks and show them how to create calendars of completion. It's a good idea to negotiate checkpoints so you can review pieces of a project and help them stay focused on the goal.

You also might try to display some of their assignments publicly. Tell the students what you plan to do in advance. If they know their science essays or art projects might be hanging in the local Jiffy Lube or the dentist's office, they will become accountable to their community, friends, and family. And most likely, they will put more effort into achieving the high standards you've set.

To that end, I recommend reducing or eliminating extra credit assignments. Instead of letting students complete additional projects to increase their grades, ask them to revise their original assignments based on the standards outlined in your rubric and the comments written in the margins of their papers. I have not allowed alternative extra credit projects for five years. As a result, students do a much better job the first time around. The difference is dramatic.

Sometimes holding students accountable involves risk-taking—yours and theirs. One year, I had a student with Tourette's syndrome. He made strange noises in class and had frequent facial and body tics. As a result, he was insecure, shy, and the butt of jokes. He also had a learning disability in language arts. So, what did I do? I encouraged him to take the lead in a school production of Romeo and Juliet. He had to memorize a tremendous number of lines, learn to fight with a sword, come to rehearsals every day, and put up with adolescent teasing about "being in love." He performed brilliantly. Not only were the tics and strange noises absent during his performance, but he demonstrated acting talent well beyond his years. His classmates marveled at a side of him they had never seen. Was casting him in the play a risk? Without a doubt. Was it worth it to hold him accountable for a higher level of performance than he had ever reached before? You bet.

Accountability is not just an academic issue. It's also a benchmark of behavior. Ask your students to describe an ethical issue they're considering, or will need to consider in the future, then put that decision through this five-question test:

1. Am I making this choice with the hope that no one will find out?

2. How will I look back on this choice 10 years from now?

3. Am I doing to others what I would want them to do to me?

4. If (an admired person) were in the same situation, what would he or she do?

5. If everyone were about to do what I'm about to do, would I want to live in the world shaped by that decision?

Dr. Michael H. Popkin, author of the seminar and book series, *Active Parenting of Teens*, reminds us that responsibility is the process of making choices and then accepting the consequences of those choices. Ask yourself who owns the problem. Who is raising the issue or making the complaint? Whose purposes are being thwarted by the problem? If the answer is the child, then the adults should let the natural consequences be the teacher, if at all possible. Popkin encourages us to let children handle their own difficulties while offering them encouragement and support. How we communicate our standards will affect the extent to which children live up to them, Popkin says.

For example, we discourage accountability when we have negative expectations; focus on mistakes, expect perfection, and provide too much protection. Conversely, we encourage accountability when we show confidence in a child's behavior; resist the temptation to rescue her; build on her strengths; value her; stimulate her independence; separate her worth from her accomplishments; and separate her worth from her misbehaviors.

Denial is the No. 1 obstacle to accepting responsibility for misbehavior. Make it easier for students to see their antics in action—videotape the class with the camera focused on the student or students who are causing trouble and ask these offenders to stay after school to view the tape with you. Focus on nonemotional questions: What were you doing? What was the effect on your learning? What was the effect on the learning of those around you? What was the effect on the teacher? I've gone through this sequence using poster boards with different-sized windows cut in them. In the first one, there is a small window revealing just the student. In the next, the window is larger, revealing the student and those immediately around him. This allows us to focus our conversation on one thing at a time as I ask the questions. It's particularly effective if you invite Mom and Dad to join you.

If you want more support from home, get a cellphone to use in your classroom. When students come to class without the required assignments or act out in inappropriate ways, hand them the telephone and tell them to call their parents. That's accountability. For tougher behavior issues, invite mom or dad to sit next to the offending student during your class period. This works every time.

For maximum impact, let's use our professional selves as the highly effective teaching tools we are. We might not like all the public pressure to boost students' scores on standardized tests and meet the requirements of various state mandates, but too many teachers are using that pressure as an excuse to stop trying anything innovative in the classroom. They claim that administrators or the tests themselves require rote memorization and workbook practice, not complex projects and high-level thinking activities. Besides, they say, innovations take too long: If we let students work on interdisciplinary projects and extend learning through the community, we won't be able to cover all the material in time for the test.

Hogwash. What parents and the public want children to do is master the material, not just cover it. Many of those "innovative" practices are the best teaching tools for learning and retaining new concepts. If students do not master the material, their test scores will plummet. Ensuring that students achieve passing scores on state tests doesn't mean we forfeit our creativity or autonomy as teachers.

Rather, it demands even greater imagination and initiative than ever before. I can teach comma placement in quotations with worksheet drills, but true learning comes by writing meaningful dialog between a black student and a white student in South Africa during apartheid, or among plant and animal cells discussing the merits of a cell membrane over a cell wall. Thinking logically and providing substantive evidence for one's opinion become paramount for all students during those mock trials in civics class. When exposed only to the descriptions of such in a textbook, however, students can remain passive and not develop.

In his book, *Reaching the Peak Performance Zone*, Gerald Kushel states that peak performers take total responsibility for their jobs. They are intrinsically motivated, they share generously, they ask for mentoring when needed, and they continually find reasons to achieve excellence. Less than peak performers blame other people or conditions for their poor performance. Former Washington Redskins coach Joe Gibbs was the model of accountability. Whenever his players made mistakes that cost the Redskins a victory, the coach's first response under questioning from reporters was to share what he did wrong and what he was going to do to fix it.

We can learn something from Gibbs's example. Try apologizing sincerely to students when you fail to live up to your standards. Vow to make corrections—and keep your promise. Come each day prepared to teach a lesson well, not just get by. Follow through on the little things like that book you promised Maria, Geoff's new family arrangement, or writing large enough for Sahisna to see from the back row. In this way, you will model the commitment you want from your students.

Successful middle school teachers feel accountable to their students. They recognize that people learn in different ways, and they're not so arrogant to assume that their preferred method of teaching is the only way. They can do more than one trick. All students can learn, but it's up to us to find the right connections. It might mean learning and trying different instructional techniques, providing extra resources, or giving students different placements entirely. Let's vow not to pass on our problem students and hope someone else will figure out how to help them. We can provide a teacher report card that students fill out about how we're doing as their teachers. Better yet, let students design the card based on what they consider to be good teaching.

When we meet or hear about successful adults who acknowledge having been undisciplined or unwilling students, we usually ask what turned them around. As author and speaker Rabbi Harold Kushner reminds us, these people often reply, "There was this teacher…" I want to be that kind of teacher and colleague—challenging, responsive, innovative, and highly effective. To be these things, we invite accountability, not avoid it. It's one of the greatest teaching tools we have.

Failure Preferred, Actually

Let's stop demonizing failure. It will be our undoing.

I'm not advocating that we celebrate low test scores or students' dashed dreams. I am calling for a shift in metaphors from failure as a student's foe to failure as a student's ally, and a move away from the presumption that giving students Fs and zeroes for inadequate performance is the best way to promote their self-discipline.

Failure can teach us in ways that consistent success cannot. Wandering down blind alleys, fumbling through half-baked ideas, and mixing the wrong ingredients often yield new insights. This is the stuff of scientific, mathematical, literary, and societal progress.

Our civilization advances because of failures. Medicine, construction, dentistry, investments, culinary arts, and space travel are some of the fields that have improved dramatically due to insights gained through past failures. In some cases, there was a horrific outcome of these failures: people died. But what an even greater loss to never have learned from those mistakes and taken steps to make sure they never happened again. Automobile companies crash cars on purpose, so they can make the car more successful—safer for human passengers. Failure here leads to the better outcome.

Take a look at *This We Believe: Keys to Educating Young Adolescents* (National Middle School Association, 2010); *Turning Points 2000: Educating Young Adolescents in the 21st Century* (Jackson. Davis, Abeel and Bordonaro, 2000); or the online research at www.amle.org. Middle grades students are in prime exploration mode. They require ample opportunities to wrestle with ideas, not have those ideas spoon-fed to them. They should feel invited to experiment and secure to fail in their middle school classroom or at home.

Making failure okay

Unfortunately, in many schools students consider academic struggle as a sign of weakness. Instead, let's make it okay to fail in the pursuit of learning. One of the most vivid ways we can do this is to model it. We set up real situations in which we do not know answers or how to solve problems—really not know something, not just fake it. Then we find the answer or solve the problem constructively in front of students, so they see what it looks like not to know something yet to handle it wisely and to remain a respected individual in the community.

Many students do not push themselves to explore different talents or new thinking because they are focused on protecting their reputations as the students who always get the right answers or who answer questions first. What potential is lost because a student needs to protect his personal status quo!

To make it acceptable to fail in the pursuit of learning, we also must remove the grade myopia we place on many of our assignments. For example, some middle school students who are struggling would rather say they forgot the homework, didn't have time to complete it, or just didn't do it rather than admit that they did not understand something. Realizing some of our students feel this way is a red flag that our classroom culture is not what we want it to be. Our students should have every confidence that their attempts to wrestle with content and skills will be met with support and encouragement; judgment and ridicule should not even be on the radar.

One of the worst perpetuators of an unhealthy avoidance of failure is the pressure we feel from state or provincial testing. Due to the nature of standardization protocols, it's almost impossible to create a test that is financially feasible, legally defensible, and also allows for more than one correct answer. As a result, schools promote the philosophy that there is just one correct answer or just one way to write an essay. We become formulaic and limit students' learning and thereby their growth.

In his 2008 book *The Global Achievement Gap*, Tony Wagner asked dozens of employers in both blue- and white-collar professions to identify the number one characteristic they want to see in potential employees. No matter the level of the job, every employer responded with the same characteristic: "They know how to ask good questions." Daniel Pink, in his 2006 book, *A Whole New Mind*, claims that high-concept, right-brain thinking that is often messy but full of "outside the box" thinking will be the new "it" skill for future employees to have on their resume as we evolve beyond left-brain protocol thinking in manufacturing and business.

If our students are going to be prepared for the 21st century professions, we have to make it safe to ask questions, to see adults and culture as fallible, and to experiment with more than a 50–50 chance of failing. Russian composer Igor Stravinsky once said, "I have learned throughout my life as a composer chiefly through my mistakes and pursuits of false assumptions, not by my exposure to founts of wisdom and knowledge." Imagine the beauty and insight that would have been lost if he had succumbed to the "correct answer" dogma or if he never allowed himself to fail in his attempts at composing. We don't want a generation of citizens to spend their days avoiding failure when it so readily leads to a positive future.

The route to failure

Let's make failure a valued route to learning in our classrooms. Here are 14 suggestions to get started:

1. Privately or publicly affirm students who attempt something initially beyond their reach regardless of their success. Make this a weekly recognition.

2. Make sure all students experience failure once during a grading period—particularly your high-performing students. Middle and high school classes are the opportunities to experience

what it's like to hit a brick wall and then develop the coping strategies to navigate around or through it. We want students to learn these skills now, while the stakes aren't so high and while they have a solid "pit crew" (us) to get them back on track again. Students who coast unchallenged in these grade levels often don't develop these skills. They fall apart in college, careers, or the military when the stakes are much higher.

3. Model how to fail at something and how to handle it constructively. Ask students who are willing to help promote this message to demonstrate it as well. Invite administrators, other teachers, and members of the community to stop by and give testimony to failure.

4. Frequently relate the stories of famous figures in history, sports, politics, entertainment, and other professions who failed in some way but learned from the experience and grew as a result. Students are consummate story-receivers; they'll remember the lessons learned.

5. Overtly teach problem-solving skills regardless of whether it's an official part of your curriculum. This is often referred to as "the hidden curriculum." It's those values and skills for living life that all citizens should have. Skills to develop in students include analyzing tasks (breaking down tasks into smaller pieces), revising one's thinking in light of new evidence, developing more than one response, looking at something from multiple angles, weighing the pros and cons of different options, using trial and error, seeking advice from trusted others, thinking critically about arguments and ideology, preparing before a challenging task, learning from mistakes, controlling impulsive thinking, considering consequences, and knowing which questions to ask.

6. Create a "Wall of Failure Success" on which you identify students (with their permission) who failed at something

initially, but learned from the experience and eventually became successful with that skill or topic. Be specific in telling their stories.

7. Frequently brainstorm constructive responses to what appear to be initial failures. Use hypothetical situations so students can safely converse about failures without feeling the added pressure of having failed at something. They'll remember some of the solutions, but even better, they'll feel comfortable asking for help when they do fail. These conversations set the tone that failure is acceptable.

8. Teach students about the formative nature of classwork and homework, then live up to that promise. This means we reduce the influence of formative assessments and assignments on the overall subject grade. This opens homework to its true role: to practice, reinforce, and expand students' skills and knowledge as they come to know our topics, not as the final declaration of proficiency. It gives students license to explore and extend themselves without worry.

9. Ask students questions to which you do not know the answer. This can be a scary thing for teachers who are used to eliciting predetermined responses from students, but it sure is a good model for students, and it builds empathy for what they are feeling as we ask them to take risks.

10. Make it possible for students to ask more questions in class than you do. We find that whoever is asking the questions is doing the learning. If we're asking the questions, we're doing the learning, and supposedly, we already know the curriculum.

11. Don't bail out students when they struggle to respond. Give them the time, including silent time for idea percolation, to come up with a worthy response. If we give them too many templates, too many hints, they quickly learn that we'll rescue them from ignorance. This doesn't mean we're insensitive, just

that we give them the tools and often let them find their way to use them without our interference.

12. Remove all posters and promotional materials that express the sentiment, "Failure is not an option." There's a popular book by Alan Blankstein with this title that I heartily recommend—it's unfortunate that the full title is not often used: *Failure Is Not an Option: Six Principles That Guide Student Achievement in High-Performing Schools* (2004). The statement means that we don't give up on students or claim our hands are tied due to circumstances beyond our control when students struggle, nor do we allow students to give up on themselves; we build resilience.

13. Allow retests, retakes, and redos for full credit. I know this will frustrate some teachers, but at some point we have to accept the fact that redoing something is one of the most powerful teaching tools we have, and in reality, competent adults are competent because they learned those advanced skills repeatedly—not in a one-shot unit at the end of February.

14. In the training for every profession, including teaching, we are encouraged to make initial attempts and, as we fail, we are given descriptive feedback on what to do differently to be successful in our subsequent attempts. This feedback is meaningful for having gone through the task at least once. For this to work, however, we have to receive full credit for what we learn. Why would we take this highly effective strategy away from students who need it most?

The opportunities of failure

Of course, this mindset about failure's positives only works if teachers don't let failure become a liability for students. For example, a student who says, "I don't care if I fail, school sucks!" is not someone who should be left in charge of his own learning and destiny. Most of our middle school students do not have the maturity and training to be given such responsibility; they can influence it, but as mature guides, we help give it direction.

Some teachers abdicate their teaching responsibilities by turning learning over to their students completely. They declare, "Students have to meet me half way," and, "An F on that quiz will teach him to straighten up." Neither statement is true. If a student doesn't "meet the teacher half way," does the teacher back off and say there's nothing he can do to help the student? No. Like a good editor working with a writer, the teacher saves the student from himself. He investigates and takes corrective action. He does not allow the students' immaturity to dictate the extent of the student's learning.

Turning Zeroes to 60s

A student does not turn in his project. You record a zero in the grade book. When it comes time to determine the student's end of the grading period mark, you have to make a decision: Do you keep the zero or turn it into a 50, 60, or 70 to make the grading scale fair?

Few aspects of grading cause as much consternation among middle school teachers as this one. If you convert the zero to a 60, it seems as if the student could literally sit on his rear end and do nothing for an entire grading period and still earn 60s. It's wrong, we think, to give students points when they didn't do anything. This is an understandable conclusion, but it's wrong.

The power of zeroes

When we turn students' zeroes into 60s in our grade books, we are not giving students something for doing nothing. We're adjusting the grade intervals so that any averaging we do is mathematically justified. More important, in the overall pattern of grades, it presents a more accurate picture of the students' ability. A zero on the 100-point scale has an undeserved and devastating effect on students and their grades—so much so that no matter what the student does, the grade distorts the final grade as a true indicator of mastery. Mathematically and ethically this is unacceptable.

Our decision should go something like this: Should we use an F grade near the top of the F range, such as 50, 59, or a 60, or should we use the bottom, most hurtful and distorting of F grades—a zero—as the indicator of failure? What purpose does it serve to use a zero to indicate a student failed to demonstrate mastery? Do we need to discern between levels of "No Evidence Presented," or, "Failure?" Does a string of perfect papers for a grading period combined with one paper not submitted, equate to a C level of mastery? No, that's two whole grade levels below an A. If we still have to average (see the previous article in this collection), a B might be more accurate, though still problematic because we're aggregating.

Also, if the zero was earned in the first half of the grading period or even just once in a consistent string of other grades and we are grading on a trend because we want to be current in our evaluation of the student's status, we might even drop that one score and use the majority and most recent grades to indicate mastery, earning the student an A for the grading period.

In the June 29 issue of *The Virginian-Pilot*, Virginia Beach School Board member Emma L. Davis compares the practice of giving zeroes to taking temperature readings over time:

> "Consider trying to find the average temperature over five days and recording 85, 82, 83 and 86, then forgetting a day and recording 0. The average temperature would be 67, a figure that does not accurately show the weather from that week. If those temperatures were grades, a student would fail after consistently earning Bs and Cs."

Being accurate

In a properly run class, we avoid any practice that compromises a grade's accuracy. Effective teachers determine grades using the mode and sometimes, median, not the mean. This means we don't average all of a student's grades to determine his or her final grade. We look instead at the most consistent level of performance, not all the performances. This is a far more accurate rendering of proficiency. Proficiency improves as the year progresses. Students are very different people in June than they were in September, and we don't hold their earlier digressions against them. For example, if a student earned a D, A, A, and A for his four quarters with me, he'd earn an A for the year.

With such a policy, some of us might be afraid that students who earn a zero that has been adjusted up to a 60 can brag about how they can get 60 points without lifting a finger. But think about that for a moment: The 60 is still an F. What sense does it make for the student to claim to classmates, "Hey, check it out everyone: I didn't do the project, and I still got an F"? The correlation between hard work, learning, and achieving success is still clear: If we act irresponsibly or don't learn, we get a failing grade.

Teachers who have trouble accepting this often push back with: "I'm not going to pay someone $60 if he doesn't do the job assigned." I agree with this, but tell these teachers that this has nothing to do with what we're discussing here with zeroes on the 100-point scale.

These teachers are mired in the "Grades are compensation" metaphor. They think grades are reward, affirmation, compensation, validation, or payment for work done. Such bartering and economic relationships make grades susceptible to falsifying and to being grounds for tedious arguments from students and their parents about what it would take to raise or lower a score by a tenth of a percentage point. To be truly evidence-based, i.e., standards-based, grades must be considered as communication, not compensation. They are an accurate, honest report of a child's performance against standards, nothing else.

Assessing for learning

At an AMLE conference in Philadelphia, assessment expert Rick Stiggins made the point with his insightful reminder that we should assess for learning, not just do assessments of learning. It's not enough to measure and report students' mastery of standards. We have to use assessment data in ways that motivate students to learn and grow. We can jump up and down, calling for higher standards and rigid accountability while presenting overwhelming data on individual students, but it all means nothing unless the failing student understands the meaning of assessments and that we are there to extend a ladder to him to help him crawl from his hole. Regardless of whether he failed because of his immaturity or cognitive readiness level, great teachers still provide the ladder.

Remember, too, that an F is not a label. It does not mean the student has failed at learning, only that he has not yet demonstrated mastery. An F on an assessment is not justification for declaring a student incapable, immature, irresponsible, or defiant. They simply mean no evidence of a standard was presented. Effective teachers investigate the reasons for the failure and then address them. So much negative emotional baggage is associated with receiving an F that we must extend an emotional bridge to each student who fails, in order to bring him back to personal investment in the class and his own future. The task becomes even more important with students who received a string of failing grades.

Adjusting zeroes to 60 is not giving students something for having done nothing. It's adjusting the grading scale so that each grade has an appropriate amount of influence on the student's summative evaluation and each grade provides information for effective decision making. Distorted and inaccurate grades that offer little more than harsh punishment with no hope for parole make students throw down the ball and go home. They see no reason to play. Grades that mitigate the negative effects of an imperfect grading system keep students in the game.

Late Work

Middletalk posting November 2010

I get asked these questions a lot:

- Colleges are not going to let students redo work or turn it in late, so why should we?

- If I don't count quizzes, homework, and classwork a lot, their grades will suffer. How can I keep up their motivation if this happens?

- How can I allow retakes and redos without students taking advantage of me so that I have to spend the last two weeks of the grading period marking papers from the whole grading period?

- How many retakes should I allow before I say, "no more?"

In a perfect world, everyone would just get "Not there yet" or "Incomplete" on their transcripts until missing work is done. "F" is often associated with failure, but these students aren't failures; they just haven't presented evidence of the standards yet. For clerical reasons only, not for educational reasons, we arbitrarily draw a line in the sand, i.e., on the calendar, and declare this is the final day we will accept particular assignments. We do it because otherwise it would get messy with everyone at different points in their learning and only one teacher orchestrating the learning of so many. As a result, successful teachers tolerate moderate hypocrisy in their pedagogy, which seems necessary. The system, as it is set up, conspires against a lot of wise teaching practices.

One thing we discovered in how humans learn is that we are hard-wired to do hard work. It's a natural part of who we are. When students don't do complex, demanding work, there's actually something wrong, perhaps something we can't see right away. Every single student desperately wants to be competent and to achieve. Helping them figure out what's going on, giving them the tools to turn their lives around, really learning the content and skills, and finding a path to recovery collectively teach more than labeling them or their work with a zero or F. There is no wavering or waffling when we do this. My students know I mean business. Redoing work is not even close to waffling or going soft. It's actually far more demanding than declaring failure with no hope of turning it around. My reputation in the schools I've served has been "If you're a slacker, you don't want Mr. Wormeli for a teacher. You can't get by not doing your work in his class. You do it over and over until you learn it."

For those who worry that we fail to teach students responsibility if we let them turn their work in late, there's a difference between holding individuals accountable for their job performance once they've achieved mastery or certified status that's very different than holding individuals accountable for something as they come to know it, especially young humans who are discovering the way the world works and who they are. The learning process is developmental and uneven, no matter how much we wish it were the factory model of schooling in which everyone learns at the same pace and in the same way. Wouldn't that be easier? But this messy process cannot be overturned and both children and adults are the same in this regard. The best preparation for students learning responsibility and performing tasks as adults comes from recovering from those times they didn't demonstrate either and from really learning what teachers have to teach. In both, there must be hope.

This is what I hope I am accomplishing by not allowing them to fail but also not allowing the late work to continue. Very few of my students have late work after the first nine weeks because of my high expectations for them. They do learn, and through asking them questions and involving them daily in discussions in class, they stay engaged and increase their confidence as well. I hope I am helping them recover as well.

What if students have not contributed to a group project?

Students sitting through all those projects others have done shouldn't get to scam off their classmates' hard work, effort, and ideas. What's stopping you from assigning something different to those students to keep this from happening? The assignment you give may include an analysis of other classmates' work and ideas, in addition to a completely original approach from each student. They should write a letter of what they've observed about themselves as learners during the course of this new and different assignment. Listening to all those projects from classmates is actually a great instructional experience—use it as one instead of being worried about it.

When students don't do something, there's usually a reason. They may have needed some ideas from others before getting their mind going. Sure, they may have been tempted by other interests and simply not done the work, too, but now they have to go on with the new curriculum; their sports, families, church/synagogue/mosque, music, scouts, etc. responsibilities; and also redo this assignment. They'll learn very quickly that they are going to have to learn it sooner or later, so they might as well learn it sooner and have a life.

Consider the type of missing work

Something else to consider is what type of assignments the missing work is. Does the missing assignment provide final, summative evidence of mastery of the standards? If so, then the student did not present clear and consistent evidence of the standard in his work or thinking, and an associated lower mark is justified. If, however, these were practice assignments such as homework, classwork, etc., and he was able to demonstrate clear and consistent evidence regarding the standards on subsequent summative assessments, then the marks for the missing assignments are irrelevant.

If the student has failed to submit clear, consistent evidence of the standard, you can tell the student and his parents that it's an F right now, but if he wants to go back and learn the material successfully in the next marking period and then resubmit evidence of his clear proficiency regarding the standard, you'd be glad to reconsider the grade. Tell them if he's definitely learned the material (while, of course, keeping up with his personal/sports/academic/family responsibilities in the new quarter—an amazing feat, actually), you will submit a request to change the grade on the official transcripts.

Catching up at lunchtime

Trying to understand the student, figuring out what can be done positively, and making sure this doesn't happen again, some teachers have students work through lunch on missing assignments. If the kids discover they could have done the assignment all along and it wasn't that bad, they gain some maturity as a result. Although they have learned to assume responsibility, it raises the question, however, of why they didn't do it properly in the first place. Was it that they had never experienced such success and now that they've tasted it and seen themselves doing it, they are willing to pursue it? Did they not have quiet small group or individual time with a caring adult in their lives to help them through it, and the lunch groups helped in this regard? If that was the problem, how could we set this sort of thing up within the regular class periods? Maybe a rotating basis after/before school? Saturday school? Summer early-back programs?

Reporting new level of mastery

Some schools have a policy of not reporting students' new levels of mastery after they have successfully completed their missing work. Why continue to report that they don't know the standards when they so clearly do? Students learn responsibility a million other ways than through grades and far more effectively, too. It was the time with their teacher and/or the parent or schoolmate, the tools and new sense of confidence they gained, and the powerful experience of personal success with the content they finally achieved that taught them responsibility, not the withholding of an accurate mark indicating full credit for learning achieved. I encourage the reporting of full credit for all that is achieved, even in these relearning sessions for the wayward students—even when students make immoral or irresponsible decisions early on. They will invest even more when they see that the hard work pays off. They're not getting away with anything here; they're not getting a treat for being irresponsible when we do this.

Cheating

MiddleTalk posting November, 2010
Cheating is an important concern in our age of technology. A lot of us bemoan the cut-and-paste-off-the-Internet approach so many students use to do papers. Of course, this can be a helpful set of skills to have: Knowing what information is important to use and weaving it into a compelling presentation can be useful, actually. That's very different than generating insight, knowledge, and learning.

For me, constructive response to cheating has three components. First, we must be proactive. Students have to know what constitutes cheating and about consequences of cheating ahead of time, and we should help them see how it breaks trust and damages reputations. Because students so often try to justify cheating during times of stress and impulsivity, we have to let them know it is perfectly okay for people not to know something or be good at something and then ask for help. This is very hard to teach, but we all have to learn it. Proactively, too, we must cultivate positive student-teacher relationships, so students will think twice about disappointing us and their classmates. When we care about each other, we are less likely to do something unethical to each other. We want to live up to others' expectations for us.

Second, there must be some way for the student to rebuild the trust he has destroyed. He needs a way to make emotional restitution to the class, teacher, family, and friends. A private and/or public apology to the teacher, class, and family may be in order; extra service to the school may need to happen; etc.

Third, there must be a clear path to recover from the digression; forgiveness must be in the picture. Otherwise, we let students' immaturity dictate all that he is, and none of us would be here if the rest of the world never forgave us our indiscretions. There has to be hope for the student that others will be able to return to normal relations with him. This might be six weeks of not trusting him to do basic everyday things like running errands, borrowing equipment, etc., but there is a finite window, not an endless window that makes him feel like there's no hope of things returning to normal. Students who don't have complete control over their impulsivities can panic if they are labeled purely by their missteps. When cornered, we fight back, and not always in the most constructive ways.

Another aspect of this is to let students redo the work on which they cheated. They will have to keep up with the new curriculum the class begins as well as everything else in their lives, but they will have to redo the work. That's a big motivator for students. They soon realize that they are going to have to do it properly sooner or later, and they might as well do it sooner and have a hassle-free life. This is a step closer to maturity.

If something is meaningful to us, we don't see it as adversarial or something so insurmountable we have to cheat in order to succeed. If what we're doing is relevant to us, we enjoy the struggle and are not threatened by it. On our myopic road focused on students getting the right answers to test questions, we don't take the time to make learning meaningful, and as result, any route to success on the final exam or project will do.

Honor Roll? Really?

I look at the 16 students in my classroom. On any other day, 35 students would be looking back at me, but today the other 19 are eating cake and being honored at the morning's honor roll assembly. What am I supposed to offer these academic castaways? Solace? How about platitudes about working harder next grading period? Maybe I could use this time to work on these left-behinds' weaker areas. Or not.

Disinvited and vividly reminded one more time why they don't measure up, these students sit, daring me to say something that makes this situation okay. I've got nothing. Instead, I silently plan the adjustments I'll need to make to the second period's lesson sequence because of the lost time due to the assembly. Then I introduce a new logic game to my remaining students and wait for the period to end.

Let's be honest

Let's put it out there and let the e-mails fly: Honor roll in middle schools serves little or no purpose, and it actually hurts the progress of some students. It is the antithesis of middle schools' mission. This is a touchy subject, so let me make my case.

In a not-very-scientific research survey, I asked 11 high school students of mostly high level academic performance whether being on the honor roll mattered in high school. Did they think about it? Was it important to get on the list? Were students who did not make the list disappointed? Was honor roll motivating in some way?

Every one of them said they never thought about honor roll, quickly adding that they did think about their GPA. "Making the honor roll doesn't get you anything," one of the high school students said. "GPA and high grades in advanced classes do. Honor roll is mostly for middle school, and it's just one more way to sort students." This is a telling statement on two fronts: First, students see grades and GPA as currency.

Second, students wonder about teachers' need to sort students into "successful" and, "not-so-successful."

The former is an unfortunate outcome of currently used but very inappropriate grading policies that create our grade bartering system: If you do this assignment, you'll get 50 points in the grade book; if you don't do this assignment, you will not have enough points to pass. Grade bartering doesn't lead to true student learning. Grades are about communication, not compensation.

Does posting a list of students who achieved straight As or some acceptable mixture of As and Bs actually motivate students to strive for honor roll status in the future? And, exactly how does an honor roll assembly motivate invitees and their disinvited classmates to learn more or work hard in the future? If we conduct an honor roll assembly with a motivational guest speaker for those honored students and their parents, shouldn't we also invite the disinvited students because they have the most to gain from listening to the speaker?

Of greater concern is the flimsy nature of the single factor used to designate those worthy of honor roll status: grades. Yikes! As most teachers know, grades are subjective, relative, and inferential at best. They are fragile things on which to base so much celebration and rejection. Grades are more a reflection of teachers than a reflection of what students know and can do regarding lesson objectives. Some teachers count homework 10%, some count it 30% or more. Some hold students accountable for one level of performance while others give As for far less proficiency. Some allow retakes for full credit, some for partial credit. Classroom assessments tend to be one-sitting "snapshot" samplings of student thinking/performance rather than clear and consistent evidence over time, which is necessary if they are to be valid.

Considering grades in conjunction with other tools, such as teacher observation, analysis of students' products, outside and objective testing, teacher recommendation, and multi-dimensional screening devices, gets us closer to accurate marks, but grades by themselves are very suspect diagnostic indicators. They are easily and frequently distorted, so much so that they should never be used as the sole criterion for determining a student's label.

Revisiting our goals

Asking why we do what we do in education is always a good idea. Many educators respond to cautions about honor roll by telling us to ease up, saying that they are just trying to affirm students' hard work and high academic achievement. These are worthy goals, of course, but we can provide affirmation without resorting to a printed list of honor roll students in the school newspaper.

Is this really what middle schools aspire to be? Is it legitimate to lift up and recognize only those whose learning capacities and development allow them to function well in conventional classrooms while the rest of our students in varying degrees of maturation, or those whose learning needs are not met by regular classrooms or with teachers who fail to provide differentiated approaches, are told one more time that they don't fit into our preconceived ideas of what constitutes being smart?

Middle school innovator Bill Ivey at Stoneleigh-Burnham School in Vermont reflected on these concerns in the April 3, 2009, AMLE MiddleTalk Listserve about his school's decision to not have an honor roll:

> If we are educating the whole child, we need not to be privileging recognition of one aspect of development over another .... When we started our middle school, we decided not to do honor roll, given what we knew of research. One reason was that honor roll at this level has less meaning, given the vastly different developmental levels of kids—someone who's well into abstract thought will be working at a totally different level than someone else who isn't there yet, no matter how motivated and hard-working both kids are.

The other reason (again, research-based) was the potential negative implications to self-concept of separating kids into honor roll and not-honor roll groups .... While I know middle school kids are more resilient than many people give them credit for, some kids apparently really do develop a permanent (or at least potentially permanent) feeling of inferiority when they work hard but don't make honor roll—again, perhaps due primarily to (temporary) developmental differences ... .

My son's school (grades 6-9) also doesn't do honor roll (nor, for that matter, do they do athletic awards). They do have a 'commendation' system which is simply recognized with a notation and explanation in the comment, whereby anyone who does something special in some way—finally masters a sticky concept, writes an outstanding paper, basically anything that makes sense to a teacher—can earn special recognition for that fact.

Affirmation for all

Affirmation is not a bad thing, but we can do so much better. Let's dismantle our increasingly narrow view of what constitutes student success—single-shot test scores and inaccurate grades—and let's find multiple ways to provide positive feedback to all students. Let's change assessment and grading practices so assessments are authentic and conducted from many angles and categories of measure, and grades are accurate reflections of mastery, undistorted by non-academic factors.

Let's privately and publicly affirm the most important skills of the 21st century we find in our students: creativity, collaboration, compassion, critical thinking, flexibility, resilience, task analysis, positive social change, ethics, courage, mental dexterity, pattern recognition and manipulation, and initiative. Most of these are not easily transferrable to most current reporting systems, but they are just as important as knowing the cubed root of 27, and thereby worthy criteria for celebration.

Affirmation for achievement in these areas and for hard work can come in many effective forms:

- Private conversation with the teacher in which the teacher highlights the student's growth and achievements, pointing to specific evidence for each and its positive effects.

- Free time to pursue personal interests during class without having to make up missed class work.

- More independence and personal choice.

- Additional privileges such as more access to the computer lab, extra court time in the gym, planning school lunches for a week.

- Letters of commendation from respected members of the community.

- Books of the student's choice purchased for the school library in the student's name, including an official bookplate indicating the honor.

- The opportunity to address younger students about life in middle school.

- A one-year subscription to an appropriate magazine of personal interest.

Notice that none of these affirmations involve food. Let's not add to the obesity issues or eating disorders that begin so often in middle school.

We are creative people, so let's find developmentally appropriate ways to affirm all students' growth, including students who are not on pace with others or whose talents aren't as clearly manifested in standard classrooms. Let's avoid programs that purposely sort students for dubious manipulation. Identifying students' levels of performance is helpful for assigning homework and determining levels of classes they should take, but to sort students for a posted list or invitation-only party makes little sense. To best teach the next generation, let's be honorable ourselves.

Conclusion

Graduation Speech
to the Class of 2012

Address for Commencement of Seniors of Oakton High School, Vienna, VA
June 19, 2012

[Note: My daughter, Lynn, was in this graduating class and introduced me
to the students and their families and friends that evening.]

Thank you, Lynn. And thank you, Dr. Banbury, faculty of Oakton
High School, parents, and honored guests. Thank you for the time,
wisdom, and dedication you put into getting the Class of 2012 to
young adulthood.

And class of 2012? If you believe the overblown media hype about the
end of the world in December of this year according to the Mayan
calendar, then YOU are the last graduating class of planet Earth, and
perhaps, our solar system! You better make this year a great one!

> *[Cell Phone rings] Yes? …Oh, hello, it's you! No, no, it's okay. I'm doing*
> *the commencement address with them right now. [Aside to the audience]*
> *It's your future calling. It can be pretty pushy.*
>
> *No, no, I'm here. "It's the year 2112 on your end," you say? Wow, that's*
> *quite a time dilation. Tell me, what's new 100 years from now? …*
> *All iPhones, tablets, laptops, apps, iPads are bundled together and*
> *are now accessed via a contact lens everyone wears…any site on the*
> *Interplanetarynet, including video and conversations, is projected just a*
> *few feet in front of your face any time you want? Wow…that's awesome.*

And what else? You figured out cold fusion and how to distribute food to poor countries equitably, but you still can't figure out what to make of Justin Beiber? What's that? As former President Gaga says... Wait a minute! President Gaga— as in Lady Gaga? Wow, it must have been her Poker Face....no, no, I'm not trying to be mean, I know she was born that way... So, what was it she said? ... That many of these graduates will live to see the year 2100? That's incredible!

What's that? Yes, all those party photos they posted on social networking sites WILL be used to judge their fitness for employment. Reputation is everything. Got it, I'll pass these along. Look, let me finish my message to the 2012 graduates, and you can take it from there, Future! [Trying to hang up] Th–th– thanks, yes, that's good, too, I'll tell them. Yes, ye...[click]

Wow, you're future is pushy, eager for you to get there. Let me briefly describe four actions to help you on your way: question, reach back, vote, and connect.

Do the thing that scares the heck out of you, dare disturb the universe. Every single invention and innovation that has bettered our civilization in some way came from someone who did not follow conventional practices. This is how we got representative government, the printing press, Cloud computing, Pepto Bismol, and Elvis.

Boldly question the status quo. Openly discuss controversial subjects like intelligent design vs. evolution, politics, religion, and for whom you would offer yourself as "Tribute." Visit the intellectually demanding world outside your echo chambers. Go ahead and eat Double-Stuff Oreos, invent new sports, accept the torch Ray Bradbury recently passed to you, and dream of impossible things.

Seriously, you will be hired for how you are similar to an organization, but you will be promoted for how you are different. Our society advances when you do something outside of normal. For those of you far, far outside of normal, thank you for all you're doing to advance humanity!

If you all learned in high school was only what we teachers and parents know, civilization will grind to a halt. Our goal was for you to surpass us, not get equal to us. No one will ever ask you to write a five-paragraph essay in the working world; they'll expect you to know how to adjust your writing to match your purpose. So transcend formulaic models. Mental agility, not conformity, will put dinner on the table.

We need people who can make connections the rest of us can't see, whether it be in figuring out why the car's engine won't start, how new architecture better insulates a home, what propellant works best to get us to Mars, or how laundry magically cleans itself by migrating to the bottom of the dirty clothes pile.

In his book *The Global Achievement Gap,* Tony Wagner asked a question of multiple CEOs of companies: "What's the #1 thing you look for in new employees?" Independent of each other, they all responded the same: "Do they know how to ask good questions?"

Yeah, where is that measured on standardized tests? Being good at taking standardized tests does not qualify you for successful citizenship and creative contribution to society. Do not fall into the feckless trap of letting your test scores and your grades define who you are. There are a whole bunch of you that were C and D grade students here in high school that will suddenly grow into your own skin, figuring out what you want in the world, and you'll earn As and Bs in college, or excel in the workforce or military. And there are some of you A and B students sitting here now who will lose yourselves in college, the workforce or military, and you will drop out.

But the past is not prologue! As you carve your own future, remember that you're here because those of us ahead of you reached back to guide you. For every parent, teacher, coach, mentor, and kind adult who ever stopped what they were doing so they could assist you with what YOU were doing, how about a round of applause?

In the American ethic, the hero we elevate in our stories and movies isn't celebrated for being the first person to cross the raging river and then just sitting there, waiting for everyone else to catch up and marvel at his accomplishment. He or she is the one who finds the route forward, then reaches back to make sure very last person—, young/old/slim/heavy/infirmed/healthy/rich/poor or mutant—fords the rushing waters successfully. Graduates, be known for reaching back as much as you are for reaching forward.

Success in our society isn't about being a multi-million dollar athlete or a reality show celebrity. True heroism is about showing up every day to fix highway potholes in the hot August sun and helping a mentally challenged person learn a new skill. Modern heroes have the courage of their convictions to do justice when it is not popular and who postpone self-gratification for a greater cause, and they don't see it as a sacrifice. Riffing on the famous psychological study: Don't eat the first marshmallow. Wait patiently for two marshmallows.

Go forth and invent, lead, achieve, fly to distant worlds, and enjoy Nutella on a cracker, but if you become a lawyer, spend some time doing legal aid work for those who cannot afford proper representation. If you're a professional athlete, volunteer to coach in children's sports leagues in impoverished areas. If you're a doctor, volunteer some time to do rotations in hospitals where there is little equipment and even less hope. If you're a financial planner, offer some free classes to families who are struggling to find their way. If you end up homeless, volunteer to build homes for others. These will be the testimonials to your character more than the money you accrue or the heights you scale. From the famous Coach John Wooden: "You can't live a perfect day without doing something for someone who will never be able to repay you."

And whatever you do, vote. Democracy requires effort. We have to spend energy understanding the issues and listening to each other's point of view. The world you're about to enter draws lines between red states and blue states too readily, for we know that whole states don't vote the exact same way, nor does every Republican and Democrat respond similarly to every issue. In a world of growing narcissism in which most of us visit only those websites that reflect our own values, we avoid complexity and anything that counters our fragile egos. It's easier to speak in sharp contrasts than to explore layered meaning, and we grow less civil as a result.

Democracy can shock our status quo, confronting unexamined notions of right and wrong and providing alternative perspectives. I cringe when I think of how long this country existed before disallowing slavery and granting full civil rights to all. Supreme Court Justice Louis Brandeis, reminded us, "The greatest menace to freedom is an inert people."

Class of 2012, YOU are NOT inert. You ARE powerful. For decades to come, you will be setting consumer policies, designing new technology, voting for congressional leaders, arguing cases in our courtrooms, rebuilding hurricane-ravaged towns, teaching our young, and navigating increasingly complex moral issues in society. But build your civic selves and do not resort to uneducated, ill-considered acts of "me first." Don't look back and have to cringe about what you once allowed.

Ambrose Redmoon, was a rock band manager who was also a quadriplegic in the 1960s. He once said, "Courage is not the absence of fear, but rather the judgment that something else is more important than fear." What do you, Class of 2012, consider so important in our world that it trumps your fears of failure, rejection, embarrassment, or being politically unpopular?

I'm indebted to *New Yorker* magazine for running a cartoon back when Lynn was five years old that to this day as a father, takes my breath away. The cartoon portrayed a dance recital hall with several dozen parents seated in bleachers to one side of the dance floor while a single, very young girl in front of them moved her body in an almost graceful manner, doing pirouettes and pliés with abandon, lost in the music, completely sure of what she was portraying in that moment: a flower. It was drawn clearly in the mind bubble above her head.

In the mind bubbles above each of the observing parents' heads, however, were very different interpretations. Was she a windmill? A dinosaur? A snowflake? A frog? A toaster? Scissors? But up on the top bleacher, sitting in the back was the beaming father of the little girl. Among all the parents, his was the only mind bubble to portray the same picture: a flower. He "got" her like no one else did, and for them, nothing else mattered.

Find people who "get" you unconditionally. They are the ones that free our better selves and reassure us that we belong, especially in those times we wonder whether or not we do. Having a companion or three with whom you can be your unguarded self is worth every sleepy work day following a late night discussion on the cultural values skewered by Stewie on Family Guy.

When those archeologists declaring the end of world would be in December of this year first came across the ancient Mayan glyphs carved in the walls of Yucatan pyramids, the wicks in their lanterns must have burned quite low, for in the fading light, they missed the clear image of a bright aura sculpted in stone around planet earth, protecting our planet from solar mishap and the misdeeds of humans. This, of course, clearly represents the power and promise of the Oakton 2012 graduating class.

As a representative of ALL generations that have existed on this planet prior to you, let me remind you of where YOU stand in the sequence of civilization: WE gave you farming, writing, Mozart, democracy, penicillin, automobiles, computers, space flight, indoor plumbing, the Rolling Stones, nutrition, the idea of quantum mechanics, National Parks, Harry Potter, and Chia Pets.

WE gave you astronomy, navigation, Susan G. Komen Race for the Cure, biology, Calvin and Hobbes, JavaScript, the Internet, Rachel Carson, engineering, baseball, nanotechnology, the Sistine Chapel, freedom, the Avengers, Dr. Cheryl Newton, and the United States of America.

What are YOU going to do? You can now join us and share the steering wheel for humanity, but no texting while driving our planet, and please, refill the tank on the way home.

You are now a legacy of Oakton High School. Be worthy of it, and enjoy the ride.

Thank you.

About the Author

One of the first Nationally Board Certified teachers in America, Rick brings innovation, energy, validity and high standards to both his presentations, and his instructional practice, which includes more than 30 years teaching math, science, English, physical education, health, and history and coaching teachers and principals. Rick's work has been reported in numerous media, including *ABC's Good Morning America, Hardball with Chris Matthews, National Geographic* and *Good Housekeeping* magazines, *What Matters Most: Teaching for the 21st Century*, and the *Washington Post*. He is a columnist for the Association for Middle Level Education's *Middle Ground*, and he is the author of the award-winning book, *Meet Me in the Middle*, as well as the best-selling books, *Day One and Beyond, Fair Isn't Always Equal: Assessment and Grading in the Differentiated Classroom, Differentiation: From Planning to Practice, Grades 6-12, Metaphors & Analogies: Power Tools for Teaching any Subject*, all five from Stenhouse Publishers, as well as *Summarization in any Subject*, published by ASCD, and the Homework foldout from Incentive Publications. His classroom practice is a showcase for ASCD's best-selling series, *At Work in the Differentiated Classroom*, and he is a contributing author to *Middle School Matters* and *Because You Teach*, published by Incentive Publications.

With his substantive presentations, sense of humor, and unconventional approaches, he's been asked to present to teachers and administrators in all 50 states, Canada, China, Europe, Japan, Vietnam, Thailand, Korea, Australia, the Middle East, and at the White House. He is a seasoned veteran of many international Web casts, and he is Disney's American Teacher Awards 1996 Outstanding English Teacher of the Nation.

He won the 2008 James P. Garvin award from the New England League of Middle Schools for Teaching Excellence, Service, and Leadership, and he has been a consultant for National Public Radio, USA Today, Court TV, and the Smithsonian Institution's Natural Partners Program and their search for the Giant Squid. In June 2012, Rick was the graduation commencement speaker for the highest performing, public high school in the Washington, D.C. area. He lives in Herndon, Virginia, with his wife and two children, who are both now in college. He is currently working on his first young adult fiction novel and a new book on homework practices in the 21st century.

CPSIA information can be obtained at www.ICGtesting.com
Printed in the USA
BVOW061901110213

312824BV00002B/3/P